MEET THE ANCIENT GREEKS

MEET
the
ANCIENT GREEKS

By
XENOPHON LEON MESSINESI

With an Introductory Note by
SPYROS MARINATOS
RECTOR, ATHENS UNIVERSITY

ILLUSTRATED WITH PHOTOGRAPHS

THE CAXTON PRINTERS, LTD.
CALDWELL, IDAHO
1959

© 1959 BY
THE CAXTON PRINTERS, LTD.
CALDWELL, IDAHO

Library of Congress Catalog Card No. 59-5485

Printed, lithographed, and bound in the United States of America by
The CAXTON PRINTERS, Ltd.
Caldwell, Idaho
84201

To my daughter
Susan Athena
and in memory of her
Godmother, Mika Skouses

INTRODUCTORY NOTE

IN OUR AGE, the age of astonishing progress in the physical sciences, it is more necessary than ever that humanistic studies should also be pursued. For two generations, all persons of higher intellect have stressed that the greatness of human civilisation evanesces when bereft of humanistic culture. Education and culture are quite different matters. Education can produce a good scientist and a good technician. The totality, however, of well-balanced learning forms the character of man and gives him his personality, just as the totality of lines can constitute a work of art. This is why such upbringing gives character to the man of intellect.

After great civilisations had flourished on our planet for thousands of years, whereby mankind emerged from a state of savageness, the civilisation of the Greeks appeared. It was of short duration, but it was the illuminating meteor which opened the way for mankind. Whatever the Greeks made, whatever they said, whatever they thought, was usually good, in part outstanding and often beyond approach in its beauty, and it became thenceforth the possession of mankind.

Mr. Messinesi, a distinguished journalist and a man of high culture, has wished to write yet another book to join the innumerable others which have been written on Greece.

He well understands the value of the humanities and also knows what the study of Greece can tell the contemporary man. The wide public to whom his book is directed often asks what possible interest Greece can have for the contemporary man and what benefit the study of ancient Greece can now offer. But he knows how to give the appropriate answer in a convincing manner.

The most recent discoveries of excavations on Greek soil are paraded in the pages of his book. The heroic shades of the early pioneers of the archaeological spade are also silhouetted. The nature and character of the Greek land and of the Greek nation are set forth. Culled blossoms from historical, philological, religious, and mythological knowledge guide the reader and help him to keep his bearings. Art, the manner and circumstances of life, and the deeds of the Greeks are presented in fitting measure so that they constitute an easy and pleasant guide to the reader.

Mr. Messinesi imparts to every page a portion of his own culture, which has been the standard of his own life, and he has properly evaluated the eternal merits of Greek civilisation. The reader of this book will find in its pages a safe and sober exposition of the subject from which he can, finally, derive only profit and pleasure.

SPYROS MARINATOS
Rector, and Professor of Archaeology,
Athens University

Athens, 1958

PREFACE

ARCHAEOLOGISTS are writing ancient history at an accelerated pace. By the time that this book had been written, a matter of several months, it was found that the beginning was becoming out of date.

Originally the writer had mentioned the hope that the scripts found in Crete and Pylos would one day be deciphered, just as the Rosetta stone of the British Museum had given the clue to Egyptian hieroglyphics. While the book was being written the late Michael Ventris had been successful in deciphering the script which is known as Linear Script B, examples of which had been found in the places mentioned. As a result it was ascertained that the Achaean inhabitants of Greece in 1600 B.C., or earlier, were Greek speaking. Then, early in 1956, Professor Arne Furumark, of Upsala University, made a start toward deciphering Linear Script A, which had been found on clay tablets and ceramics in Aghia Triada and elsewhere in Crete. He was able, partly, to read the hitherto unknown language, which he thinks was related to the Hittite. But Professor Cyrus Gordon, in the United States, believes he can read the Akkadian Semitic language in the same tablets.

Meantime, John L. Caskey, director of the American School of Classical Studies in Athens, was digging up relics of Neolithic times in Lerna of the Peloponnesos and had demonstrated that in the years 3000 to 2500 B.C. there was a relatively advanced culture in the Peloponnesos with a well-developed sense of proportion and rhythm.

Simultaneously Spyros Marinatos, the then head of the Archaeological Department of the Greek State, as well as many of his ephors, made remarkable finds, bringing new localities and sites to the light of day, including the treasures found by Professor Marinatos in Crete, Pylos, and elsewhere.

In gratitude I must thank the last two named professors for their continual assistance which they have given with a charm that rivals their vast erudition and sagacity.

However much one wants to be impartial, it is inescapable that one should lean to one theory or another. I must make it clear, therefore, that I do not wish to implicate any of the above, or any other of my many archaeological friends who have helped me, in any theories that I may have appeared to sponsor.

Opinions regarding the historical accuracy of what has occurred only a generation ago can be most contradictory. Opinions regarding the history we are actually living through can be fundamentally controversial. How, then, can it be but there should be differences of opinions on historical matters which have been buried for centuries upon centuries before being brought to light? I have tried to avoid assertions on what might be controversial matters.

X. L. M.

Athens
June, 1958

ORTHOGRAPHICAL NOTE

ONE OF THE problems has been that of the spelling of Greek names. One of the legacies of the Middle Ages is that learning was in the hands of monastic institutions and the Church. The Church, under the influence of Rome, not only gave Greek names a Latin spelling but even converted them to Latin declensions. Generally speaking, this has been rectified in this book. The letter *C* is not Greek, and has been replaced by *K*, a tendency which has been accepted by archaeologists. Greek masculine words ending in *os* have been kept as such and not converted to *us*. Similarly, "Symposion" has not been latinized to "Symposium."

Certain exceptions have been made, as is customary, for particularly well-known names. "Athinai" has been kept as "Athens." "Corinth" and "Acropolis" have been left as such.

In Greece itself the tourist organization is now writing Greek names with Latin letters according to modern pronunciation. No doubt it has its purpose for motorists and tourists, but this does not affect any enquiry into ancient Greece.

TABLE OF CONTENTS

PART I
THE BACKGROUND

Chapter	Page
I. General Perspective	1
II. Pre-Classical Times	12
III. Archaeologists and Myths	23
IV. Goddesses and Gods	33
V. Early Spartan Supremacy	45
VI. The Greek Colonies	51
VII. The Olympic Games and the Oracle at Delphi	58
VIII. Athens, Up To the Persian Wars	70
IX. The War with the Medes and the Persians	80
X. From the Persian Wars to Alexander	94

PART II
GREEK CULTURE AND THOUGHT

I. Greek Culture	111

Chapter   *Page*

   II. SCULPTURE - - - - - - - - - - 117
  III. ARCHITECTURE - - - - - - - - - 128
  IV. THE THEATRE AND OTHER ART - - - - - 140
   V. PHILOSOPHY AND THOUGHT - - - - - - 158
  VI. THE ACADEMY, THE LYCEUM, THE MUSEUM - 171

PART III
EVERYDAY LIFE

    I. POPULATION, ORGANIZATION, AND JUSTICE - 181
   II. CHARACTER AND CHARACTERISTICS - - - 197
  III. THE AGORA - - - - - - - - - - 212
  IV. THE HOME — FOOD AND DRESS - - - - - 220
   V. THE HOME — THE WOMEN AND THE SLAVES - 231

PART IV
ALEXANDER AND AFTER

    I. THE SPREAD OF GREEK CIVILISATION - - - 245

INDEX - - - - - - - - - - - - - - 255

LIST OF ILLUSTRATIONS

Picture Section - - - - - - *Following Book Page* 44	
	Plate
Terra cotta eight-inch-high Neolithic figurine -	I
Clay tablets, Linear Script A - - - - -	I
Interior of the reconstructed Minoan Palace at Knossos - - - - - - - - - - -	I
Mycenaean gold cups of around 1400 B.C. - -	II
The upper cup shows wild bulls, the lower, tame ones - - - - - - - - - - - -	II
The Prince. A coloured fresco from Knossos -	III
Knossos. The Throne Room in the Minoan Palace	III
Minoan mural at Knossos known as the "Blue Ladies" - - - - - - - - - - - -	IV
Model of around 2000 B.C. of the chryselephantine statue of Athena - - - - - - -	V
The eight-thousand-foot Taygetos Range - -	VI
Delphi, looking down onto the Temple of Apollon	VII
Olympia and the verdant valley of the Alpheos -	VIII
Delphi. The circular temple of Athena Pronoia	IX

LIST OF ILLUSTRATIONS

	Plate
Delphi. Looking down on the theatre and temple	IX
Mycenae. Lion's Gate, which leads to the Acropolis	X
Sounion. The gleaming columns of Poseidon's Temple	XI
Mournful Athena. A sepulchral stele	XII
The mountains of Thessaly and the Rocks of Meteora	XIII
Delphi. Frieze of the Siphnian Treasury	XIV
Bronze statue of Poseidon, about 460 B.C.	XIV
Bronze head of youth, fourth century B.C.	XV
Archaic Kouros	XV
Marble head of the god Asklepios, god of Healing	XV
The bronze statue of the Charioteer at Delphi Museum	XVI

Picture Section	*Following Book Page* 140
The Parthenon crowns the Acropolis	XVII
Corinthian columns of the temple to Olympian Zeus	XVIII
Ionian columns of the Erechtheion on the Acropolis	XVIII
Late black-figured lekythos, circa 510-500 B.C.	XIX
Apollon with lyre leads, followed by Hermes	XIX
Athena, and Herakles comes last	XIX
The theatre at Epidauros held seventeen thousand	XX
The temple of Athena Nike on the Acropolis	XXI
Bas-relief of Bacchos on proscenium of the theatre of Dionysos	XXI
Acropolis. The Caryatids of the Erechtheion	XXII

LIST OF ILLUSTRATIONS

	Plate
The Erechtheion from the west	XXII
The Hermes of Praxiteles at the Olympia Museum	XXIII
The site of the ancient Agora, the Acropolis at the right	XXIV
Sides of two rectangular bases for archaic Kouros	XXV
All eight sides have sporting scenes from the palaestra	XXV
On some there is still the pink background paint	XXV
A model of the civic centre of the Athens Agora	XXVI
Plan of the ancient Agora in Hellenistic times	XXVI
The use of this nursery utensil could not be understood until a similar pottery drawing was found	XXVII
Gold earrings of the fourth century B.C.	XXVIII
Gold bracelet of the third century B.C.	XXVIII
Above, gold forehead ribbon from Kos, seventh century B.C. Below, gold belt of the first century B.C.	XXVIII
Victory loosening her sandal	XXIX
The head of Hygeia, believed to be by Scopas	XXX
Lindos, on the Isle of Rhodes. Temples on the Acropolis	XXXI
The Democracy Stele, 337/6 B.C.	XXXII
Stele inscription	XXXII

PART I
THE BACKGROUND

CHAPTER I

GENERAL PERSPECTIVE

Introduction

THIS BOOK has been written because I wanted to give a book to a friend, who was visiting Greece, which would serve as an introduction to the ancient Greeks. Some books were bought and others read, but none could be found that gave an all-round picture, without being far too long. Some books had too much about battles and history and were full of names, all of which claimed just and right due to appear, but had little about the culture and less about the ancient Greeks themselves. Others dealt only with their culture and art, their architecture, or else their gods and goddesses, yet included nothing about their history and character.

A start was thus made to write this book. When a good lady was told what was being done, she replied, "And who wants to know about the ancient Greeks?" The first answer to this is that the subject is interesting, entertaining, and very fascinating. The dear lady, however, went on to say, "And what good can the ancient Greeks do for us now?"

There is much that we owe to the ancient Greeks, and there is hardly a phase of life in which their influence cannot be felt today. Not only in our language, but also in how we talk and write, and still more in how we think and in what we think about. Their influence runs through our art and architecture, our laws, our administration and system of government, our system of money, our theatres and athletic games, most of our science, and, in general, our culture and ethics. The important fact is that we can still learn from them, and today we are reverting to their outlook on life. We appreciate their tolerance and their "humanism" more than our forefathers did less than a hundred years ago. We are getting rid of many of our inhibitions.

To know them we must examine their history, for the culture of Greece is so much the reflection of momentous events that included these must be, though every possible endeavour will be made to curtail them as much as possible.

Our knowledge of the history of the Classical Period is to a large extent due to two outstanding historians of ancient Greece, than whom the world has produced none greater. The first, Herodotos, who describes the deeds of valour and the glories of the Persian wars, was a supreme narrator and an artist. The other, Thucydides, who delves into the unpleasant squalidness of the civil wars, was more of a historiographic professor, yet how wise he was, for he tells us that he writes these things, "for human nature being what it is, such things are bound to happen again."

In many aspects the Greeks were up to date, if not in advance of us.

They produced art which has never been surpassed, and probably has never been equaled. Such art cannot be produced by technical skill alone. It requires inspiration, and inspiration cannot exist without ideals, and such ideals depend on the way people think and live. It is generally considered, however, that at the time that the Greek sculptors had attained their highest perfection of technical skill, the vitality of their artistic inspiration was on the wane, and that this period in the fourth century B.C. was therefore not the very greatest of their art.

A clue to their outlook on life is that the Greeks believed that what was good was beautiful, and what was beautiful was good.

In being introduced to them we must also not forget the work carried out by the experts in putting the bits and pieces together to build up the picture of those bygone days, for it is as absorbing as any detective story could be, the main difference being that, instead of dealing with clues to a crime, we are dealing with clues about the people who gave us our culture.

Most of us already know something of the legends and myths of ancient Greece. In the last eighty years, that is, since the discovery of ancient Troy and Mycenae by Schliemann, so much has been unearthed, and so much reconstructed by the use of such clues, that we now know that all those legends have a solid basis of truth. Even the descriptions in the epics of Homer of a period three thousand years ago are proved to be accurate.

The Greeks, nonetheless, whom we want to meet through these pages, are principally the men and women of Athens of the Golden Age of Perikles, for this is the time of the greatest culture of ancient Greece, but of course we shall meet others, of other cities and other times.

Before meeting them we shall first enquire as to when they lived and whence they came; for they were not all the original inhabitants of the shores of Greece, but a mixture. In a sense, perhaps, they were mongrels, and with the full intelligence of the mongrel. It is only by understanding their origin that we can fully understand their religion and therefore their culture. To the Greeks their gods and goddesses were real people, for whom they cared as if they were their own supernatural family. Even if they were somewhat distant and supernatural relations, many of the great families did believe that they had gods and goddesses among their ancestors. The important point is that it is from their devotion to their deities that the finest inspiration in art found its source and strength.

We must hear about their environment and something about their history and their reactions, for these all are reflected in their inspiration. When we have heard of the deeds of valour of their warriors, of their oracles, and of their athletic games and festivals, we shall also be ready to follow them to the Agora, that is, the civic centre and market place, and examine their daily lives. We shall also endeavour to enter their homes, and find how unpretentious and simple they were. In Classical times there was no approval of luxury or ostentation in private life. The famous maxim that was followed in Classical Athens was that "Excellency is only to be found in moderation."

In visiting their homes we are likely to get a shock in one respect, as regards the Classical Period in Athens, for we will find how low the legal standing of women gradually became. Even though there may have been the highest respect for their reputations, we may feel that it can hardly have compensated for the tragically secluded lives that they were forced to live in order to have the privilege, whether they wished it or not, of being considered "ladies."

In Greece, as well as the wives of the free men, there were other women who were neither slaves nor concubines, but still free, and known as the "other women," the "hetairae." A balanced account of the Greeks should not entirely omit the hetairae, though in this respect they practised their precept of moderation as in everything else. Whereas this subject is curtailed as having no great significance, it does not mean that it might have embraced any undue sensualities.

The Greek called "a fig a fig," to use his own expression; he had few if any inhibitions, but quite a good measure of superstitions.

Their Background

We can now have a look at their background of time, environment, and race. So let us take our imaginary time telescope and get them into focus. When we have them in perspective we will place them in a suitable frame and have a look at the picture.

It is worth pondering just a while on exactly what distance value of time separates us from them. From the time of the Trojan War to the final conquest by the Romans, which was about a century and a half before Christ, there is a span of time a little longer than that from the landing of William the Conqueror in England in A.D. 1066 to the present day. What is more, in the last

three or four years so very much has been excavated that
goes back to a period at least equally distant from the
Classical era as we are at present removed from that era.
The period of greatest culture is much shorter, in all
about two centuries, from about 500 B.C. to before 300 B.C.
Can you conceive how very long ago all this was? It
is some twenty-five centuries ago. To understand this try
to think how very far back was the time when Napoleon
was master of Europe, when not even trains or steamers
existed, and when the American Declaration of Independence had only just been signed. If you repeat that process
of looking back another fifteen times, each time span of
the same duration, you will meet the ancient Greeks of
the Golden Age of Perikles. If you repeat it yet another
fifteen times, you will meet the ancient Greeks of the
Peloponnesos and of the Aegean islands who were making
beautiful ceramic vases and figurines. Alternatively, think
how very long ago in the remote past was the time when
Queen Elizabeth ruled in all her glory, and the might of
Spain had been laid low by the valiant seamen of England.
You will have to go back about seven times as much as
that to be in the time of the Golden Age of Perikles, when
the seamen of Athens had just overcome the armadas of
Persia. You will have to go still much further back to
the time when the men from the North descended upon
Greece and partly ousted and partly mingled with the
previous inhabitants, whose civilisation had already been
an old one.

The Environment

With the time element in focus, let us have a first glance
at the country itself.

Greece is a fair land. Some of it is strikingly beautiful,
but its beauty is never ostentatious. In many ways its
scenery matched well with the Greek character—or is it
the other way round? But why it tended to make Greek
art take the form of sculpture we will leave to another
chapter.

Though the sky line is rugged, the outlook is ever serene,

yet with a quality which whispers that man's destiny is to be up and doing. It instills a feeling of yearning which sent her sons then, and still does today, to the ends of the earth to find that intangible something which they experience in the soothing murmurs of the ripples of the sea caressing their shores—something too softly mellow to explain. Sunlight there always is, as also the blue of the sea and the sky, a richly royal blue, which is always asking you to accept it in compensation for the paucity of verdure of a sun-bathed but rather barren land.

Flying in an aeroplane over mountainous areas, and over the level of the clouds, one can gauge that purity of atmosphere which makes the horizon the only limit of visibility, and in Greece, particularly in Attica, such a pellucid air has been brought down by the gods from their abode on Mount Olympos, down to the very shores. Small wonder then that the goddesses and gods should have found it congenial to descend to these shores to mingle with humanity, share in its pleasures, and be avid for divine adventures. The goddesses and gods were well satisfied to have their temples built squarely on solid earth, blending with the scenery, erected on sites which they themselves chose in their divine knowledge of the perfection of suitability. At the altars of these temples they would come invisibly to the open-air festive ceremonies to inhale the savoury aroma of the sacrifices offered to them. For them there was no need of Gothic spires groping blindly skywards for men's prayers to reach them.

Should you visit Greece, do not lie in waiting to catch a glimpse of some goddess or god who may have taken mortal form, and do not pry into their affairs, for no man can look upon the gods without their assent and live. Content yourself then with some fleeting glimpse of some woodland or mountain nymph, or should you go to Mount Helikon, luck may favour you by the apparition of one of the Muses. It is perhaps unlikely that you will visit the byways of Arcadia, the more the pity, for there you could scarcely fail to see some centaur, half horse, half man, of whom, 't is said, that some were very wise, and in the very olden days of yore were the tutors of heroes and demigods.

If, however, you happen to be in Greece, you will find some supernatural force trying to tear you away from the relentless spirit of the age, which is ever avid to crush us in the grinding cogs of progress, forcing us on and on without pause for rest or quietude. You might climb some mountain, and there, as the sun has just dipped over the horizon, you might halt in tranquility of thought. The knowledge will dawn upon you that you have left the land where time exists and, from the remote distance, you will hear sounds from Pan ascending upwards. Pan is playing upon his reeds to the flocks. Every single note will rise to you crystalline pure and clear, and each note itself will be a song that needs not the artifice of music.

Where would you choose to go to hear these magic pastoral notes? Make your choice, and as Apollon and his chariot are drawing the sun over the western horizon, you may tell which part of Hellas you have chosen. If you see the pink-toned mountains opposite reflecting the light of the setting sun, gradually changing it into a wine-coloured glow, which, even as you look, becomes purple, you will be ready for a guess. The light has a quality which has taken all the body out of the mountains, either leaving them but a silhouette of cardboard through which you might like to push the point of a pencil, just to see if it is real, or creating them into a stage setting conjectured by the gods. If you see them then becoming mauve, you will know that you are in Attica. Look down, with me, to the centre of the plain; you will surely see the Parthenon, the temple which is the crowning jewel on the summit of the eternal rock of the Acropolis. Just look at its serenity, its hues changing in the centre of the stage, a pillared hall of crystal facets refracting the celestial light until everything is bathed in amethyst, the sea, the sky, the mountains, and the land; and, finally, before bidding us return homewards for the night, granting us to see that all-pervading miracle of colour which of old caused the citizens of Athens to call her the "City of the Violet Crown."

Perchance it will not be Attica that you choose in which to contemplate the glory of an Hellenic sunset. If the heavens are flushed with the rubicund blush of a chaste country maiden, then it is likely you will have chosen the western shores of Greece. You will know and aver this for certain when you see that roseate blush give way to a diaphanous yellow creeping upwards from the horizon, to meet the darkening blue of the sky in a horizontal stretch of emerald green, bright as the stone, but without its hardness.

If, perchance, you wish to travel north to the mountains overlooking the broad plain of Thessaly, you will have travelled beyond the lands where the culture of Greece had its finest blooms, but at sunset you will see the gaudy reds of the sky changing their tones to burnt sienna and precious amber before the farewell of parting day, as they give way to the gradual birth of myriads of bright blue diamond-scintillating stars.

You need not hasten to bed even long hours after nightfall, especially if you are in Athens, for you will need little sleep to rest a weary brain and body. Pray, do not worry what colour the sunset has been, for the land of Greece knows not of the "Red sunset at night, shepherd's delight; red sunset in the morning, shepherd's warning," for tomorrow will be another bright and sunny day, and you will rise early, as Homer says, "When early-rising rosy-fingered Dawn appears."

Perhaps you have been asked, in the last page or two, to let your fancy run away with you. It may have taken your mind away, we hope, from history and facts, and prepared you to populate this land with the men and women of old, who lived and thought very much as we do, though they wore garments (may Apollon protect me, and Fifth Avenue and Saville Row forgive me) more comfortable and certainly less hideous than those of the present days. Let us think of Athens, Athens of the Golden Age, when one comparatively small city produced, in about the span of two generations, more great names in art and philosophy, in tragedy and comedy, in science and strategy, and upon the rolls of history, than the whole of the world, with possibly the exception of our own age, has produced in one century.

The Ordinary People

Let us now consider the peoples of ancient Greece. Some difference of outlook there certainly was in different places and times, just as there was between the Edwardian times of fifty years ago and the present day, or between Hitlerite Germany, Soviet Russia, and the United States. With these differences we will deal later, but here let us try to populate these lands with people who were once alive. They were not all creative artists and philosophers, for some were barbers and hairdressers who made conversation to their clients in like manner as today, and others were stallkeepers who tried to water their fish, but only when the market policemen were not looking, for such an offense was an infringement of the law.

There were country gentlemen who preferred their country estate to city life, and this was habitual. There were some men who were too fond of gambling or drink, but of these there were few. Some gloried in wrestling and athletics, and of these, some, perhaps the less skilful, were the more boastful, while others were ever so careful about the way the folds of their himatia were adjusted, and asked, "Dear boy, do you think the colour of these Corinthian shoes tones correctly with my cloak? Just too divine, isn't it?" They were careful, too, of their table manners, as they reclined on their couches. They always washed their hands before and after meals with a special piece of doughy substance, which we, too, would do if there were no soap and we ate with our fingers. They had their pride and their vainglory, but also their humility, and the Athenian was always ready to give sympathy and assist another in need, for he was far more humane and more kindly than the citizens of ancient Rome.

So let us think of the ancient Greeks as men and women of flesh and blood, like ourselves, probably gesticulating in the fashion of the Mediterranean folk, but on the whole with more of a leaning to reason than to sentiment. The Athenians in particular had a greater sense of art, even among the common people, but a lesser of creature comforts, and in whatever they did avoiding the excessive. They were quick-witted, loving an argument, but prone to litigation. They loved the gaiety of youth and would not allow advancing age to quench it. The pomposity of a Victorian paterfamilias would have fitted ill with their character, but the memory of a departed relative was deeply cherished and sacred. They were vigorous and healthy, and lived to a ripe old age, with mental faculties unimpaired.

The Greek Scene

What of the land of Greece? It would be well to take more than an occasional look at the map, for thus we will get a better idea of their exploits and their battles, for sometimes the enemy city or state was but a few hours distant and sometimes several days' march away. The Greek himself preferred to walk. Looking at the map will also tell us how important shipping was, and how mastery of the seas was the key to power.

There surely cannot be a book about the ancient Greeks without a sentence in some form or other implying that "Greece never was one country." The nearest approach to such a conception was the early federation of the Hexapolis, the Six Cities, of Asia Minor, and even more so the interesting second Achaean League, prototypes of federated states or cities such as the United States of America or Switzerland of today. The Achaean League, however, was at a later date, and though before the Roman conquest, was, nevertheless, after the greatest days of ancient Greek history.

The reason why Greece was divided into many small cities and states can be ascribed to many causes, but the reason generally given is geographical, for Greece is very mountainous, and the mountain ranges either come straight down to the sea or leave only a narrow coastal plain. There are so many deep inlets and gulfs stretching tortuously far inland, and the islands are innumerable and, for the most part, of a fairly small size. Certainly such a country would have made central government more difficult, but not impossible, as is proved by Athens, which later held sway over an empire, and by Alexander the

Great who controlled a very much vaster territory than Greece alone. Nonetheless, in the mountainous country of Greece, which has many similarities with Scotland, though the mountains average over twice the height of the latter, there was a very strong sense of clanship which was inimical to centralisation.

The climate of Greece is indeed enviable, and though it is said that parts of Greece were more wooded than they are today, which may have meant more precipitation, rain must have still been comparatively rare, and only in the spring and winter months. During most of the year no Greek would have thought of making an appointment and adding the words, "weather permitting." Summer is hot, but has not the heat of the tropics, and in the pure, dry atmosphere, especially of Athens, the heat is quite bearable. The Greeks rose early, and even the theatres filled "dawn onwards," and so, when the sun was at its meridian, they already had had a lengthy day, and then the market place closed and they went home to their midday meal.

In this climate the vine and the olive grow to perfection. So do wheat, flax, and cotton. Fruits and vegetables are plentiful, but citrus fruit, which now prospers in Greece, was then unknown, and so, too, was the potato.

The northeast of Greece is different. Before Mount Olympos, which towers on the east coast to almost ten thousand feet, lies the broad plain of Thessaly. Beyond Thessaly to the north is the extensive land of Macedonia, with many mountains, but with rich pasture land. Here lived a people akin to the Greeks, in a land of severe winters. They tended to their cattle and to their husbandry; their civilisation lagged behind that of the south.

To the east of Macedonia lies Thrace, which stretches afar to the Dardanelles and the Black Sea. The men of Thrace were definitely reckoned as barbarians. We must not, however, get a wrong idea of what the Greeks meant when they originated this word, for there were many peoples whose civilisation they knew to be equal to their own in many aspects, and yet who were still called barbarians. Largely it implied that they had different gods, but the actual meaning of the word was of a people who had a strange language, which sounded, when they talked, like "bar-bar-bar."

CHAPTER II

PRE-CLASSICAL TIMES

IN OUR purpose of meeting the ancient Greeks, we have but one principal desire: to know how and when they attained such a supreme standard of culture, and whence came their inspiration which so cultivated their minds. In the previous chapter we dealt with the soil in which this culture grew, but in this chapter, and the next, we have to take stock of the seed that was planted, for from the quality and selection of the seed will come the flower and the fruit. We will find that this enquiry, that is to say, an examination of the human element, is by no means a simple matter, for the seed was diverse and mixed.

Two generations ago the history books on ancient Greece began with the traditional date of 776 B.C., the date of the first Olympiad, and the year one in the Greek way of reckoning dates between one city and another. We can now go very much further back, for first of all we now know that the siege of Troy was not a legend or merely a ballad, and that it took place close to, and, possibly, immediately after the year 1200 B.C., whereas, previously, many had asserted that it was completely a myth and had never occurred.

Even before Troy, in the very old days, as far removed from the Greeks of Classical times as we are from them,

PRE-CLASSICAL TIMES

there were, of course many advanced civilisations in the eastern Mediterranean lands. Sumerians and Akkadians, Babylonians, Egyptians, Cretans, Aegean Islanders, and even Peloponnesians, were people who knew and traded with each other.

The Greek historians mentioned in the last chapter have given us accounts as to what was believed in their times about the remote past, and they have told us something about the connections of Greece with the traders of these other lands. Writing about them would have been to these historians like our talking about the Saxon kings and the Vikings, or even of the Roman conquests of Gaul and Britain, but with this significant difference. Whereas we have had the existence of writing during the whole of the period subsequent to the Vikings, they only knew of its existence for a few generations prior to their own time. The knowledge of writing had faded out in Greece for well over five hundred years, and for all that period the knowledge of history was based only on hearsay.

These old historians tell us of the various princes and traders who are said to have come to Greece from other lands and founded cities, or brought knowledge and learning. We have been given the names of most of these, and they came chiefly from Egypt, Asia Minor, and Phoenicia, but the only three whom we will mention are Kekrops, who is said to have come from Egypt and founded the city of Athens on the rock of the Acropolis in Attica; Danaos, who went to Argos; and Kadmos, who is said to have come from Phoenicia and to have brought the alphabet to the Greeks.

All that we previously knew of the earlier period was chiefly contained in the two great epics of Homer, the *Iliad* and the *Odyssey*, and these have been considered among the greatest works ever composed. Indeed, there are many well qualified to judge who maintain, without any hesitation, that they are the greatest. There has been, and there still is, great controversy about Homer, and whether he even existed at all, but now it is generally accepted that he flourished in Asia Minor after 850 B.C., and that he composed his epics some three or four hundred years after the fall of Troy. These epics had the most profound influence on the Greeks, and practically up to the Christian era formed part of the education of all Greek youths, but we will revert later to the reason for their importance.

We shall not deal with the stories of these two epics, except to give the following shortest possible reminder: The *Iliad* is an episode in the great story of a prince of Troy, Paris by name, who visited King Menelaos in the Peloponnesos and was made welcome. While the king was absent on a journey, Paris fell in love with the queen, Helen, the most beautiful of all mortals. He abducted her and took her to Troy, which was close to the southern shores of the Hellespont (the Dardanelles) in Asia Minor. The Greeks were sore angered at this affront to the sacred laws of hospitality, and under the leadership of the king's brother, Agamemnon, king of Mycenae, sailed forth for Troy to avenge the wrong and bring the fair Helen back to her husband.

It took ten years to capture Troy, for the Greeks had incurred the disfavour of the gods. Finally, the well-known device of the Wooden Horse brought them victory. The story of the fight is largely that of personal challenges issued by the knightly heroes to those of the opposing camp, and in the fights the goddesses would lend aid to the hero they favoured.

The *Odyssey* tells of the ten long years that the wily and heroic Odysseus took to return from Troy to his native isle of Ithaca, of which he was the king. It tells of the extraordinary places he visited on the way, of the one-eyed Cyclopean giants, of the witch Circe who changed men into swine, of the lotus-eaters, and others. Also, it tells of how, when he finally reached his domain, he found his wife Penelope still loyally awaiting his return, and how he slew all her suitors and re-established himself.

Both epics, though recognising the inevitability of Fate and the divine order of things, require of humanity a high sense of tradition and ethics.

We know of times even far earlier than the Homeric, and we owed until quite recently all our knowledge of these times to two great archaeologists who had faith in that which the Greeks of Classical times had written about the remote past. These two backed their faith by undertaking excavations, which not only belied those who considered Troy to be a myth, but brought the site of that city to the light of day, and also unearthed remains of earlier and great civilisations. Today, even if we do not know the names of the kings and of the battles and their dates, we are accumulating a vast knowledge of the Bronze Age, which started somewhere around 2800 B.C., when the Minoan civilisation was born in Crete, the Cycladic in the Aegean Islands, and the Helladic in the mainland of Greece. We are getting to know about their art and about their habitations, and we are also gradually unearthing knowledge of the period prior to the Bronze Age, the Neolithic.

The first of the two great archaeologists whom we mentioned above was Dr. Heinrich Schliemann, who started to excavate the site of Troy in 1870. Later he went to the mainland of Greece where he excavated the ancient stronghold and "palace" of Mycenae in 1876. This was the city of Agamemnon, the king who had led the Greek host against Troy. He found in Mycenae evidence of a highly developed civilisation which had existed even prior to the Trojan War. He discovered royal graves, which he first thought were of King Agamemnon and his princes, but which are now known to have been of the sixteenth century B.C.

The other great archaeologist was Sir Arthur Evans who, in the spring of 1900, started to excavate the site of Knossos, the main ancient city of the island of Crete. He discovered what is known as the Minoan civilisation, which flourished from about 3000 B.C. till about 1450 B.C., shortly after which Knossos fell. This civilisation was already as advanced in many material and artistic ways as that of the Greeks of the mainland of the seventh century B.C., and perhaps in some ways more so.

As a result of these extraordinary discoveries more faith was given to the old legends and myths, and we feel confident that most of them, if not all of them, have solid foundations of truth.

Let us first of all examine what Sir Arthur Evans found, though it is only recently that we are starting to build up some idea of the old civilisation, and get some notion of the ancient trade of the eastern Mediterranean, so that we will not go on groping in the entire dark.

When Evans unearthed Knossos he found the palace of the king, who was known as the Minos, in the same way as the king of Egypt was known as the Pharaoh. The palace of Knossos was far larger and more elaborate than any palace or residence that has so far been found in Greece or elsewhere. The palace of Nebuchadnezzar at Babylon covered an area of 40,000 square metres but had only a single floor. That of Knossos covered 20,000 square metres but is surely believed to have had three, or even four, floors. It is reckoned that Knossos was destroyed a little before 1400 B.C., after which its power and influence fade.

The end that befell Knossos was cataclysmatic in its dire swiftness. There was not a sign that there had been even a moment's warning, and it came as a thunderbolt hurled from Zeus to the unsuspecting king and courtiers, to the retinue of workers and slaves, to the guard and soldiers. Everything, every spear dropped on the floor, every sheath of arrows which the Minoans had not even time to collect, tell, almost in speech, of this devastating nemesis which came upon them before they could even collect their thoughts. The palace of Knossos was extensive, with halls and with pillars of stone, with stairs, and with more than one floor. Their walls were painted with scenes of daily life, and they had pottery which was beautifully made and decorated, principally with marine subjects and flowers, with Minoan traditional designs, and with pictures of bull sports. There was also fine gold ware and inlaid work. They had large jars for wine and oil, and water was laid on as well, there being sanitary arrangements.

The Cretans were fond of athletics of all kinds, and especially racing on bulls; they liked dancing and music, and their art was of a high standard, some of it exquisite. The soldiers had bows and arrows and fine implements of bronze. Their ships were swift and their trade far and wide. The men wore very little, but the women had flounced skirts which we would call modern. In some instances it would seem that they wore little above the waist and did not cover their breasts.

As a result of the excavations we know that Knossos had been sacked more than once, and that at the time of its final destruction its art had already passed its prime.

The Minoans had their own forms of writing. The earliest, which first appeared around 2000 B.C., was hieroglyphic, that is, of a pictorial nature, irrespective of sound value, though it included some sound signs. The other two were of a linear script type, the earlier, being known as Linear Script A, must have evolved in Crete around 1700 B.C., or earlier, as a simplification of the hieroglyphic form of writing. It is purely a phonetic-syllabic type.

A somewhat similar script was also found in Crete when Knossos was unearthed by Evans in A.D. 1900, and this is known as Linear Script B. Clay tablets were found with a similar script in the last few years at Pylos, in the southwest of the Peloponnesos, where the palace of King Nestor, of whom the Homeric bard sung, was brought to light. These were recognised as being in the same Linear Script B, and also matched script found at Mycenae, of about 1300 B.C.

Michael Ventris was principally responsible for deciphering the script found at Pylos around 1953, but, unfortunately, he died in a motor accident not so long afterwards. There were some five thousand examples of Linear Script B, and these are accepted to be in the Greek language, although recently some quarters have stated that this is not positive.

Professor Arne Furumark, of Upsala University (Sweden), reckons that Linear Script B was probably evolved in the Peloponnesos around 1600 B.C. by the Achaeans in order to utilise the basis of Linear Script A to render the Greek language. Early in 1956 he was able partly to decipher the Minoan Linear Script A and was satisfied that this script was not in Greek. The first conclusion, hitherto a surmise, was that since the language was not Greek, the inhabitants of the island were also not Greek. Their language, according to Professor Furumark, was undoubtedly Indo-European with a basis analogous to Hittite, but including other elements. There is every reason to believe that this language was introduced to Crete by a people who migrated from southwest Asia Minor about 3000 B.C.

Linear Script B was also found in Knossos. The explanation given for this is that it was used by the Greeks when they had captured the island, and that they had brought it with them. In Script B, found in Crete, there are both Greek and non-Greek personal names, but the Cretan names are mostly of those in menial positions, possibly slaves.

The partial deciphering of Script A has already told us something about the Minoan religion, and has even given us the names of some of their deities, which were previously not known. It also offers an explanation regarding the legend that Zeus, father of the gods, was born in Crete, in the Dictaean cave. These would not have been Greek gods, but old Indo-European gods, and the Greeks, after capturing Crete, called them by the names of their own Achaean gods.

From the findings in the graves opened by Dr. Schliemann at Mycenae it was clear that Knossos had traded with Greece, since art which was undoubtedly Minoan was uncovered there. Some of the articles found in the early tombs of the Peloponnesos may possibly not have been from trade with Crete but spoil brought back at the time of the fall of Knossos. Contrarily, from the finds at Mycenae it had not been clear as to what influence Crete had had on Greece. It had originally been the opinion that, whereas the two civilisations had progressed contemporaneously, Greece was definitely not so far advanced. Very recent discoveries, however, show that Greek culture and civilisation was advanced many centuries before both the fall of Troy and the fall of Knossos. It would seem that, in the Peloponnesos, administration was well regulated, and in all probability there was a central government at Mycenae.

It is surmised that the inhabitants of Greece, in the very early civilization, before 2000 B.C., were short of stature, swarthy, with black hair, long foreheads, and brown eyes. These early Mediterranean people probably thought highly of their women, as can be judged by their deities, but there is no evidence that they were matriarchs, as has been stated, and that succession was through the female line.

Into this hazy picture came the Achaeans, and they started to trickle into Greek lands even further back than around 2000 B.C. It was hitherto believed that their full weight must have descended into Greece about 1300 B.C., but it would seem that the Achaeans were fully established well before then, having traded with Crete some three centuries earlier. The Achaeans, it is believed, were tall, athletic, white-skinned, fair-haired, with broad foreheads and blue or grey eyes.

Throughout European history there have been waves of peoples moving from central Asia and advancing westwards, then southwards, and this movement has never ceased, even if the interludes are measured in centuries. The first wave that concerns us came to Greek lands from the north and were of Aryan, or Indo-European stock. They may have come from the Danube basin, but before that they may have come from farther north, after travelling first westwards. It is really very much conjecture, but apparently they came in tribes and waves, not in any centrally organised body. These were the Achaeans, and we are now satisfied that they were Greek-speaking people. These Achaeans were less civilised than the existing inhabitants, but they had the best of it, though we do not know what fighting took place. Many of the existing inhabitants would have been killed, but in spite of this the Achaeans would have mingled with them and had children with the native womenfolk.

We are learning almost daily about these times of the remoter past. Neolithic tombs are being discovered all over Greece, including those in the Athens area. Professor John L. Caskey, director of the American School of Classical Studies in Athens, has been undertaking excavations in Lerna in the Argive Plain. Starting around 1950 and culminating in 1957, he found many proofs of an early civilisation in the Peloponnesos which was more advanced than was hitherto believed. Even in Neolithic times the foundations of the houses showed an astonishing rectangular geometric accuracy. Pottery was of cultured balance and shape, while an eight-inch-high terra-cotta figurine, unfortunately with its head and feet missing, displayed a high degree of sensitivity as well as some sensuality. Lerna is the place where, by tradition, Herakles slew the Hydra monster in performance of his second allotted labour.

Of the Achaeans there were two main branches, and these were the Ionians and the Aeolians. They settled in different parts of Greece, but it is beyond our purpose to delve into this other than noting that in Attica the civilisation became known as Ionian, though the Athenians always boasted, even with arrogance, that they had always withstood the invaders and were born from the very soil itself. The Ionian branch of the Achaeans did come to Athens, but, possibly, only two or three centuries later, when the Dorians descended upon Greece, around 1100 B.C. They would have come then as escapees from other parts of Greece, and in particular from the southern shores of the Gulf of Corinth.

Several centuries later than the bulk of the Achaean influx, there came more waves of Northerners, the Dorians. A dark age descended upon Greece which lasted many decades, during which culture was mostly dormant. These new incursions were made by the Dorians who were a little different from the Achaeans, for they were mountain folk. They came down upon Greece, descending through the central Pindos Range, and in many parts they fought and ousted the Achaeans, for they were better armed, since they had spears of iron, a metal which until then had been a rare and precious ore.

The Dorian arrival was a dark age from two points of view, one in that we know little about it and the other in that civilisation took many backward steps. Where the Dorians passed, culture withered, though they had very little influence on Greek religion, which stood its ground. It is well to take note, however, of the fact that the Homeric religion of the Trojan War was of a period prior to the Dorian invasion, but was described by Homer who lived after their advent.

The first stronghold of the Dorians was along the north

coast of the Gulf of Corinth where the massive mountains, including the prongs of Mount Parnassos, stretch out and down to the sea. On their southern slopes lies Delphi, and its Pythian Oracle henceforth showed a slight benevolent leaning towards the Doric folk.
The Dorians then built ships, and where the Gulf of Corinth is at its narrowest, crossed into the Peloponnesos. They spread over most of the peninsula, by the iron spear and the sword, and advanced to the southeast, to the valley of the Eurotas, where there were five villages clustered together, and these later formed the city of Sparta. This was the region of Lakedaimonia, also known as Lakonia, and the warlike Dorians made it theirs. It remained theirs, unpolluted by non-Dorian blood until the second century B.C., when it fell to the Romans. Later the Dorians spread still further, and Crete became theirs. They did not, however, conquer the land of Attica, which, as far as is known, was not highly developed, though it must be stressed that geometric and Helladic period tombs are being found regularly throughout its land.
Earlier, we considered the myths and legends of Greece, and expressed the opinion that most of them had a solid foundation in fact. Possibly, however, the most doubtful myths are those concerning Athens. The Athenians had their traditions and their beliefs regarding their antecedents, but there must have been a temptation to their leaders to embroider their legends of past history to suit political propaganda. Bearing this in mind, we can read the story of the attempt of the Dorians to conquer the land of Attica, which would have occurred before the year 1000 B.C.
Kodros, of the royal and noble house of Matondidae, king of Athens, heard that an army from Sparta had crossed the Isthmus of Corinth and was advancing towards the frontiers of Attica. Hastily Kodros sent runners to consult the Pythian Oracle at Delphi, and they brought back the oracular pronouncement that that army would win whose king was slain. Without hesitation King Kodros made his plans and, disguising himself as a peasant, took an ax and made for the Attic borderland close to the Isth-

mus of Corinth, where the Spartans were now encamped. There he started to fell a tree within sight of some Spartan soldiers, so that they came and told him to move away. He not only refused by asserting that he had a perfect right to chop his own tree, but so insulted and goaded a soldier that they struck him and he was slain. When, later, the Athenians came and found his body, they asked for that truce which would be granted in accordance with honoured custom, so that the body could be decently buried, adding, "for he was our king." As soon as the Spartans learned this, they became afraid, for they, too, had heard of the prophecy of the oracle, and so, of one mind, they decided that it were better to return to Sparta.

King Kodros, 't is said, was duly buried with reverence and great honour was done to his memory. So that his name should live forever in the annals of the city of Athens, it was decided that none should succeed him as king, so that all should know that Kodros was the last king of Athens, and had given his life for his city.

CHAPTER III

ARCHAEOLOGISTS AND MYTHS

WHEN THE Dorians invaded Greece there must have been much strife, and many of the previous inhabitants were killed. Some fought a losing battle and escaped to the mountain strongholds, while others were able to take to their ships, and, with whatever chattels they could collect, escape to other lands. It may be that many went to Athens, and thence (or direct from the Peloponnesos) sailed to Asia Minor, which they could easily reach by stages of short trips from island to island. Culture found its rebirth among the Achaeans who fled to Asia Minor, where the Aeolians settled in the north while the Ionians established themselves in the south.

The Achaeans thought with nostalgia of the happier, bygone days when they had been established in Greece, yet they did not remain idle and gradually built fine cities, with temples to the gods they had always worshipped. They overcame the incursions of the wild tribes from the Crimea and the north, as well as those of the "barbarians" from the south.

At night, or on holidays, they would foregather and the bard would sing to them of the heroic deeds of their forefathers. Above all they liked to hear the bard string his lyre and sing epics by Homer, stories which glorified the deeds of the heroic Achaean warriors at the siege of

Troy and told of the long wanderings of the mighty and wise Odysseus in his ardent desire to return to his homeland. To the Achaeans of Asia Minor these epics were not only the stories of their glorious past but, in a sense, they were the Sacred Unwritten Volumes from which their religion was crystallized into a final form. The attributes of the goddesses and gods, as recounted by Homer, remained undisturbed even in Classical times some eight hundred years after the fall of Troy, and even for centuries beyond that.

We have comparatively few major problems regarding the historical facts of Classical Greece, for we have such reliance on the great Greek historians, who recorded the truth as they saw it. The matter is quite different regarding pre-Classical times. For historical facts of these earlier periods we have to draw our conclusions from the excavations and the interpretations of the archaeologists.

The work of Dr. Schliemann in this field is so memorable, so original, and so interesting because it is an account of ambitions fulfilled, that his life story in short is worth recounting. We will follow it up with the myth of Theseus, which, if perhaps the least historical of the Greek myths, gives more food for thought, for ruminating, and for forming our own theories.

The Story of Dr. Schliemann

Over a hundred years ago there was a young German boy who was a poor grocer's assistant at a store. Here he sometimes served a certain customer who was an impecunious schoolteacher with a good knowledge of Homer and a great liking for drink. The lad, Heinrich Schliemann by name, had heard the bibulous schoolmaster recite Homer, and the sonorous rhythm of the hexameters was music to his ears. His imagination was fired with the exploits of the glorious past, just as the imaginations of the Achaeans had been. The few coppers that the lad saved, and could ill spare, he gave to the schoolmaster so that the spirit should move him to recite again favourite passages from

Homer. Schliemann allowed his imagination to carry him to the land where men had been so noble that the gods and goddesses themselves mingled with them and they were almost equal to the gods. Such had been their deeds of valour as to make them immortal.

Schliemann made up his mind that he would visit those lands which had inspired this heroic race, and to this ambition he decided to dedicate his whole life. In his spare time the lad learned his Homer. He also read Pausanias, a Greek of the second century A.D. who had travelled all over the Hellenic lands and who had written a guidebook account of what he had seen. Schliemann's conviction grew strong that Pausanias knew what he was talking about. If only he could faithfully follow up the guidance of Pausanias, the site of Troy might yet be found, and of other places, too, such as that of the palace of King Agamemnon, king and leader of the valiant host of the Greek heroes.

Once Schliemann's mind was made up, he devoted his life to his objective with German dogged thoroughness. The first requisite was to make himself wealthy enough to be able to carry out his ambitions, but the process was slow. For a long time it was anything but encouraging, so that there did not even seem a rift of sunshine in the skies.

After some years his chances seemed to recede and he reached the lowest ebb, for, when working as a seaman, his ship was wrecked off the coast of Holland, and though he was rescued, even his very scanty possessions were lost. In Holland he managed to find work, and his luck turned, for he was now in commerce. Here, he thought, was the threshold of vast possibilities, where instead of being employed by others, hard work and intelligence could open the doors to wealth. Avidly he learned all that he could about trade, but it took many years before fortune even began to smile on him. When at last he was prospering, and had sufficient funds to visit Homeric lands, he still held himself in check, and continued increasing his fortune, working in St. Petersburg, in Russia, where he had finally established his business.

At last he reckoned that he had a sufficient fortune. He had visited many continents and lands, but to Greece he had not yet been, nor did he go at once. He went to Paris, and for three long years, which seemed an eternity, he studied archaeology and everything that he thought could be useful for his task.

In 1870, the year when his native land of Germany was ready to strike the land of France which he had made the home of his studies, Schliemann announced to the world that he was going to find Troy. He was laughed at, and all the more so when he took his excavators to the spot which he understood Pausanias to have meant, and not to the spot, not so far distant, which had hitherto been accepted as the traditional site.

Patiently and persistently they worked, with only Schliemann's unflagging faith to urge them on. After many a weary month they were rewarded, and their efforts were crowned with complete success. Troy was found; it was brought to light. Problems, of course, there were, for, as they dug, they found not only one city, but many cities, even of a far remoter period than the "Troy of the broad Avenues," the Troy that had been besieged somewhere between 1189 and 1184 B.C. Finally it was decided that one of these prehistoric cities, the sixth or seventh, was the Homeric one, and the evidence was accepted as conclusive.

Encouraged by his success, Schliemann now had implicit faith in the descriptions of Pausanias regarding the "Homeric" city of Mycenae, for Pausanias had been told that a circle of stones within the ancient "Lion Gateway" marked the site of the tombs of King Agamemnon, and of the heroes of his household who had accompanied him on the expedition to Troy. This required more faith than the matter of Troy, for Pausanias had not seen the graves, only the stones which marked the site. Schliemann thought that Pausanias would not have reported this unless he had confidence in the story, and so he embarked on the task of finding them. He found the stones, and by systematic excavations he discovered the tombs referred to well below, and in due course these were opened.

Not only were the actual bones of the dead brought to

light, but, as Homer had said, Mycenae was wealthy in gold. There were death masks of gold, plates, drinking cups, earrings, ornaments, sword hilts, diadems and much else, all of gold. There were armour of bronze and also vessels. There were silver, ivory, alabaster, amber, crystal and enamel. There was pottery, too.

In some of the graves the artistic work was of a higher and finer quality than in others, showing a different period, but the decorative emblems and the art were analogous to that which was subsequently found when Knossos was excavated a quarter of a century later. Some of the treasures no doubt came from Crete, while others may have been by local artists of the period of the sack of Knossos, or of an earlier period. Much fitted in with the descriptions of similar things in the Homeric epics.

At the time it was believed that the tombs were those of King Agamemnon and his entourage, but this has been discounted, and generally the tombs are ascribed to the sixteenth century B.C.

And Schliemann, now the world-famous Dr. Schliemann, his ambitions being fulfilled, built himself a house in Athens and took a Greek lady for his wife. But not being immortal like the Homeric heroes, he finally died in this land of Greece.

Later, at Vaphio, near Sparta, a Greek archaeologist discovered an intact grave which had not been plundered. Among the interesting treasures were two gold drinking cups. The workmanship of these is superb, and we can be confident that they are Cretan. The embossed designs of the one show the catching of wild bulls in a net. One bull is escaping, but another has managed to impale a man on his horns. The other cup depicts bulls which are apparently tame. Perhaps the dead man had taken part in the sacking of Knossos.

Recent discoveries have thrown quite a new light on the myths of ancient Greece which previously had been treated as fairy stories of next to no value. The twelve labours which were assigned to Herakles may have been the stories of trade expeditions, and they might even be analysed as either expeditions to bring back the merchandise, or tasks to eliminate the pirates and robbers on the trade routes. The story of Jason and the Golden Fleece, for instance, might well be interpreted as an expedition to the Black Sea to bring back the "golden" corn, though the myth refers to the "Golden Fleece."

Of these myths possibly the least historically accurate is that of Theseus, but it is a myth of historic conjecture. Athens was not of much importance in the pre-Classical times and especially in the Helladic era. It does not seem to have been a civilisation centre like the Peloponnesos. The story of Theseus was more likely to have been promoted in order to kindle the civic pride of the Athenians and give lustre to their traditions, yet however much it was invented it would still have to fit in in conformity to the historic traditional beliefs. The myth of Theseus does seem to fit in with what we know of the fall of Knossos, but, apart from that, it is worth recounting as an example of the Greek genius of narration and imagery.

Aegeus, father of Theseus, was king of Athens, and one guess has been made that it would have been about 1250 B.C., but this would be wrong if it is to fit in with the sack of Knossos, which took place over a century and a half earlier. Aegeus had married a daughter of the king of Troezen, a city state on the northeast coast of the Peloponnesos. The queen preferred to live with her father at Troezen, and there the lad Theseus was brought up.

When Theseus had grown into young manhood, his mother called him one day and imparted the message which his father, the king of Athens, had entrusted to her. "Before you were born," she told him, "your father, on leaving for Athens, placed his sandals and his sword under a heavy rock. He required of me that so soon as you had grown strong enough to lift the rock and secure the sandals and the sword, to tell you that you were to go to Athens and join him, and that he would recognize you as his son by the token of these possessions."

All impatience and excitement, Theseus went to the rock, and, as we might expect, had no difficulty in lifting it.

His mother and grandfather tried to persuade Theseus to proceed to Athens by the safe sea route. Theseus, how-

ever, who knew that the overland route, by way of the
Isthmus of Corinth, was infested by highwaymen, robbers,
and wicked innkeepers, was all agog for adventure, and
insisted on proceeding by land.

Once again our hero came up to all expectations and
made short shrift of all the various terrible brigands. Included was one wicked innkeeper close to the end of the
route, who accommodated his victims in a bed, and if
they were too long for the bed and their feet protruded
at the end, he cut them off. If, however, they were too
short, he stretched them to the bed's length. This time,
however, Theseus did unto the wicked innkeeper that which
he had been practising upon others.

Theseus duly reached Athens where, without revealing
himself, he asked the king to grant him hospitality in his
palace. The king readily granted this request to the noble-looking youth, and was overjoyed later when his glance
fell on the sandals and the sword, and he realised that
Theseus was indeed his son. The king in his gladness presented Theseus to the people as his heir, and the Athenians
rejoiced, for the fame of his mighty exploits on his way
to Athens was already known to them.

Theseus had not been long in Athens before he was
yearning for deeds of valour. He went to Marathon, close
to Athens to the north, and captured the powerful wild
bull that Herakles had brought from Crete, and which
had been ravaging the countryside.

One day, a short time after this exploit, Theseus found
the whole city lamenting and mourning. He discovered
that the days were drawing near the time when Athens
had to send seven youths and seven maidens, chosen by
lot from the best families of the land, to Crete as food
for the Minotaur. This was a ferocious being in human
form, but with a bull's head, and quartered in an incredible maze at Knossos, known as the Labyrinth.

Minos, the king of Crete, had imposed this cruel punishment on Athens because, when his son had come to the
city to take part in athletic contests, he had actually
been victorious but had been slain by a possibly jealous

competitor. This was the third year in which this ghastly mission had had to sail for Crete.

When Theseus learned of the dire imposition, he insisted that he should be included as one of the youths, and he finally persuaded his reluctant father to allow him to join the others. In due course, with much lamentation, the ship sailed forth with a black sail of mourning. The king, however, gave the captain of the ship white sails and enjoined him to hoist these on his return journey, should, perchance, his son survive and be returning alive.

On arriving at Knossos, Theseus went to the Minos and asked his permission to slay the monster. This was readily granted, for not only did the Minos deem this an impossibility but he considered it was equally impossible for anyone who went into the depths of the Labyrinth to be able to find his way out unaided.

Theseus, full of heroic courage, set forth for the dread task. The Minos' daughter, however, the Princess Ariadne, had seen Theseus, and what fair princess could but fall for such a gay, handsome, and debonair prince. So she gave him a princely sword, and a reel of thread, her blessing, and, we may be allowed to guess, a kiss. She told him to tie the end of the thread to the entrance of the Labyrinth, and to unwind the reel as he proceeded so that he could find his way back whence he had come, if he were successful.

Guided by the unholy bellowing, Theseus reached the centre and came face to face with the monster and, after a long and superhuman struggle, slew it. With the help of the thread he made his way out, where he was embraced by the other would-be victims with tears of joy and gratitude.

As in most Greek plays which have a liking for the tragic, stern Fate always lurks around the corner, and so the myth terminates with the sad fact that with the rejoicing the worthy captain forgot to hoist the white sails. King Aegeus, who daily went to the sea front to look for the returning vessel, saw it coming in with the sails still black. In his distress he threw himself into the sea, which henceforth has been called the Aegean Sea.

And of Ariadne? Well, perhaps Theseus was not quite such a gentleman after all, for either he left her behind, or dropped her en route at one of the islands.

Probably the story has been too well known to you, but it has been recounted so that it can be considered in relation to the excavations at Crete. First of all the story indicates that Knossos had been mistress of the seas, and that at some period she had been able to impose her will on at least some coastal towns in Greece. From the story of the athletic games we might gather that Crete had at least some suzerainty over Athens, but also that there had once been friendly relations between Greece and Crete.

The palace that was excavated by Sir Arthur Evans was of such a size that, by Athenian standards, it could well have been described as a maze in which one could not find the way out. In Crete, too, there were emblems encountered most frequently, and obviously of a holy nature, in the shape of a double-headed ax, known as the "labrys." We can safely assume that the Labyrinth was but the Hall of the Double Axes, which could have been expected to be in the palace. It is interesting to note that these emblems were also found at Mycenae, though probably in this case the emblems were on loot or merchandise from Crete.

The bull was also holy to Crete, and coloured murals of bulls have been found in the Knossos palace. The story of the Minotaur may have shown that the Cretans worshipped some god similar to Moloch, god of an Asiatic religion in which a bull-headed monster claimed human sacrifices.

This story could fit in well to be an elaboration of an expedition from Greece to terminate Cretan supremacy, and the slaying of the Minotaur figurative of the elimination of Knossos and its power. At the time, however, when Knossos was overcome, Athens was a townlet of no significance, while might and sovereignty lay in the Peloponnesos. The story, it is noted, accepts the compromise that Theseus was educated in Troezen of the Peloponnesos and, what is more, it borrows some of the legends of Herakles to cloak the Athenian hero, Theseus.

Almost daily, archaeologists are digging up the past, and the more they do so the more we are astonished at the historic foundation of even the more improbable ancient myths.

CHAPTER IV

GODDESSES AND GODS

THE LIFE of the Greek was devoted to his city, and this was not only his first duty but his first thought, for his city held the sacred temples of the goddesses and gods. This came before everything else. He would take no action before consulting his gods, or before propitiating them by offerings or sacrifices, or perhaps pouring a libation. Generally the city, or in earlier days the kings, would consult the oracle for any action of importance, especially if war were involved.

In the historical times in which we are principally interested we note a difference between the behaviour of the Greeks themselves and that of the gods and goddesses, and yet it was the Greeks who created their deities. The Old Testament teaches that God made man in His image. With the Greeks, unlike the Hebrews, it was quite different, for they imagined their gods in their own image, but being, of course, immortal, and more noble in those matters to which they attached importance, physical perfection ranking very high.

Since the Greeks modelled their goddesses and gods on themselves, the latter had many of the human weaknesses and many of the better human qualities, and in a sense they were more human than the gods of other lands. They did punish those deserving of punishment, but not as avenging gods, for they acted with much the same tolerance, kindliness, forgiveness, and affection that parents, even if stern, show their children. We can therefore expect that the Greeks had the love for their goddesses and gods such as children have for their parents. There appears also to have been, especially in the earlier days, some feeling that even above the gods there was something to which they, too, had to bow, something which we can call Stern Necessity.

The gods and goddesses were immortal, and as a body all-powerful. We do not often hear of them quarrelling very seriously among themselves, even when they took opposite sides, so that there were only rare cases of one treading on another's toes. The gods belonged to the Olympian family, and Zeus, the "Father of the Gods," had the same say as any father of a family. We all know this would mean that, even if he had a right to a final say, there were still Mother, Uncle, and the grown-up children, who had very much their own way.

The goddesses and gods were much more tolerant than most gods of other lands, who might demand that only they, and they alone, were to be worshipped. There was no curse from God for worshipping false gods. The Greeks looked to their gods as if they were the superhuman aristocracy of their city, and, just as nobles from other lands might establish themselves in their cities, so, too, could gods visit them from other climes. If they behaved themselves and followed the established customs of the new country, they might be welcomed. Many such gods undoubtedly did come to Greece, and they all behaved themselves very much as they should. They either married into the family of Greek gods, or else they did something much more subtle—such as getting themselves merged into one of the older gods or goddesses so that, finally, you could not tell which was which.

At the very first, of course, it was somewhat complicated, for it was not quite clear whether a goddess was the wife or the sister of another god. But, as we have said, they were a happy family, and in the end they got their relationships pretty well sorted out, and in this Homer was an invaluable arbiter. An occasional divorce did take place, but it was generally done in a friendly fashion, without undue resentment, and without the existence of any gossip columns of the press to lend sensationalism.

The gods and goddesses of importance were twelve. They lived on Mount Olympos. Each had a separate residence or palace, and each had a sphere of human conduct or some quality to look after. Zeus was in the nature of a president or prime minister. The gods usually acted on their own initiative, but sometimes they held a council with joint responsibilities.

When the Achaeans started filtering into Greece they would have put many of the previous inhabitants to the sword, but they would have enslaved the women or married them. Resistance to the Achaeans would not have ceased at once, especially considering the mountain strongholds of the Peloponnesos. While, therefore, the men were fighting, the women had the care of the children. The children would first learn to worship the gods of their mothers. When the children grew up they would be taught to worship the gods that the Achaeans brought with them, and thus the gods would acquire the characteristics of both races. The influence of the Dorian gods of the later incursions into Greece does not seem to be so pronounced.

The deities of the earlier inhabitants were mostly feminine. They were earth goddesses. It is the woman who gives birth and therefore the fecundity of the soil will also be attributed to a goddess. Woman was an equal in the pre-Achaean Greek world, and possibly even a superior partner, so that it is not astonishing that their deity was the Great Goddess. As we speak of our Lord, they spoke of their Lady. They called her by the feminine name for Lord, or "Hero," which is Hera. In other parts of Greece they called her "Goddess Mother" and that became known as Demeter, the first syllable of the word being of the same root as "deus" or god. Demeter was also the Corn Goddess and the Goddess of the Fruits of the Earth. Hera and Demeter gradually became quite separate goddesses, for whereas Hera married Zeus, and therefore became his wife, Demeter appears as the daughter of Rhea, mother of Zeus, and therefore his sister.

The deities of the Achaeans were mostly male, or at least masculine. They were Sky Gods, just as was the God of the Hebrews, and just as the Lord's Prayer says today, "Our Father which art in heaven." The first Great God was Ouranos (*Latin:* Uranus), which is Greek for "sky." Heir to him came his son, Kronos (*Latin:* Saturn), whose name implies that he was the god of the Weather and Time. Kronos was married to Rhea and they had children who eliminated them. The new supreme god was Zeus (compare the Latin *Deus*), or Poseidon, the Lord God. Gradually they became separate gods, both sons of Kronos, and although Zeus became Zeus the father of the gods, or Zeus-pater (*Latin:* Jupiter), it was nonetheless Poseidon who was the elder brother.

The Twelve Olympian Gods (with their Latin equivalents) are the following:

ZEUS (Jupiter) — God of Heaven and Father of the Gods.

HERA (Juno) — Wife of Zeus. Goddess of the sanctity of Marriage.

POSEIDON (Neptune) — Originally the Horse God. The God of the Seas. Elder brother of Zeus.

APOLLON (Apollo) — God of the Sun. God of Fine Arts and Music, of Law and Order, of Moderation, and of Prophecy. Twin brother of Artemis, the children of Zeus.

DEMETER (Ceres) — Goddess of the Corn and the Crops, and of Fertility. Wife of Poseidon (who later left her). Mother of Persephone (Proserpine), who was married to Hades, king of the Underworld. Also mother of Pegasos, the winged horse. Sister of Zeus.

HEPHAISTOS (Vulcan)	The God of the Forges and metalsmiths, and the God of the Artisans.
ATHENA (Minerva)	The Maiden Goddess and Warrior Goddess. Goddess of Wisdom. Goddess of Peace. Daughter of Zeus. Athene is an older form.
ARTEMIS (Diana)	Goddess of the Hunt and of Woodland Animals, of Girlhood and of Womanhood. The twin sister of Apollon.
APHRODITE (Venus)	Goddess of Feminine Beauty and Virtue. Mother of Eros (Cupid), the youthful God of Love.
ARES (Mars)	The God of War.
HERMES (Mercury)	God of Commerce and of Heralds. God of Landmarks. Conductor of souls to the Underworld. Guardian of children. Son of Zeus.
HESTIA (Vesta)	Goddess of the Hearth and of the Home.

Of the other gods the most important, especially at a later period in Athens, was Dionysos (Bacchus), a nature god and the God of Wine. He was accredited as a son of Zeus, and seems finally to have supplanted Hestia and become the twelfth Olympian.

Plouton (Pluto) was the God of the Underworld, known as Hades, by which name he himself is often called, and was a brother of Zeus. Plouton, as the "thirteenth" god, had no celestial mansions.

Pan, the God of the Woodland Satyrs and Nymphs, had his worshippers, especially among the shepherds, and he was thus also the God of Flocks, as opposed to Artemis, who was the Goddess of Wild Animals.

There were also demigods, of whom only one parent was divine. Of these Asklepios (Aesculapius) later rose to the full rank of a god, the God of Healing. That was at a later period when more respect was being paid to science. Of the demigods and heroes, the most famous were Herakles (Hercules), Theseus, and Orpheus.

Eros, the impish God of Love, with the bow and arrows, lived on Mount Parnassos, the massive mountain towering over Delphi, where Apollon had his oracle.

The Muses lived on Mount Helikon, not so far to the west of Athens.

Satyrs and nymphs populated the wooded vales; there were the dryads who were tree nymphs, oreads of the mountains, and nereids of the springs and bubbling brooks.

And now a little about the dramatis personae of the gods, starting with Zeus.

Zeus it was who flashed the lightning and hurled his thunderbolts, which Hephaistos fashioned for him, yet Zeus it was who took hospitality under his patronage, a quality so cherished in the lands of Greece. Zeus was truly majestic, but he had a twinkle in his eye, and he was not averse to escapades, which gave his good wife, the Lady Hera, no little concern. Of such frailty and concupiscience was the occasion when the attractions of Leda proved more than divine flesh and blood could withstand, and Zeus proved himself no exception. Zeus had full-grown sons glorious to look upon, so we can well understand that his suit did not meet with instant response, for even in those days there were things that neither power nor money could buy. Zeus, however, was an old hand, and transforming himself into a swan, was soon able to bring his wooing to a successful denouement.

Hera was majestic but not matronly. She was the original Great Goddess and her conduct was such that she set a royal example to mortals. Hers was the Sanctity of Marriage, and she was worshipped in those strongholds of the Peloponnesos where the original inhabitants had strongly resisted the invaders. Thus we see her worshipped in Argos and at Olympia.

Poseidon first appears as the Horse God, and with his trident he would smite the earth and cause it to quake, but later he took to the sea and became its god. To him the mariners would pray, and Homer tells us that he was not the wrecker but the savior of ships. As a young man

Poseidon had married Demeter, and as the Sea God we can well understand that there would be incompatability of temperament with the Corn Goddess. But this was easily settled for he took unto himself as a new wife, Amphitrite, most alluring of sea nymphs, without apparently even bothering about a divorce.

Apollon, the far-shooting Apollon of Homer, he of the silver bow, was Phoibos Apollon, the shining driver of the Sun Chariot which daily traversed the vault of the heavens from east to west. As such he was worshipped with his twin sister Artemis in Delos, the small isle in the Aegean which was sacred to them. His greatest fame, however, was at Delphi where his oracle was the most famous of antiquity. Here he was Pythian Apollon, for it is said that he slew a monster serpent named Python.

Artemis was a truly feminine goddess, and though in her youth she, too, had some slight amorous propensities, she soon became the chaste goddess whose main attribute was that of Goddess of the Hunt, the Goddess of the Woodland and the Glade. In her later statues we see her tall and lithe, graceful in movement, more gliding than running, giving her protection to all wild animals. Though Hera was the Goddess of Sacred Marriage, it was Artemis who was invoked by women in childbirth. The goddess was much worshipped in Asia Minor, and "Great was Artemis of the Ephesians."

Aphrodite was born, according to the Greeks, in the semi-Semitic isle of Cyprus, and there she came from the foam (in Greek, "aphros") of the rippling waves breaking on the seashore, and at her birth the Graces anointed her with unguents. Later, even in the time of Homer, she transferred her domicile to the isle of Cythera, which lies close to the southern shores of the Peloponnesos, on the route to Crete. She is known as the Cyprian, or as the Paphian from the locality of Paphos where she is reputed to have been born, and later she is known as the Cytherean.

She has also been identified with the Oriental goddess Astarte, and this is not astonishing, for at Paphos, as also at Corinth, whose patron goddess she became, she was worshipped with un-Hellenic rites. These included the offering of maidens, during the Great Festival, to the highest bidder, the proceeds therefrom enriching the coffers of the temple. Corinth, however, was the great port of seamen, and the rich centre of the entrepôt trade, and as such was a port as all ports are today.

When Aphrodite Hellenized herself and behaved as a lady of the land should do, she was taken to the bosom of the Olympian aristocracy. Aphrodite was the Goddess of Feminine Beauty, but like all Greek goddesses who inspired the Athenians, her statues were draped, anyhow until the end of the fourth century B.C. Apart from Corinth, her feminine beauty was essentially that of the spirit as well as that of the body. She was not a disdainful goddess, for in Athens she was Aphrodite Pandemos, "of all the People."

It was more the perquisite of her son Eros to be the God of Love than her special care, but Eros surely took after his mother, whose emblem was the dove, a creature with most amorous proclivities. Aphrodite, if not the Goddess of Love, was not so far removed, for she was the Goddess of Procreation. She was also known as "The Lover of Laughter."

Hephaistos was the God of the Forge, both for the gods and for mortals. He was a helpful god and a human one, but he had not physical perfection, which made it rather unwise for him to have married Aphrodite, the divine beauty. No wonder that Homer tells us that she fell to the inducements of that warrior Ares, and that the suspecting and wily Hephaistos laid a trap by making a metal net of such incredible delicate texture as to be invisible. In this net Aphrodite and Ares were enmeshed and caught *flagrante delicto* on the sudden return of Hephaistos, for Ares to become the laughing stock, and envy, of the gods. Hephaistos was up to all sorts of such pranks and on one occasion he so fashioned the throne of Hera that once she was seated thereon she could not be removed, for he had a grudge against her. Zeus had to send Dionysos, the God of Wine, to use his persuasion with Hephaistos to undo the wrong, and Dionysos, with his intoxicating wiles, made Hephaistos relent.

Ares is a god to whom, in the kindness of our hearts, we can extend a little sympathy, for he was somewhat of an outsider, possibly even a Thracian, and so he was very lucky to have obtained an abode among the elite of Mount Olympos. His were not attributes which would call for beautiful temples to be built to him, and few were the festivals at which there would arise for his savouring the succulent aroma of burnt sacrificial offerings which might be palatable to him.

Hestia is the goddess for whom we can have sympathy, for she tended the hearth of the gods and likewise the home fires of mortals. No gay outings for her, but only the humdrum life of domesticity. The poor little Cinderella of the gods finished up with an incertitude of residence on Mount Olympos, where she was finally replaced by Dionysos.

Dionysos was a younger brother of Apollon, and when Apollon paid his annual three-months' visit to the lands of the Far North, it was Dionysos who was left to deputize for him at Delphi. Dionysos did not resemble his elder brother Apollon, who was the God of Good Order and Regulation, for Dionysos was the bibulous black sheep of the Olympian family. He was the God of the Vine, and the vine and the ivy were sacred to him. His other name is Iacchos, which is also known as Bacchus. During the Great Dionysia Festivals celebrated in his honour at Athens, wine flowed freely and the Athenians disported themselves with merriment and frenzy. Owing to a curious development, the Theatre came under his wing. The cult of Dionysos, however, has a deeper significance, for his worship increased as faith in the other gods was beginning to wane. There was an uneasy attraction towards the unknown, the mysteries of which the other gods could not explain, nor allay the fear of the "Ghoulies, and beasties, and things that go bump in the night."

Hermes, with the exception of Athena, we have left to the last, for he was a god of many parts. Like Dionysos, he, too, was a brother of Apollon, and he was a well-loved god, but he did not have the distinction of quite the same aristocratic breed as Apollon, nor could his attributes permit this, for as well as being everybody's god, he even included the thieves and brigands as those who especially worshipped him.

Far in the remote past, when the ordinary things of nature such as trees were divine manifestations, the humans would erect a mound, a stump, or a post, as a landmark, and these landmarks soon began to be something sacred under the auspices of some god, gradually becoming known as "herms."

Hermes had so many other duties and assignments that we will just record them. He was the God of Heralds and the Messenger of the Gods, supplanting Iris, who had held this appointment in Homeric times. He was the God of Travellers and the God of Commerce and Trade, and this, we imagine, is how he became the God of Thieves, for if he were the God of Trade, this would include retail trade and also pedlers, who were not of good repute in those days, for, in order to make a profit, they were not too honest.

It was Hermes who conducted the departed to meet Charon, who would row them across the Styx to the Underworld Land of the Shades. Hermes was also Hermes Epikouros, under whom came the care of young children.

Athena, or Athene, we have left to the last, for she is by no means least, and gladly will we place her on a pedestal and worship her, whether we are women or men, for she is the magnificent embodiment of all that is finest in her sex. Was not Athene of the Cretan Palaces also Athene Promachos, ever at the forefront of the array of battle? Yet-Pallas Athena was the Goddess of Wisdom, of whom the owl was her symbol, and even if she were the intrepid warrior of the spear and the shield it was but to safeguard the liberty of her citizens. Though she might avenge any wrong to her city, as she certainly did, she was also the Goddess of Peace.

Athene, the miraculously conceived daughter of Zeus, born from his brain, was the Parthenos, or Maiden, after whom her temple is named. If in the times of Homer she was but the "Kore," or girl, in the more Classical times her youthful majesty called from the Athenians the deepest respect mingled with the most profound affection. Proudly they called their city after her, "Athinai," or, as we know it, "Athens" (in the plural). To the Athenians she gave her blessing as Athena Ergane ("worker"), who teaches that however noble you may be, however exalted your position, there is no shame in labour, be it of the brain or the craft of the hands.

There are variations of the symbolic story of how she was elected to be the Patron Goddess of Athens, but they only vary in detail:

When the good folk of Attica found that the hamlet on the Rock of the Acropolis, which Kekrops is said to have founded, was spreading beyond its former narrow confines, and was becoming a beautiful and worthy city of distinction, they deemed that it was fitting for some patron deity to give it their blessing and protection. The Olympian gods therefore assembled for a choice to be made, and to vie for the honour. The Greeks, ever good traders that they were, asked for some sign, or some gift partly in exchange for the honour and partly as a criterion on which judgment could be made.

The gods and goddesses duly assembled, and by elimination it was left to Poseidon and Athena for the final choice.

Poseidon, elder brother of Zeus, the Horseman, and King of the Oceans and Seas, had the privilege of precedence. It was up to him to produce some gift, or show some token, so that the citizens could judge that he had proved himself worthy and was the god with the best qualification.

Poseidon struck the rock of the Acropolis with his trident, the marks of which can be seen to this very day, and from that spot salt water gushed forth whence arose a truly noble steed. A murmur of admiration arose, and the citizens were truly impressed; surely Poseidon would be the winner, for this beautiful horse was a gift of merit inestimable in warfare.

Now it is Athena's turn and there is a hush. With her spear she too struck the rock of the Acropolis, and on that spot there flourished an olive tree, and the admiration and approval of the citizens knew no bounds, for here was the supply of their cooking material, and their lighting fuel, and their soap, great and practical gifts. So they said to themselves, "This olive tree is an emblem of the cultivation of the soil, and prosperity-bringing peace, whereas the steed is an emblem of war." Thus, then, they voted, and they chose Athena.

Now some aver that the Athenians with one voice acclaimed Athena, as well they might and should, but there is an apocryphal story that she was elected by one vote, and that it was the women's vote that elected her. Henceforth the men no longer allowed the women to vote and disfranchised them. But this we do not believe.

Photo by *American School of Classical Studies*

Terra cotta eight-inch-high Neolithic figurine found at Lerna. Now at Corinth Museum.

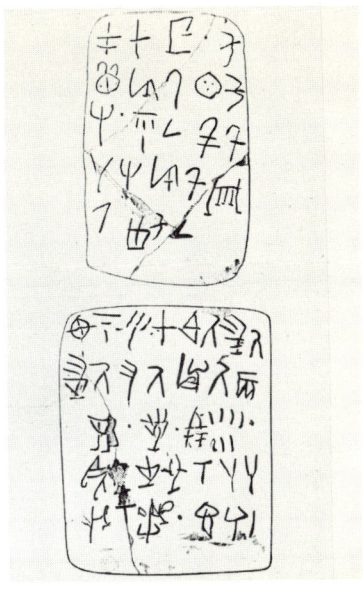

Clay tablets, Linear Script A, found at Aghia Traida, Crete.

Interior of the reconstructed Minoan Palace at Knossos

Plate I

Mycenaean gold cups of around 1400 B.C. found in an intact grave at Vaphio. The upper cup shows wild bulls, the lower, tame ones

The Prince. A coloured fresco from Knossos

Knossos. The Throne Room in the Minoan Palace

Plate III

Plate IV

Minoan mural at Knossos known as the "Blue Ladies." Heraklion Museum

Model of around 2000 B.C. of the chryselephantine statue of Athena which stood in the Parthenon.

Plate V

The eight-thousand-foot Taygetos Range dominates the Eurotas Valley and Sparta

Plate VI

Photo by Alison Frantz
Delhi, looking down from the theatre onto the Temple of Apollon

Plate VII

Photo by German Institute Olympia and the verdant valley of the Alpheos. The Sacred Grove of the Altis is among the fir trees

Delphi. The circular temple of Athena Pronoia

Delphi. Looking down on the theatre and temple

Plate IX

Mycenae. The massive Lion's Gate which leads to the Acropolis and the royal graves

Photo by N. Stournaras
Sounion. The gleaming columns of Poseidon's Temple

Plate XI

Courtesy National Archaeological Museum (Athens)
Mournful Athena. A sepulchral stele

Plate XII

Photo by Spyros Meletzis   The mountains of Thessaly and the Rocks of Meteora, a formidable northern barrier

Plate XIII

Delphi. Frieze of the Siphnian Treasury depicting the battle of the giants against the gods.

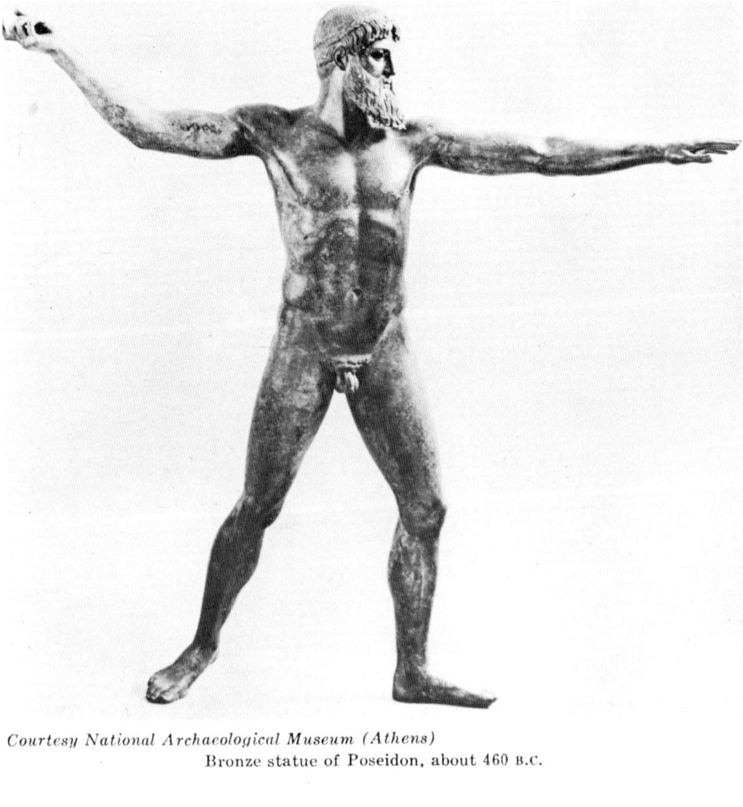

Courtesy National Archaeological Museum (Athens)
Bronze statue of Poseidon, about 460 B.C.

Plate XIV

Courtesy National Archaeological Museum (Athens)
Bronze head of youth, fourth century B.C.

Courtesy National Archaeological Museum (Athens)
Archaic Kouros

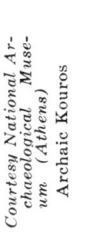

Marble head of the god Asklepios, god of Healing

Plate XV

The bronze statue of the Charioteer at Delphi Museum. Circa 470 B.C.

Plate XVI

CHAPTER V

EARLY SPARTAN SUPREMACY

AFTER THE early Dorian invasion of Greece, which probably started around 1100 B.C., or possibly a little earlier, we hear nothing of historical interest for a very long time. Athens had not yet attained any importance like that of some of the Peloponnesian cities, and in a small way was pursuing the peaceful path of expansion.

We must bear in mind that the art of writing, as in Linear Script B, had become extinct in Greece and for some five or six centuries was unknown. Further, on two occasions, Athens was sacked by the Persians and therefore there is comparatively little to be found of the days previous to 479 B.C. which the Persians had not destroyed in Attica, though much pottery and other vestiges of this earlier period have been unearthed in the last few years. These recent finds throw much light on this dark age, which followed the Mycenaean era, known as the Geometric Period, that is, from about 1100 B.C. to 600 B.C. These vestiges show art of a struggling but fair standard, yet still below that of the Mycenaean Age, as well as that of the Minoan culture.

After the somewhat mythical King Kodros, the last Athenian king, archons, or rulers, were elected. At first they were chosen for life and, later, for ten years, but they were elected only from the royal family of Kodros (the Matondidae). Then they were elected annually, but only from the nobles, until about 500 B.C., after which they were elected by lot.

Let us now, however, turn to Sparta, stronghold of the Dorians. They differed so much from the Achaeans, yet they had the same gods and the same language, differing only in dialect. They also participated in the Olympic Games, which, indeed, they first revived and sponsored. Their ideals were different, so too their customs and culture. Sparta, unlike almost all other Greek cities, was situated away from the sea.

The Dorians took their lands by the sword and the spear. Those who offered resistance they made slaves, as also those who tilled the soil. They called their slaves "Helots." Those who had not resisted had a measure of freedom, but they were not allowed to be citizens; they paid heavy taxes and became the artisans and merchants.

The citizens of Sparta were always only a few, whereas the artisans, and especially the Helots, were very many. The Spartans treated the Helots harshly and their hate smouldered. When the Helots rose in rebellion, their insurrections were quelled unmercifully, and many were slaughtered. Thus their resentment grew all the stronger, so that the Spartans, whether they liked it or not, were forced to live on the alert, as soldiers, ever ready for battle against a foreign foe, or against insurrection within their midst.

Sparta had a famous lawgiver, Lykourgos, of whom there are many stories. He is said to have been of royal descent, and to have acted as regent until the heir to the throne reached manhood. He then travelled to many places of the then known world, including Egypt and Asia, always learning. On his return to Greece, after many years abroad, the Spartans, who now found themselves in a chaotic state, their king having been killed in battle, sent for Lykourgos and begged him to come and restore order in their city.

Lykurgos first consulted the oracle at Delphi. The seer pronounced that the laws that he would give to the Spartans would make their city strong so long as they kept them. Thus assured, he went to Sparta and gave the city laws which regulated the whole of Spartan life and to which it always adhered.

Sparta had previously been a kingdom, with nobles and landed gentry. Now Lykourgos divided the land into equal lots, one of which was assigned to each Spartan family, not to be their property, but that of the city. They did not till the land themselves; this was done by the Helots, though the Spartans got the produce.

The government of Sparta consisted of a Senate of twenty-eight members, all over sixty years of age, and the Senate elected five ephors who were the real governors and had great power. The ephors even controlled a secret police which could kill any Helot on mere suspicion. There were also two kings who were the generals in time of war and the high priests in time of peace, but the power of the kings depended very much on their personality. For any decision, however, of real importance, such as the choice of war or peace, all the Spartans over the age of thirty were called to a meeting of the Senate and allowed to cast their votes.

The most important legislation by Lykourgos was on the upbringing of the Spartan children. At birth, if a child were defective, it was not allowed to live, but was hurled over a chasm, the *Kaida*. The boys were brought up to be good soldiers and, at the age of seven, were taken away from their parents and quartered in barracks. Their lessons, if we can call them such, were entirely for military purposes and consisted of physical exercises, war songs, and the like. They were taught to be hardy and were not encouraged to read or write. They had to sleep out of doors on beds made of reeds.

After the day's exercise and work, all male Spartans ate at communal feeding rooms, and this even applied to the two kings. Their food consisted of a "black broth," mostly of pork meat, which in the opinion of non-Spartans was not very appetizing.

The Spartans did not have walls to their city, for they

said that the valour of their sons should be their safest protection.

The Spartan women, too, were brought up to be tough, and they did physical exercises; the management of the estates was left to them. When the Spartan men went to battle the women handed them their shields and told them to return either with the shields or upon them. They were to return victors, or with their bodies on the shields.

When the Dorians overran the Peloponnesos they made the five villages of which the city of Sparta was constituted their own. We do not know, however, quite what happened to all the other famous cities. Argos, under a certain King Pheidon before the year 700 B.C., grew powerful for a time. Corinth, which became Dorian, prospered, too, and founded the colony of Kerkyra (Corcyra, or the modern Corfu). We also have knowledge of the independence of the men of Elis in the west, where Olympia is situated. They were distinct from the Dorians.

In the centre of the Peloponnesos, however, are the rugged mountains, some well wooded, and the land of phantasy of ancient Greece, Arcadia. Here there were ravines, glens, and many springs, all populated by the imaginery nymphs and satyrs, where Pan made fairy music to them on his reeds. It was free of Spartans.

The whole of the south of the Peloponnesos is divided by a mighty range, Mount Taygetos, stretching from the centre to the sea. To the east of this range is the region of Lakedaimonia, or Lakonia, which is the Spartan region, while to the west is Messenia, with broad, coastal, fertile land, as well as an interior plain surrounded by mountains. This land had not been overcome by the Spartans.

Many years had gone by after the Dorian invasion, perhaps three hundred, and the Messenians were living peacefully as good farmers. They even attended, jointly with the Lacedaemonians, a temple that lay midway between their two lands, and here, at the temple of Artemis, the Spartans who were hankering after the rich Messenian lands, found the pretext for a quarrel and tried to seize their neighbours' lands by force of arms.

The peaceful Messenians were not prepared for war

and had to seek refuge in their mountain stronghold of Ithome, where they were besieged, and soon were sore pressed by hunger. The story tells us that they managed to get a messenger through the besieging army to go and consult the oracle at Delphi, but that the oracle announced that for the Messenians to obtain victory they would have to sacrifice a maiden of the nobility. King Aristodemos of the Messenians, with a heavy heart thereupon sacrificed his only daughter. Some say that he then immediately committed suicide, while others report that he finally died of sorrow and a broken heart.

The king's sacrifice, however, gave such ardour to the Messenians, that they sallied forth from their stronghold, attacked the Spartans, beat them, and were even successful in killing one of their two kings.

Their success was of short duration, for on the death of the Messenian king, the Spartans attacked again, overran the Messenian fertile lands and divided them among themselves, while the Messenians were made Helots and were obliged to cultivate the soil for the Spartans.

The Spartans kept the Messenians underfoot, and they grew to resent their harsh overlords more and more, until some eighty years later Aristomenes decided to put an end to their bondage and went clandestinely from village to village preparing the ground until the Messenians were ready to rise. He was successful and the Spartans were turned out of the lands of Messenia, and were chased to the outskirts of their own city. One night Aristomenes was even able to creep into the city, enter the temple of the Goddess Athene, and hang a shield which he had captured and which he dedicated to the goddess.

The Spartans were now in difficulties, for as well as losing the rich lands of the Messenians they were afraid that the other Helots would rise up against them. In their perplexity they did a curious thing, for they sent to Athens to ask for assistance, though there was no love lost between these two cities.

The Athenians, in order to make fun of the Spartans, sent them a deformed poet, or bard, named Tyrtaeos, who, however, took his task seriously and composed stirring patriotic war songs which so aroused their patriotism, and kindled their ardour, that they set forth aglow with courage, and beat the Messenians.

The Spartans treated their captives harshly and threw the captured men over the *Kaida* chasm, including Aristomenes. Legend says that somehow he was not killed, but escaped through holding onto the tail of a fox which had come to prey, and that he thus found the aperture by which the fox had entered. Aristomenes regrouped the Messenians, but the struggle was hopeless and, after ten years, he gave up and finally died on the Isle of Rhodes, while the Messenians remained Helots.

Sparta, by this time, had virtually become the overlord of all the Peloponnesos. These battles, which took place during the seventh century B.C., gave a still further impetus for men to flee overseas, and this resulted in the colonisation of Sicily and southern Italy.

CHAPTER VI

THE GREEK COLONIES

NOW WE CAN consider the Dorian invasion and Spartan supremacy from the viewpoint of being chief causes of the Achaeans leaving the mainland of Greece and seeking other lands. First in Asia Minor, and later in eastern Sicily and southern Italy, renewed culture and civilisation had their infant nurture and adolescence, later to bloom in Athens. Because it was in Athens that culture blossomed, and because Herodotos tells us the story of the Persian wars with such details and as a supreme and masterly artist, we consider that the foundation of European civilisation and its history were laid at the Athenian battles of Marathon and Salamis. Indeed it was, yet events took place in Sicily which were equally momentous, but these are not usually given such prominence.

From early years there had been settlements of Greeks on Mediterranean shores, principally to the east and extending to the Black Sea, but the Greeks also pushed into the western Mediterranean. We are fairly confident that Minoan Crete even traded with Britain. Crete certainly possessed amber which is believed to have come from the North Sea coast of Germany. Britain was well known to Herodotos, who calls it the "White Iron Islands," that is, the Cassiderean Isles, for tin was of the utmost importance to the Greeks. There were few known available sources, yet its admixture is essential for the manufacture of bronze.

The first movement of consequence of Greeks to lands overseas came soon after the fall of Troy, on the arrival of the Dorians. First went the Aeolians to the shores and islands of the northwest coast of Asia Minor. About a hundred years later, the Ionians followed them and settled on the southwest shores of Asia Minor and among its coastal islands.

The settlements and "Colonies" on the other side of Greece were not founded till two or three centuries later. As we have already mentioned, Corinth was among the first to sponsor these, which was natural, since she lay astride the isthmus which was the main juncture of the east-west trade of ancient Greece.

Later, in more historic times, colonies were founded from an impulse of a more economic nature, "for poverty was ever a sister to Greece." As the cities of Greece were trading and expanding, and population was fast outgrowing the productivity of the barren and mountainous lands, many would have decided to try their luck and seek their fortunes in the "new," undeveloped lands overseas.

These expeditions were no longer settlements, but organised "Colonies," and the contemporary "Pilgrim Fathers" sailed with the full blessing of the "Mother City," which was astute enough to know that trade would follow the establishment of these offshoots.

No colony would normally be founded unless the organiser first visited the oracle at Delphi, the purpose not being so much to gain a glimpse into the future prospects that the gods might have in store for the adventure as to have the assurance that it was undertaken with the gods' blessings and was not contrary to their will. The Pythian Oracle would receive the munificence of their votive offerings, and then pronounce the organiser as the founder of the prospective new colony. Here, too, in Delphi was the central pivot, whither suppliants came from near and distant lands, so that in essence it would become the Central Bureau of Information and Military Intelligence, the value of whose advice would be beyond compare as

THE GREEK COLONIES

to the nature and fertility of prospective foreign lands, and the proximity or danger of hostile tribes.

On returning from Delphi to the Mother City, the founder of the new colony would be a man whose name would be reverenced, as duly approved by the gods. Later, when he died, and prosperity was dawning upon the new city, he might even be deified.

The founder would get on apace with the organisation and on the appointed day for the departure there would be festivities. With pomp and ceremony the colons would go in procession to where the Sacred Flame of the Mother City burned, and there a torch would be kindled, after which friends and relations would join and in a body go down to the sea to wish them Godspeed. The torch would be borne unextinguished to distant lands to light the flame of the new city and to keep the fire of kinship in sacred union with the Mother City. In their turn the new cities might found other colonies of their own, and the same flame would sanctify the close ties between the Mother City and her grandchildren.

In the meantime in Asia Minor the rising Greek cities were warding off wild tribes from the Crimea. These tribes were yet a further example of those Northern races propelled with a surge to move westwards and southwards. In the south of Asia Minor there was the king of Lydia, and beyond him the king of the Medes and the Persians, whose eyes were attracted by the glitter and the magnificence with which the Greek cities of Ionia were beginning to shine. They noticed, too, that these Greek cities were becoming such mistresses of the seas that their own trade was being constricted, and so they stretched forth to seize them and possess them and to curb their interference. For these and other reasons we next find the Greek cities of Asia Minor founding colonies themselves and extending far afield. We find a colony being founded at Byzantium (later Constantinople), one in Cyrene in North Africa, and even one in Egypt itself, with the permission of the Pharaoh, whom the Greeks had helped with such military power as to earn his gratitude. Especially we note that, about 600 B.C., the men of Phokaia, in Ionia, founded the city of Massilia in the south of France, the present-day Marseilles.

The Greeks were, however, by no means the only pebbles on the beach. There were others who contended for these new lands, for the Phoenicians, too, were great seafarers and colonizers, and they had founded the proud and mighty city of Queen Dido on the north coast of Africa in what is present-day Tunis. This city of Carthage was as mighty as any city of her day. Carthage held in her sway both Sardinia and Corsica, and she had settlements on the west coast of Sicily, with which, however, the Greek colonies of eastern Sicily at first did not clash, for as yet there was ample room for both.

At this time in central Italy there was another race of Northerners who may even have descended upon Italy at the time when the Achaeans were coming down upon Greece, and who were vaguely known to the Greeks, even from the time of Homer, as the Tyrseni. They were a seafaring as well as a warlike race and they traded with Greece, having a great liking for the Athenian ceramics. Their ships were in friendly relation with the Carthaginians, and had sided with them in somewhat piratical fights to capture trade.

These Tyrseni, or Etruscans, had a famous king, Lars Porsena of Clusium, who had come into contact with a townlet in central Italy, which, although it had not yet risen to the ranks of the high and mighty, had yet given foretaste of her military prowess, for this city of Rome had been able to withstand and survive the onslaught of the Etruscans.

We might think of Rome in those days and remember the old English saying that "fools build houses for others to live in them," for while Rome was fully occupied with the Etruscan danger, Syracuse, the Corinthian colony on the east Sicilian shores, was keeping at bay the far greater menace to Rome, and keeping free the lands for Rome eventually to build her empire.

We can well imagine that when a petty quarrel arose among the Greek cities of Sicily, and one of these appealed to Carthage, the latter was delighted with the opportunity to try to add the whole of Sicily to her dominions.

At this very time the Athenians were in great distress, for a fleet the size of which the world had never seen before, and an army reckoned at two and a half million combatants, had been led into Athens itself under the command of the king of Persia, who had vowed to have revenge on the Athenians. The Athenians sent to Syracuse for help, but Syracuse refused and gave a haughty reply, but the real reason for its refusal surely was that it was in similar peril itself.

Hamilcar the Carthaginian had set sail with a fleet of hundreds upon hundreds of ships, and in them was an army of three hundred thousand soldiers. They landed in Sicily at the Greek city of Panorma (present-day Palermo) and made ready to seize the island.

His opponent was Gelo the "tyrant" (Greek for governor) of Syracuse, who enlisted the help of his father-in-law the tyrant of Akragas (the present-day Agrigento) and one of the greatest battles of the world's history ensued.

Hamilcar, whose mother is believed to have been Greek, was hardly a great general, for he spent most of the day of battle in prayer and sacrifice to the gods, but the gods help those who help themselves, and his prayers were of no avail. By nightfall there was but one solitary surviving Carthaginian ship which escaped and returned home to tell the tale. Of Hamilcar and the three hundred thousand men it is reckoned that about half, including Hamilcar, were slain, and the other half were taken into captivity.

And so this battle of Himera occurred in the year 480 B.C., at the very same time, and possibly on the selfsame day, as the battle of Salamis, which latter assured that the future of European civilisation should be Greek and not Persian. The battle of Himera gave the breathing space during which Rome could grow powerful and finally add a Roman civilisation to the future of Europe.

In the south of Italy the Greeks also had powerful cities, and it had become so Hellenised as to be known as Megale Hellas, or Great Greece. Of these cities the best known today is the "New City" or Nea Polis, which we now call Naples. Here in southern Italy, six years later, the brother of Gelo, who had succeeded him, came to the assistance of one of the Greek cities and smote the Etruscan fleet.

He shattered it out of existence, thus rendering yet another service to Rome and enabling her to live another day.

Carthage had vitality, and she still had enough power to interfere with Greek trading ships in the western Mediterranean. Over one hundred years later her roots had sprouted again, and in 347 B.C. she was able to follow up her ambitions and launch another attack to try to capture Sicily. One thousand Carthaginian ships sailed forth with 70,000 foot soldiers and 10,000 horse, and they were opposed by Syracuse with but ten thousand men, yet at the battle of Krimissa the Carthaginians suffered another defeat which was as devastating as before.

In the meantime Rome continued to grow powerful, while Syracuse had passed its zenith. Hannibal now led his Carthaginians through Spain and across France. Then he crossed over to Italy and prepared to attack Rome, and though the fate of Rome was truly precarious, yet the balance was tipped in her favour. When Rome was finally victorious over Carthage, she considered that the Punic City had been so dangerous and had shown such vitality that she decided "Destroyed Carthage must be," and Rome tore out the Carthaginian roots so that there would not be a stone standing, and Carthage would be no more.

Of the history of the Greek colonies of Sicily and Megale Hellas we shall refer no more, but we will encounter the citizens of these lands when we deal with the birth of Greek philosophy.

We will have, now, a further glance at the adventurous, seafaring spirit of the Greeks, and we will take our thoughts to the more distant city of Massilia (Marseilles) in the south of France. It had little trade with Greece, and this might be ascribed to Carthaginian interference, or to the fact that its Mother City, Phokaia, was now under the suzerainty of the Great King, as the king of the Medes and the Persians was known to the ancient Greeks. That which is of especial interest to us is that the Greeks of Massilia were trading with Britain soon after the foundation of their city, and we even have the name of one of these very early traders. Our knowledge, however, of this period is scanty.

Here we may well tell the story of Pytheas, a worthy

THE GREEK COLONIES   57

sea captain of Marseilles, who set out one early spring morning to visit the land of Albion, as Britain was then called, at about the time that Alexander the Great was conquering the East, towards the end of the fourth century B.C. Pytheas went for pleasure and profit, his pleasure being that of the explorer, and he reported his whole voyage, though we do not have his direct account. Strabo, an Ionian who lived just before the time that Julius Caesar landed in Britain, gives us much of this report, but Strabo himself did not believe it and says so, with the result that this most interesting "discovery" of Britain has been given no prominence.

Pytheas was a sea captain, well skilled in the art of navigation, learned, and with an up-to-date knowledge of astronomy. He was known, by repute, to one of Aristoteles' pupils. He visited the tin mines of Cornwall and found the natives of Britain of a friendly disposition and hospitable. He did whatever trade he had come to do with the people of the West Country where the tin was collected and transferred to the Isle of Ictis, which may have been the Scilly Isles, or more likely Saint Michael's Mount, and then set sail along the Irish Sea on discovery bent.

Pytheas rounded the north of Scotland, and reports that the headland which stretches into the sea is called Orca, which we can recognize as the Orkneys. Thence he sailed southwards until he reached that part of Britain which is nearest to the continent of Europe, and which he tells us was called Kantion, and which surely was Kent. He was told that it lay eleven miles from the mainland and that the sea forms a strong current.

Britain, he reported, was triangular and of a similar shape to Sicily. Beyond Britain to the far north, was the Isle of Thule, which was six days sailing distance to the north, which was the same sailing time that he gives from the north of Brittany to Cornwall. It is unlikely that he was referring to Iceland, but more likely to the Orkneys.

From Britain Pytheas sailed to the German shores for amber, and finally returned to Marseilles before the bad weather set in, before the end of October.

CHAPTER VII

THE OLYMPIC GAMES AND THE ORACLE AT DELPHI

WE HAVE grouped together into one chapter these two diverse subjects, not because they were peculiar manifestations of the Greek religion but because they were the magnetic points whither all Greeks might convene and there be conscious of their common language, religion, and affinity.

Both institutions had well established pre-Dorian roots, and both underwent strong Dorian influence in their early days. Both flourished for well over a thousand years.

Athletic games were held in many cities, and in Athens we saw that there had been games before the times of Theseus, for at these the son of the Cretan Minos had been killed. There were games in Arcadia, and in Corinth to the honour of Poseidon; especially there were many games in Asia Minor, whence attendance at Olympia would have been somewhat distant. After the games at Olympia, the Pythian Games at Delphi ranked highest in esteem and popularity. The games were definitely of great religious significance, and they were backed by institutions which aimed at peace for the Hellenic world.

The localities at which these two great gatherings were held could scarcely be more scenically contrasting. Olympia, which is near the west coast of the Peloponnesos, is set in gently undulating land, broadly smiling with the gay verdure of bright vine leaves, and with the silvery ripple of its two humble rivers. Delphi, facing southwards, is set high on a fairly narrow ridge over a deep gorge. Above it is the menacing grey-blue wall of a high cliff which rises precipitously and continues upwards, though out of sight, eight thousand feet and more to the summit of bulky Parnassos. Delphi nestles in a cleft on this ridge, close to the Kastalian Spring, while opposite is the sloping wall of another but less ambitious mountain. It would almost seem that Apollon, the "Hyperborean" of the extreme North, himself chose the spot, built by nature into a natural majestic cathedral, for the mountains rise to meet the blue vault of the heavens in a manner almost Gothic in conception. A few minutes' walk away, round the corner to the west, and you are high above the valley of Amphissa, or Krissa, a grey-green sea of dully shimmering olive, and beyond the Krissean Plain rise more mountains, range upon range, into infinity, capping even Parnassos in height. From your vantage point, just around the bend, you can also get a view of the deep blue of the Corinthian Gulf, backed by the Peloponnesian mountain ranges.

At Delphi you are on hallowed ground, and you will get that peculiar feeling, common to most of Greece, but far more pronounced here than anywhere else, that time has stood still, that you are neither in the present nor in the past, nor in the future either, and that the epoch of the oracle and of the Pythian Games are removed by only a matter of days.

The festivals of each, of Olympia and of Delphi, are of a sacred nature, but when we try to visualize them as living scenes, let us rather think of the concourse of vast fairs, or of multitudes that might assemble for the great racing event of the year.

The athletes are already there, but so, too, are the lords of Hellenic lands, for the horse chariot owners have come in force to see how their entries will fare. Should they win a race it is they who will get the honour and inflate themselves with pride, and not the skillful chariot drivers.

Delegations are now arriving composed of the most illustrious members of the Greek-speaking cities, and for them the organizing committees have reserved seats. Each delegation vies to reflect the magnificence of its own city by the show of its individual splendour and the munificence of its votive offerings. Sparta will be strongly represented, but alone of all the delegations it will avoid all ostentation, yet impose by its Laconic aloofness. The Athenians will vie with the plutocratic mercantile Corinthians whom they will try to outdo in good taste, and with the courtiers of Megale Hellas and Sicily.

It is a mighty crowd, thousands upon thousands, pitched in their tents for miles around. It is fair game for every performing huckster, for the owners of the dancing bears, for the vendors of dried figs, salted marrow seeds, roasted chick-peas, unmixed Chian wine and local Elian wine, of finest Sicilian cloth, of unguents from the East, of salted and pickled olives, and of beribboned garlands. Of such would be the scene spreading around the central temples and the stadium, but remember that the beribboned garlands are for the men's evening wear and not to grace any fair feminine heads, for women may not attend the games, and on no account, for in the case of the Olympic Games, should they even cross the river Alpheos, death is the penalty.

The Olympic Games

First let us proceed to Olympia, for this year is that of the Olympiad. Every fifth year it is held, according to their way of reckoning; that is, with four years intervening, and thus, according to our way of speaking, every fourth year. So, too, are the Pythian Games, but three years after the Olympic Games. You may well ask if it were not simpler to describe the Pythian as taking place in the preceding year, but that would not be the correct way, for Greek chronology is based on the Olympiad.

It was probably nothing to do with any religious import that made the Greeks choose the Olympiads as the method of reckoning their dates, but the fact that each city had its own calendar, its own months with totally different names, and the New Year of each might start in any of the seasons. Thus, for inter-Hellenic understanding, what better choice than one based upon the pan-Hellenic venue? The Olympic Games were, supposedly, originally founded by the demigod Herakles and his apogeny, and traditionally refounded around 884 B.C., but the official date from which records were kept, and the one which was made the Basic Year, was 776 B.C., and this was Olympiad the First. Thus, then, as an example, the year 490 B.C. would be the third year of the seventy-second Olympiad. In practice the Olympiads were not named by their arithmetic order, but by the winner of the first man's race, the sprint of one length of the stadium, some two hundred yards, in which Koroebos attained everlasting fame by winning this event in the first Olympiad.

As the time for the games drew near, peace heralds were sent to all lands of the Hellenic world. They announced the games and demanded that there should be a truce from fighting during the whole of the month in which the games were held—fourteen days before and after the full moon. During that month the whole region of Elis, in which Olympia is situated, would be sacred and in it no man must bear arms. In the early Olympiads entries were almost entirely confined to the Peloponnesos, to judge from the provenance of the victors as recorded, but after about 600 B.C. there are entries from all Greece, and from Sicily and Megale Hellas. Even later, most victors hail from overseas cities.

The total duration of the games was for five days, the first being devoted to ritual and organization. The judges, ten in number, were chosen from the people of Elis, and very proud they were of the purple robes which distinguished them, nor was their task a sinecure, for first they had been tutored and trained for ten months by the Elian magistrates. The period of training for the athletes compulsorily was the same, and the last of these ten months was spent in supervised training at Olympia itself.

At the beginning of the games the athletes underwent close scrutiny and had not only to swear but also to prove to the satisfaction of the committee that they were of pure Hellenic blood, that they had not been convicted of any crime which was considered a disgrace, and that, further, they had fulfilled the correct period of preliminary training according to the rules. During the last month the athletes were fed on beef, probably raw, though such meat was not to the liking of the Hellenes who had no predilection for meat at all. They had to swear that they would keep the rules and play fair.

The programme of contests did not vary very much in scope from Olympiad to Olympiad, but occasionally there were innovations. It is doubtful whether there were any actual contests on the fifth day, which would be taken up with prize giving, processions, sacrifices, and the banquets given by the Elians to the city delegates and the victors.

Of the games themselves there were normally twenty-four, six of which were for boys, and these were held on the first days. The blue ribbon was given for the sprint of one length of the stadium, and the winner of this event gave his name to the Olympiad. Of importance, too, was the pentathlon composed of five contests, which events do not appear to have been included separately. The javelin throwing and the discus were part of the pentathlon. Running included races of medium and long distances, and also one wearing full armour. Other events were wrestling, boxing, and the pankration, which was an all-in-catch-as-catch-can affair with but very few limitations. It was viewed with disapproval and was prohibited for boys.

The chariot races, of which there were several, were differentiated as to full-grown horses, or foals, and as to fours or pairs, and they seem to have been more important than the horse races, one of which was for mares only. There was no high jump, but the leap was an event peculiar to the Greeks. They took but a fairly short run and held halters, and by somehow swinging these they were able to increase the length of their jump. We find it hard to believe that in the leap they recorded jumps of fifty feet or over, and yet we have no reason to discredit their accuracy, for we can also take into account the prodigious performances of some of their feats of running on missions on historic occasions, which showed an endurance far greater than that of today.

The prize for the victor was a garland made of olive

THE OLYMPIC GAMES AND THE ORACLE AT DELPHI 63

branches cut by an Elian boy whose both parents were living. It was cut with a golden knife from the olive tree which Herakles himself is credited to have planted. In parenthesis it is interesting to note that there is still a famous olive tree in that olive grove at which Platon taught and which went by the name of *Akadēmeia*, and which botanists aver was a contemporary of his, some twenty-four centuries ago.

The honour of prize winning gave glory incomparable. The victor would make a thanksgiving sacrifice at the altar of Zeus in that magnificent temple in which Pheidias had spent five years, around 450 B.C., in his sculpture of Almighty Zeus. This was a seated statue with the sceptre and the eagle, and of such proportions that the head reached the roof of the temple, the face and body being of ivory and the robes of gold. The victor would also be a highly honoured guest at the official banquet, among the elite of the Hellenic world, and in all probability his fellow citizens would commission a statue to be erected in the grove sacred to Zeus. Still greater honours would await him on his return to his Mother City, and surely there would be a procession formed to meet and welcome him. Some cities might even make a token demolition of their walls through which the heroic victor might enter, thus to show that with such sons, his city required no walls for its protection. No doubt, too, prize money would be voted for him, and almost certainly, if he so wished, there would be free meals for him for life, at the city's expense.

Before concluding with the Olympic Games we must note that in Classical times there were at least some who disapproved of the overadulation of the athletes, especially among the philosophers, and for various reasons. One such reason was that excessive training did not result in that perfection of the human figure which, all said and done, was the cause of the inception of the games as an act of religious expression, since overdeveloped muscles are neither graceful nor artistic. Another reason was that philosophers and others deplored the glorification of brawn over brain. Some considered that the type of training and its heavy demands caused it to be supported by a type that became professional, and egad, not your amateur gentleman. Of this last opinion there was good ground for complaint in its application to the boxers, wrestlers, and pankratists, for their training grounds—that is, the palaestra (wrestling clubs), as opposed to the gymnasia (athletic clubs), were not frequented by most gentlemen. Besides, for the pankratists especially, a powerful, stocky figure had advantages.

The games themselves were called *agones* and participation demanded such effort, endeavour, and strain that we can understand the meaning now given in English to the word derived therefrom, "agony."

The Pythian Games

The Pythian Games at Delphi did not have quite such an early origin as those of Olympia, and, indeed, there is a legend that the games at Olympia were re-established on the advice of the oracle at Delphi as a means of pacification among the Greeks. The Pythian Games were held at the Delphic Stadium close and above the oracle, but the site imposed many limitations as to size, so that the long-distance races and the chariot races were held down on the Krissean Plain. The scope of the games did not differ much from those at Olympia, except that originally they were instituted for poetry and music, and these two contests were always prominent in the Pythian Games, but were excluded from the Olympic, which, however, had contests for heralds and for trumpeters.

Although athletes visited Delphi from all Hellenic lands, it was not quite so pan-Hellenic in significance and did not require a truce from all Greeks.

The temple of the god at Delphi served many surrounding villages and hamlets too poor or too small to have their own, or having temples devoted only to some local goddess or god. This fact can be well understood owing to the particularly mountainous country in which Delphi perches, where, with the exception of the Krissean Plain, there is no fertile valley for many a mile. The surrounding communities whose worshippers visited Delphi sent two representatives to the temple to participate in its management. Gradually it evolved that the committee of management, which was known as the Amphictyonic Council, was divided into two sections, and the representatives were so elected as to serve for the specific duties of their section. The one section dealt with religious rites and the games and the management of the treasure of the temple, whereas the other dealt with the relationship between the member cities and states, which took vows not to fight each other. The Amphictyonic Council would therefore sit in arbitration and its decisions must be obeyed. There were elsewhere amphictyonic councils, but that of Delphi became extended to embrace distant cities, and in order to enforce its decisions, if necessary, it controlled an armed force. There were also famous amphictyonies in the Peloponnesos and also in Asia Minor.

The Delphic Oracle

The earliest oracle of Greece was in the mountain-girt oak forests of Dodona where whined the wind and rolled the thunder. Here, to the northwest, in Epiros, the descending northerners would first have established their institutions. Thus, too, they placed the abode of their gods to the north, though on the eastern side of Greece, on Mount Olympos. Dodona, however, faded out in quite early times, as a tribe of Illyrians, who were non-Hellenic in race and religion, settled on the northwestern shores.

Delphi was an ancient, hallowed site, and Mother Earth was worshipped there before Apollon made it his own. As father of the gods, it was in Zeus that prophetic lore resided, and thus Apollon, in one sense, was an intermediary or deputy for Zeus.

Apollon was called Pythian because he is said to have slain the serpent Python, and there is a legend that the vaporous exhalations which came from the rock in earliest times were interpreted as the breath of the monster.

The management of the oracle was in the hands of five of the noble old Dorian families of Delphi, or Krissa. The five prophets were chosen from them, and they selected the women to be chosen as Pythia, of which at the height of the oracle's fame there were two alternating and one reserve. The women were chosen from the village. After an unfortunate experience of the dangers of selecting a youthful and attractive Pythia, they were invariably at least of middle age.

There were set days of consultation, precedence being by lot, but exceptions were made. The suppliants would bring rich gifts, and thus Delphi became the storehouse of great wealth. Suppliants would also have to make burnt sacrificial offerings, after the priest had satisfied himself that the animal was a fitting and healthy one whose condition would be acceptable to the god, and perhaps whose savour would be acceptable to his own supper. A certain fee was also charged.

The suppliant would finally be introduced to the innermost sanctuary of the temple, whither the Pythia had been brought by the prophets. She would already have prepared herself by fasting for three days and have cleansed herself by bathing in the waters of the sacred Kastalian Spring. In the sanctuary burned the eternal flame, fed by fir wood, and there, too, was a golden statue of the god. The eyes of the suppliant would at once be attracted to the Pythia, for in the centre of the temple was a small opening, or chasm, in the ground, above which a high tripod was placed, and over this the Pythia had her seat. The Pythia would be chewing laurel leaves, the toxic juices of which affected her and aided the intoxicant of the natural gasses which arose from the opening, or rather (and more likely) the fumes from burnt laurel leaves stage-managed from below.

Soon the Pythia would become giddy; then she would be convulsed with tremors, finally going into a trance punctuated with delirious shouting. These incomprehensible utterances of the Pythia would be noted by the attendant prophets, and collected and co-ordinated, while the suppliant would then await their interpretation, which, after due consultation, no doubt, by the back-room intelligence, would be issued in hexameter form.

The whole essence of the soothsaying was in ambiguity so that whatever the future turn of events, the prophecy would fit in and not belie the oracle. The suppliant would not come so often to enquire as to what would happen, but for approval of action to be taken, and so the nature of the reply would be a problem less taxing upon the ingenuity of the soothsayers. It is clear that a very high standard of intelligence was required and maintained, but it is not necessary to imagine that agents were required for the priests far and wide, since the continual stream of suppliants from every part of the Hellenic lands would centralize all foreign-affairs knowledge in their hands. Most enquiries which were posed to the oracle would in themselves be of a nature giving information of use in answering others. Close relationship with the colonies, founded with their advice and blessing, and for whom they acted as arbiters in differences with the Mother City, was another invaluable source of knowledge.

The controlling Dorian families must have performed with great sagacity and ability, for the oracle secured universal respect. There were but one or two occasions when the oracle lapsed in pure integrity, and that is very little when the vast span of time is considered in which it held sway. The one blemish of the oracle was its slight partisanship for the Spartans, which we can appreciate when it is realised that the Delphians were sufficiently Doric to pronounce the hexametric soothsaying in Doric dialect. This leaning became unduly pronounced during the thirty-year Peloponnesian War when Athens and Sparta were fighting each other to the death, and the Athenians began to lose some faith in the Pythian impartiality.

We shall not collect any examples of oracular pronouncements here, for reference will be made in the later historic context, yet all in all we can consider that the oracle had a beneficial effect, for it would maintain religious precept which universally demands probity and decries evil. Gone were the days of human sacrifice. With very few exceptions, religion was not maintained by a professional priesthood, sacerdotal rites being an honour performed by people who, apart from festive days, attended to their professional or lay occupations in the same manner as everybody else.

Let us return to giving Delphi and Olympia joint consideration as we did at the beginning of the chapter, and in that unconscious function in which their influence was identical. Unless we give these festive meetings most thoughtful attention, we may fail to realise how tremendously important they were to the Hellenic world.

We must always bear in mind that writing itself was a slow process and that printed books did not exist. Of still greater consequence, anything in the nature of a newspaper was completely unknown. To these festivities therefore would come all merchant magnates, all financiers, to find out what was brewing in other lands, what was wanted in any particular land, and what could be got in exchange. Perhaps at an evening meal with an opposite number of some other city, a deal might be discussed and concluded. A shipload of Athenian ceramics might be sent to Sicily in exchange for a freight of some fabrics, and it might be through the intervention of a Corinthian middleman that the deal is promoted. Possibly it might be an arrangement whereby Thebes, a city of gourmands and gourmets, might exchange fat eels from the Kopais marshland for the preserved sturgeon roe which the men of Byzantium (Constantinople) would get from the northern shores of the Euxine (Black Sea), since the sturgeon roe (caviar) was a delicacy for which the Athenians and Thebans had a partiality.

Should a man wish to get renown for some work he had written on philosophy, or for some history, his means of publicity would be limited beyond his own city, and his best method would be to attend these festivities, and there to read it to those who had a disposition to be interested.

Here, too, would the fashion for men take root, and gallants like Alkibiades might return to their city and describe to their cobbler a shoe of a certain type, colour, or material that had taken their fancy, and order a pair to be made. More than likely, however, they would have been able to buy such a pair from a traveller visiting the festival with an eye to business.

At the festival, too, the sculptors would see the statues erected and inspired by artists of other cities and with other techniques, and they might learn and modify their own future statues. Perhaps a tyrant from Sicily who wished to commission a statue would find the festival

THE OLYMPIC GAMES AND THE ORACLE AT DELPHI 69

the best exhibition ground from which to select the style that pleased him most, and thus choose the sculptor.

Before concluding with matters athletic and gymnastic, we will mention that in Sparta, where women had more freedom, as also in some other cities, there were games for women, and in particular unmarried maidens. We also note that whereas Koroebos, in 776 B.C., had won his sprint wearing, appropriately, very short pants, at one of the early Olympiads shortly afterwards a competitor wore nothing at all, and since he won, his example was followed by others, so that henceforth the Greeks took part at all athletic contests entirely in the nude. It is not clear whether at the athletic contests for women that they too made themselves *gymnos;* it might possibly have meant only that they divested themselves of outer clothing. The accepted belief is that they wore nothing. We might note that our present word gymnastics merely means exercising in the nude.

CHAPTER VIII

ATHENS, UP TO THE PERSIAN WARS

WE NOW COME to the pre-Classical period of Greece. An explanation is called for as to the nature of what will be included, and what will be the standard of guidance for such inclusion.

Many authorities attribute the outstanding height to which Greek culture was elevated to the tremendous events which gave Athens her survival against the Persian onslaughts. Twice the Athenians sacrificed their city and homes to secure their freedom and that of their brother Hellenes, and their elation was commensurate with the magnitude and the miracle of their victories. When they started to hit back at their mighty foe, and scored a telling blow with every hit, they began to feel that indeed they were transcending above the paths of mere and ordinary mortals. Perikles, in orchestrating the building of the Parthenon, was but interpreting the feeling of the populace. The people were devoted to its superb and adored goddess who had wrapped them in her peplos and raised them in it, so that they were no longer mere earth-bound mortals of mortal clay. The inspiration was that of those who are as demigods.

This is surely very true, but you can no more inspire a man to be a great artist than you can a carthorse to win a classic race. Breeding is all-important.

In selecting our segments of Greek history, we can take the victories over the Persians as our focal point, but we will give more attention than is habitual to what preceded them than to what followed historically. The battles of Marathon, Thermopylae, and Salamis must get some consideration, for it was the very nature of these that fanned the feeling of glory and gave inspiration.

Before the Persian wars the history of Athens is that of private politics and constitutional experimentation. Yet it was these domestic circumstances of Athenian politics that developed the Athenians into men whose civic pride came before their individual sense of personality.

Not so very long after the Persian wars we come to internecine strife, to struggles between city and city. Great names emerge; some are traitors, but most are great patriots, great generals, such as the two who raised Thebes to be the supreme city of Greece, or the Athenian Kimon, of whom it has been said that his only rival to be saluted as the greatest admiral of all times would be Lord Nelson. These battles, as such, are scarcely of interest to us, and thus, for our purpose, we may select for inclusion some who possibly might not have the right to precedence in the indelible scrolls of history, as against others the names of whom we pass over. Those, however, who get our mention will be of greater consequence in their effect on the development of culture.

The inclusion of Alexander the Great is another matter. He was one of the world's most outstanding and greatest figures. Only Napoleon and Caesar can bear comparison (we exclude any claim to those at present living) and, like them, left their influence on the world other than through their military victories. Alexander the Great caused Greek civilisation to spread to all the Middle East, including the great Greek city of Alexandria which kept the torch of Greek learning living for many a century, and produced great names in science and erudition.

In going back to the earliest history of Athens it would seem that there was a coalescence of the squires of the Attica villages and that the squire of Athens became their leader as *primus inter pares* ("the first among equals"). Very little is known about the period of early Athenian kingship. More interesting is the period after the death of King Kodros, for though we then have a period of some four hundred years with but very slow advance, the constitution of Athens was becoming little by little more democratic in form.

At first governors, or archons, were elected, but they were still chosen only from among the landed gentry. Then, in 621 B.C., the archon Drakon had the laws codified and put into writing, and he reformed them. They were harsh, since personal debtors who could not meet their obligations might be enslaved. The grievance of the population gradually came to a head, and a generation later the Athenians succeeded in electing Solon as archon, giving him unlimited powers to reform the laws. Solon gave Athens real democracy, which underwent many vicissitudes, was suppressed many times, but always came again to the surface and finally triumphed.

Whether this was a good thing or not is entirely a different matter, and though we must be careful not to make any undue incursions into the realms of political theory, it could not be otherwise than that at times it should result in dismal failure. Let us be extremely careful not to consider that last sentence as implying any comment on present-day institutions. What we call Democracy today is rule by delegated authority, but the government of Athens was ultimately the direct rule of the people, which was no longer possible when the city outgrew the possibility of its application.

Solon started by wiping out all debts and granting freedom to all who had been enslaved through them. He then divided the citizens into four classes according to wealth, the three first of which paid taxes according to their category, while the fourth, which was too poor to pay any taxes, was precluded from participation in any official government position. There was a Senate of four hundred members which could legislate, but all its decrees had to be ratified by a convocation of all citizens, in which every free male citizen of mature age, whatever his standing, could have his say and his vote.

Solon made many other laws, including those for protection of trade, but the most significant one for the future greatness of Athens was that not only was compulsory education instituted for every boy up to the age of sixteen, but also that they had to be taught at least one trade. His most unusual decree was to the effect that if there were any political uprisings, it would be a penal offense to remain neutral.

Solon prided himself on his descent from King Kodros, and incidentally from the god Poseidon. His mother was equally well connected, being of a family which later became famous, as through her he was a cousin of Peisistratos, of whom more later. When Solon was still a young man the family fortunes were at first at a low ebb, and so Solon travelled extensively, not only to see and learn from foreign lands, but also to trade. He succeeded in both objectives for he became a man of wide knowledge and accumulated a considerable fortune. He was of the gentry, but as a seafaring man he knew of the hardships of the working classes, all of which factors were assets which resulted in his being elected as archon at the age of forty-four with full powers to reform the laws.

Having drawn up his laws, Solon made the Athenians swear that they would maintain them for a number of years, and then he set forth again on his travels.

There is a story told of Solon, though it is not clear whether it was prior to his archonship or whether it occurred later. Athens had been at war with the neighbouring city of Megara for possession of the island of Salamis which, though it lies close by, opposite to Megara, stretches to the very entrance to the Piraeus, the port of Athens. After many years the Athenians had still been unable to capture it from Megara, and in weariness had not only given up the attempt but had passed a law imposing the penalty of death on whomsoever even mentioned war with Megara for Salamis. Solon considered this insulting to his city and decided that such shame should be wiped out. He pondered much over this and at last decided upon a stratagem. He clothed himself as if about to retire for the night and then went out to the Agora, acting as one possessed. Being a gifted poet of outstanding merit, he had first composed a stirring poem, and when a large crowd had foregathered to stare at the unfortunate Solon, he launched forth into his inspired poem urging them to expunge the disgrace to their city and to rise up and fight for the beautiful island. He fired them with such enthusiasm that they took to arms, and with the assistance of Solon, who distinguished himself, fought the men of Megara and captured the island.

Solon, after his archonship, travelled again, but how long he stayed away we do not know, or whether he offered himself again as a candidate for archon. When he returned to Athens he found an unhappy state of affairs, for the question of debts was cropping up again and the wealthy landowners were becoming rapacious once more. He strongly opposed his cousin Peisistratos and advised his fellow citizens not to elect the latter, who, he said, would become a dictator, but in vain.

In the travels of his last years, and within two years before his death in 558 B.C., Solon visited Lydia in Asia Minor, and Herodotos tells a story of this visit which we shall recount for two reasons, firstly, because it introduces that rise to power of the kings of the Medes and the Persians who later clashed with Greece, and, secondly, because it is so very applicable to almost every Greek who indulged in politics, or came to the fore in the service of his city.

The Story of Solon and King Croesus

Croesus came to the throne of Lydia when he was a comparatively young man. He was exceedingly proud of his riches which were fabulous, and he believed himself to be, probably with justification, the richest man alive. When Solon visited his country, Croesus welcomed him and also gave instructions that Solon should be shown over his magnificent palace, and in particular his vast treasures. After Solon had seen the extent and opulence of these, Croesus spoke to him. "Visitor from Athens!" he said. "We have heard much of your fame, and that you have travelled far and wide and seen much, and are known to be a very wise man. Tell us, then, whom do you consider to be the happiest of mortals?"

"Indeed," replied Solon, "I knew a certain Tellon, in

Athens. He was a man blessed with happiness. He lived to a ripe old age. He begat good and worthy children, and he himself died in battle, fighting for his city. He was well loved by his fellow citizens, who respected him, and they buried him with great honours."

Croesus was taken aback by this unexpected answer and was displeased, for he had fully hoped to be informed that assuredly he should be reckoned the most blessedly happy of mortals, since he had such fabulous wealth. Croesus contrived to hide his annoyance, and asked again, "After Tellon, whom do you think the next happiest of mortals?"

Solon gave the matter his consideration, and then replied: "Kleobis and Bito. They were brothers of the city of Argos. They were noble youths and very fine athletes, too. Their mother was the priestess to the Goddess Hera, but one day, after she was ready to go to the temple to perform the rites, she was forced to wait for her carriage, for the oxen were late in being brought from the meadows. So that she should not be upset, her two sons yoked themselves to the carriage and drew it to the temple, some forty-five furlongs distant. The priestess was in time for the festival, but after reaching the temple the young men died from exhaustion. The Argives greatly admired such an act of devotion, and they ordered statues of the brothers to be made which were erected at Delphi."

Croesus was annoyed with this reply and could no longer contain his irritation. "And me?" he asked, "who has such immense wealth? Do you not reckon me among the most blessedly happy of mortals?"

"Oh!" exclaimed Solon. "Nobody should be deemed happy before his end, for it is so in every matter in that first we should know the conclusion!"

It was not long before Croesus was to learn the wisdom of Solon's words, for his vast wealth was unable to save the life of his favourite son. Later still, some ten years afterwards, he was to learn even more bitterly how wise was this saying of Solon. The kingdom of Croesus was great and it embraced many other lands than the kingdom of Lydia alone, and he was vexed when he learned that Cyrus, king of the Medes and Persians, whom he considered to be an upstart and an usurper, was interfering with his authority in the remoter parts of his empire. Such insolence, he thought, should be punished, and he ordered that a mighty army should be assembled and an expedition arranged against Cyrus.

Croesus thereupon sent messengers to the oracle at Delphi, loaded with gifts of a munificence which hitherto were quite unknown to the poorer cities of Greece. This consultation by a "barbarian" is believed to be the first of its kind known to Delphi. It is understandable, however, for Apollon was one of those hybrid gods who was partly of Asiatic origin. As Phoibus Apollon he was the Sun God, and the Lydians, as well as the Medes and Persians, were Sun worshippers.

The Pythian Oracle made a pronouncement which satisfied Croesus, for the oracle gave the assurance that if Croesus attacked Cyrus he would destroy a mighty empire.

The battle went badly for Croesus and he was forced to retreat to his capital, Sardis, whither Cyrus followed him, besieged the city and captured it, and took him prisoner.

Cyrus ordered a great funeral pyre to be built, upon which Croesus, as well as some of the young Lydian nobles, should be burned alive. As the flames were gaining and the end seemed imminent, Croesus was heard to exclaim thrice "Solon! Solon! Solon!" Cyrus heard this and was perplexed, so he approached close to the pyre and asked Croesus what was the significance of the exclamation. Croesus, in spite of his dire position, told Cyrus of the wise words of Solon, and how at that moment he appreciated very fully the wisdom of them.

The words of Croesus profoundly impressed Cyrus, for he thought that such a calamity could even have happened to him, and he relented. He ordered the fire to be extinguished, but it was too late, for the flames had gained too strong a hold of the pyre. Cyrus was greatly distressed so he prayed fervently to Apollon (or rather to the Persian equivalent god), whereupon, so we are told, a sudden torrential rain fell, which extinguished the fire. Cyrus marvelled at the miracle and thereafter made Croesus his close and trusted friend and his constant adviser.

And what about the oracle at Delphi, whose soothsaying

had led Croesus so astray? Naturally he complained bitterly, but the oracle informed him that it was his own fault, for the pronouncement had but said that a mighty empire would be destroyed, and before embarking on such an expedition he should have stopped first to think which empire might be destroyed—his own, or that of his enemy?

In the meantime in Athens, at about the moment that Solon was visiting Croesus, Solon's cousin Peisistratos had managed to seize power and set himself up as dictator, or tyrant. Twice he was banished, but in 554 B.C. he re-established himself and remained in control until his death twenty-seven years later.

Peisistratos, though a dictator, devoted his life to the glorification of Athens. He was a patron of the arts and invited many of the great poets and philosophers to his "court." He revived many of the festivals which thereafter were such a prominent feature of Athenian life. Among these was the great four-yearly festival of the great Panathenaea, dedicated to the great Goddess Athene. He also revived and transformed the annual festival dedicated to the Wine God, the Lenaea, which thereafter was known as the Great Dionysia, under the direction of Thespis, whom he put in charge. The festival was originally a rustic affair, at which villagers garbed in goatskins, in imitation of satyrs, performed their dances in honour of the Wine God. This festival now became the foundation of the Attic stage and theatre. The Greek word for a male goat is *tragos* and it is therefore from these original goatskin-garbed dances that we get the word "tragedy," for it was from these that the original theatrical productions were evolved.

Of other works of the time of Peisistratos the most practical was the installation of a piped water-supply system for Athens. He also started the building of the most ambitious of all temples, that of Olympian Zeus, which, though more work was done on it later, was not completed, and in another form, till the time of the philhellene Emperor Hadrian.

One further act attributed to Peisistratos was the collection of the Homeric epics, which were classified into books of the *Iliad* and the *Odyssey* and set out in writing.

Such an act would have given lustre to Athens in the eyes of the Greek world of Ionia, and contributed much to her ascendancy. There is, however, no verification of the truth of this.

On the death of Peisistratos in 527 B.C., his eldest son Hippias, assisted by his brothers, became ruler. They, too, were patrons of the arts, but as is ever the case, a dictatorship is bound to engender hates and consequent repressions. As a result of a quarrel, two youths determined to kill Hippias, but were only able to kill his brother, who actually was the particular one against whom they had a grievance. After the death of his brother, Hippias became even more dictatorial, and four years later, in 510 B.C., had caused such general animosity that he was obliged to call for the help of a member of one of the most aristocratic but exiled Athenian families. The latter, who was staying in pro-Doric Delphi, enlisted the assistance of the Spartans. As a result, the Athenians forced Hippias to seek refuge on the rock of the Acropolis. The Athenians then took the children of Hippias as hostages, whereupon Hippias capitulated on condition that he be allowed to take his children and go into exile. Hippias found refuge with the king of the Medes and the Persians, who was now King Darius. Twenty years later we find Hippias among the Persians invading Greece at Marathon.

When the dictator Hippias was ousted, turbulent party politics broke out afresh in Athens. Kleisthenes was the head of that aristocratic family that had intrigued to get Hippias out, and he now sought popular support to establish his rule in Athens. After a first failure, the intervention of the Spartans was again sought and he was eventually successful.

Kleisthenes proved a wise archon and, in order to prevent political feuds, he reformed the constitution, making Athens a real democracy. His system remained unchanged until the conquest of Athens by the Macedonian kings almost two centuries later. He divided Athens into ten tribes, constituted from different parts of the city. Each tribe elected fifty members of parliament by lot, and each group of fifty took its turn as an acting committee of the parliament for thirty-six days. All laws initiated by parliament had to be sanctioned by the ekklesia, or convocation, of the people.

At first this pure democracy worked well, for the citizens were still devout and believed in their gods. They practised moderation in all things, disliked ostentation, and considered themselves rather as part of the city than as individuals. Still, it was pure democracy, or rather ochlocracy. They did not delegate members to decide for them as is the parliamentary rule today. They themselves —the *hoi polloi*—listened to the proposals, or could make them themselves, but they, the people, made the decisions. It was hardly a system which would secure the election of the best brains or the greatest integrity.

Of the Athenians of this period, however, it must be said that, though they were ever ready to listen to reason, they also had good orators who could easily sway the mob. It worked well at first, but when Athens prospered and grew, the individual sense of responsibility became submerged in the impersonal feeling of the mob. The affairs of state, too, became more involved as the city spread into an empire, and the ignorant mob was not fit to be entrusted with decisions about matters of which it knew nothing. Such must have been the essence of its disastrous decision one hundred years later to send an expedition against Syracuse, which sapped the power of Athens beyond repair. What could the populace know of Syracuse and its power, when few knew ought about it? There were neither newspapers, radio, nor television to tell them.

Yet at this time Athens was on the threshold of events which were the most outstanding of ancient Greek history, events which decided what the future civilisation of Europe was to be. The Athenians rose to the occasion with complete abnegation of self, and under brilliant leadership, and of course the immortal assistance of Promachos Athene, emerged the resplendent savior of Hellenic freedom, shining in the reflected admiration of the other, and not ungrateful, cities of Hellas.

CHAPTER IX

THE WAR WITH THE MEDES AND THE PERSIANS

BEFORE we relate the events of the Persian wars, let us consider some of the peculiarities of the Greeks and their institutions, which make some of their actions appear so contradictory and frequently not to their credit. One cannot help thinking of the appositeness and the wisdom of Solon's judgment that no one may be deemed happy until his end is known.

So many who distinguished themselves in the service of their city, and had been ready to sacrifice their lives, finally fell into disfavour and then turned to the enemy for sympathy and assistance. The Athenians themselves acknowledged that they were fickle, and probably they were, but this shows up to an undue extent because the people were given the political power to translate any mood into immediate and uncontrolled action. So often we read of a famous Athenian being exiled, and we are amazed at the ingratitude, yet there was no disgrace in that banishment which was known as ostracism. The "ostrakon" meant a shell, and voting originally took place by recording the name written on such a shell, but later a piece of pottery was used, and many such pieces still exist at the Agora Museum of Athens and some at the British Museum.

Ostracism generally was for five years, and it did not

THE WAR WITH THE MEDES AND THE PERSIANS

involve loss of citizenship or expropriation of property, and it bore no disgrace. A vote of six thousand or more at the convocation of the people would secure such ostracism. It was a device to get someone out of the way whom a large percentage of the public thought was injurious, or merely a nuisance to the city, and did not imply that the man to be banished had committed some improper act, for if he had the law would have taken its normal course. It was just because they thought that his presence prevented the smooth working of the constitution, or merely because they objected to him. The electoral roll of Athens at the time of the Persian wars was about thirty thousand, but this included the voters of greater Athens and not merely the city, and unless there were any matter of exceptional importance, nothing like that number might be expected to turn up. There is probably, however, some confusion as to the exact meaning of a vote of six thousand or more, because it is most unlikely that the position could be that a possible six thousand could vote for banishment, and a possible twenty-four thousand against it, and yet secure ostracism. Possibly the reference was to the necessity of a majority adverse vote with a quorum of at least six thousand.

Just as in mediaeval times in Europe, the cultured classes of one country felt much more akin to those of another country than they did to the lower masses of their own, in spite of their common language, so, too, did many of the Greeks of one city feel closer affinity and sentiment with the similar social strata of another. The nobles or great landowners of Corinth, Argos, or Thebes would consort with those of Athens when they went to the Olympic Games, or came to Athens for the races of the Great Panathenaic Festival. In modern language, they would have been members of the same clubs.

We may find it harder to understand how Greeks were ready to plot with the Great King, as the king of the Medes and the Persians was known, for they were barbarians. Barbarians, indeed, they were, but only in the narrow meaning of the Greek word. The civilisation of the Persians was a great one in many respects, and an anterior one to that of the Greeks, and even if it did not produce the culture of the Greeks, it did not lag behind in material civilisation, or in integrity of character. It was the Medes rather than the Persians whom the Greeks disliked and despised.

Darius, the Great King of the Medes and the Persians, was in all senses an emperor, and shortly after the Lydian Emperor Croesus had been beaten, the Aeolian and Ionian cities of Asia Minor had been added to the Persian king's empire. This empire was of prodigious wealth and consisted of an agglomoration of nations, controlled through provincial governors called "satraps." The Greek cities had not been treated with undue harshness and they retained a fair measure of freedom, having their own institutions and at their head a Greek tyrant who lived in more Oriental splendour than was customary in Greece itself.

In 499 B.C. the Greek cities of Asia Minor revolted against the Great King, and this they had been induced to do by the Greek governor of Miletos, the most powerful of the cities, for personal reasons of his own. The revolting cities had sent to Greece itself to ask for assistance and, whereas Sparta refused, Athens and the little city of Eretria in the Euboea agreed to send aid. It was a more nominal aid than otherwise, for Athens sent twenty ships and Eretria contributed only five triremes. The Greek cities of Ionia were not united, however, for if they had been they might have succeeded. As it was they had only an initial success as they took the great Persian city of Sardis, which, probably unintentionally, was burnt to the ground. It was this, more than anything else, that kindled the anger of the Great King, so that he sent an army and took the cities under his control again, Miletos being the only one to offer effective resistance, capitulating six years later, it is said, through treason.

Darius was informed that the Greek cities of Asia Minor had been helped by the Athenians and the Eretrians, and he could not brook such outside interference. Herodotos tells us that he asked, "Who are these Athenians?" and when he was told, he vowed to punish them too, and instructed one of his servitors to say to him thrice, before his dinner was served, "Lord and master, remember the

THE WAR WITH THE MEDES AND THE PERSIANS

Athenians!" This he was to say until such time as Darius had fulfilled his vow.

We must recount the main incidents of these wars, for Athens finally emerged triumphant, resplendent in shining glory, with the inner satisfaction that she had been ready to sacrifice everything for her honour and her freedom. When the Persians had made tempting offers of appeasement to Athens, and Sparta was afraid that Athens might accept, she had sent to find out her intentions and was told "Not all the gold that the world produced would induce Athens to betray their brother Greeks to the Mede."

It was the greatness of the ordeal, the magnitude of the sacrifice, the incredible odds over which they triumphed as much as the victories themselves which inspired the Athenians to glorify themselves. They were united in the brotherhood of the city, and later it fell to Perikles to synthetize their feeling of apotheosis into the "Golden Age."

In 492 B.C., the year after the fall of Miletos, Darius sent a mighty fleet against Greece, followed on land by an army of similar strength, and he put in charge his youthful son-in-law Mardonius. The fleet sailed the long way round, up the coast of Asia Minor where it helped the army across the Hellespont, after which it followed close by the shores of Thrace. The Thracians harried the Persians and inflicted severe losses on their army, but the real disaster came when their fleet reached Mount Athos, the eastern prong of the three-fingered Chalkidicean Peninsula. It was similar to the disaster that befell the Spanish Armada two thousand years later, for at least three hundred Persian vessels were sunk by a storm. Mardonius and his Persians never reached Greece, and he returned to Darius in shame and disgrace.

We are not told whether the servitor continued to intone his unappetizing introduction to the mealtime of Darius, but the latter was keener than ever for revenge, and the next year, in 490 B.C., a mighty fleet sailed for Greece with an army of over two hundred thousand on board, this time under the command of two admirals who set forth directly across the Aegean Sea. They sailed from island to island, demanding earth and water as the sign of submission, which they either got or else they enslaved the population of any resisting island or city.

The mighty fleet first went to Eretria, which resisted for six days. The Eretrians, on whom Darius had vowed revenge, were taken captive and, in accordance with his orders, were sent to him at his capital at Susa. Darius, when he saw them—ordinary men, women, and children—merely gave instructions that they should be allotted land not so far away from his capital, where they could found a colony, and this they did, keeping their own institutions and language, an act of magnanimity such as Darius also showed on other occasions.

From Eretria the Persians also made for Athens, and landed at Marathon, to the north, this being the nearest possible accessible beach. Almost at the last moment the Athenians sent a runner to Sparta to ask for help and he covered the distance, which is over a hundred and fifty miles each way, in two days. The Spartans were willing, but they would not act contrary to their beliefs and would not set forth before the full moon, which was two or three days hence. This incredible adherence to superstition was obviously genuine, for so soon as the moon was full they sent an advance force of two thousand, who had but one thought, that of hastening to participate in the pending battle, but they arrived too late.

The Athenian forces that marched to encounter the enemy at Marathon were nine thousand, and they were assisted by one thousand from the city of Plataea. They were commanded by ten generals, one for each tribe, and one of whom would be the general commanding officer, the polemarch. The system of his election varied at different periods, though it is probable that it was based on a daily rota. Be that as it may, the generals had a conference before the battle and, with full concurrence of the actual polemarch, who later distinguished himself and was slain in the battle, they all relinquished their rights and appointed Miltiades as leader. Miltiades had more military experience than the others, but what was more, he had intimate knowledge of the Persians and their military tactics.

The strategy adopted by Miltiades proved brilliant, for

THE WAR WITH THE MEDES AND THE PERSIANS

he called for an immediate attack, at the run, in spite of their heavy armour, and chanting their battle songs. Miltiades further arranged that the centre of the line, which would receive the brunt of the enemy's counterattack, should be the weakest point and be forced to yield. It planned out perfectly, for the Greek centre gave way and was pursued by the Persian centre, while the Greek wings shattered those of the Persians and then returned to the help of their own centre, catching the Persians from the front and from the rear. Soon the whole of the Persian forces were in flight and in frenzied panic, trying to clamber into their ships and escape, and here many more were slaughtered.

It is said that a runner was at once sent to Athens which was palpitating with anxiety to learn its fate. The runner was in heavy armour and was so exhausted when he reached the city and the gates were opened to him that all he was able to say was "Rejoice! We win!" before he collapsed and died. This runner was Phidipides, and his noble performance in giving all that he had to allay the anxiety of his fellow citizens is commemorated to this very day, for the distance of the present Olympic Games marathon race is calculated on the distance from Marathon to Athens, which is just over twenty-six miles.

The Persian fleet now sailed for the beach at Phaleron, which is only some five miles to the south of Athens, and thus some thirty miles from Marathon, though by sea, around the cape at Sounion, the distance would be at least double. The Persians knew that Athens would be undefended since its army was at Marathon, but Miltiades guessed their intention and gave orders for his battle-weary men to march throughout the night without halting, so that at dawn, when the Persian fleet arrived at Phaleron, they found the Greeks already there. The Persian fleet, which had also had, in the meantime, the worst of the skirmishes with the Greeks and with Poseidon, and had no more heart for further battle, turned tail for home, with the consolation that they had revenged themselves on Eretria. The Greeks had survived the first round.

Darius did not give up his purpose, but he died five years later, and his son Xerxes, who by no means had his father's magnanimity, finally decided to pursue the punishment of the Athenians. He became more determined than even his father had been to do so.

In Athens Miltiades was bathed in glory, and most exceptionally honoured. In the following year Miltiades asked that a fleet should be voted for him to lead against a very rich land, but he would not name it for security reasons, and the Athenians readily granted the request of their hero. The expedition went to the isle of Paros, which, however, it failed to take, and Miltiades injured his leg when escaping from a building on the island, and returned to Athens incapacitated. The Athenians were angry with Miltiades, for they considered that the attack on Paros had been a matter of personal interest to him, and that he had therefore deceived them. In view, however, of his previous great services he was let off with a very light fine, which was paid by his son Kimon, who later rendered such signal services to Athens and the Greeks. The injured leg of Miltiades turned gangrenous and he soon died.

Solon! Solon! Solon!

Meanwhile there were many in Athens who were under no delusion that they had heard the last of the Medes and the Persians. Of these, Aristeides and Xanthippos, the father of Perikles, were the leaders of the aristocratic party, and they wished to strengthen the forces of the army, which had proved so effective at Marathon. Opposed to the aristocratic party was Themistokles, a brilliant young politician and statesman who had risen to prominence entirely through his own merits as his father was very much of the middle classes and his mother was a foreigner. Themistokles had the support of the party of the coast, and therefore of the port of the Piraeus, of the seamen and of the traders. Finally he obtained ascendancy so that his plans were adopted, including the building of docks and a project for long walls to surround and join Athens and the Piraeus. Above all he had great foresight and his main plan was to build up Athens as a naval power.

In 483 B.C., that is, seven years after Marathon, he succeeded in persuading the people to budget a sum which had been obtained from the revenues of the silver mines of Laurion for the building of a fleet, which would bring up its strength to two hundred war vessels. This was the very year when Xerxes, who had previously been absorbed in the conquest of Egypt, started his preparations for a renewed attack against the Greeks.

The plans of Xerxes can only be described as stupendous and fantastic. Firstly he ordered that a canal should be constructed through the isthmus that separates the towering Mount Athos from the mainland, so that his fleet should avoid circumnavigating that part where the turbulent seas had destroyed the fleet under Mardonius. It took two years, under forced labour, to finish the canal. At the same time he ordered a fleet to be built, the size of which seemed invincible, for when it set out there were one thousand two hundred battleships, or triremes, and three thousand auxiliary vessels, manned by half a million seamen. Herodotos gives a fascinating and delightful picture of the heterogeneous army that was collected from many lands, and they were counted by being passed through an enclosure that could hold ten thousand at a time. They took seven days to pass through it, and Herodotos reckoned the combatants as 2,641,610, and about an equal number of noncombatant camp followers.

This vast army advanced like a plague of locusts and finally reached the plain of Thessaly to the north of the Greek cities. The Greek cities were conscious this time of the magnitude of their peril and they held two representative meetings at the Isthmus of Corinth. There were some cities that believed that discretion was the better part of valour, but on the whole they worked in harmony and decided that all feuds between them must cease and that a stand should be made at the Pass of Thermopylae, through which the Medes and the Persians had to come in order to reach Athens and the south. It was further decided that the Spartans should have the leadership both on land and at sea. It is very much to the credit of Athenian patriotism that they accepted this without demur, for at sea the whole of the Greek fleet was well under four hundred vessels and of these Athens owned at least two hundred.

The Greek army at Thermopylae was a comparatively small one, although Athens had contributed all she could.

Some of the Greek cities that had been convened to the Isthmus of Corinth under the "chairmanship" of Sparta had not realised the imminence of battle. Many cities were still giving undue attention to the Olympic Games which were being held. Sparta was preoccupied with a religious festival which it intended finishing before sending the bulk of its forces, and she had therefore sent but three hundred veterans under King Leonidas.

It is difficult to assess what the actual number of the Greek forces were. In Athens at least the soldier provided his own armour, whence to be in the cavalry showed some standing, financial anyhow. The "Hoplites" were heavily armed and therefore would take at least one servitor with them to carry the armour. We gather that the Spartan soldier took with him to battle, on the average, seven Helots, who would not be counted in the computations of strength. In the case of the Spartans, however, it may have been the principle of reducing the number of fit Helots that would be left behind in a city denuded of its military strength.

Xerxes was utterly amazed when he learned that a Greek army had had the temerity to establish itself at Thermopylae, and he therefore sent scouts to find out what it was all about. They returned and informed him that the Greeks were very few, and that they were passing their time in exercising, bathing, and combing their hair. So Xerxes sent his representatives to demand that they should surrender their arms. In typical Laconic fashion Leonidas replied *"Molon, labe!"* which means "Come, take them (if you dare and are able to do so)."

The legates of Xerxes were taken aback by such foolhardiness, and they told Leonidas that the army of Xerxes was so vast that the sun would be darkened by the number of their arrows. "So much the better, then we will fight in the shade" was all the satisfaction that Leonidas would give them. This was hardly a soothing answer to the youthful and impetuous Xerxes, so he sent a powerful army to exterminate them, only to suffer the ingnominy of a very thorough trouncing. Xerxes now realised the problem that was confronting him, and sent his very best troops, including his crack regiment of the Immortals, and he viewed the battle from a throne placed on heights that overlooked the pass. There he jumped up and down in trepidation for the safety of his army, which fared no better than the soldiers in the first attack. Within three days, however, he had found the solution by bribery and had obtained information as to a little-known mountain path along which an army could be sent to the rear of the Greeks.

When Leonidas heard that his army was being surrounded, he ordered the bulk of the Greek forces to escape so that they might live on and be more useful in continuing the fight for Hellas. He himself kept his three hundred Spartans (and the Helots) and also seven hundred Thespians, as well as five hundred Thebans who were suspected of being in collusion with the Persians. In the battle that ensued the five hundred Thebans surrendered, but the remainder fought valiantly to the last man, doing such havoc to the Persian army so that even two of the brothers of Xerxes were included among the slain. Leonidas considered it his duty to the laws of Sparta that he and all his men should thus face the enemy to the last and bitter end.

We can imagine how very busy Delphi must have been at this stage for its Intelligence Department must have been well primed from the north as to Persian strength and intentions. The cities must have sent their suppliants into a frenzied queue for consultation. The oracle must have been in an invidious position, and it is difficult to know whether one should approve or disapprove of its attitude, for it did nothing to rally the Greeks. Rather it depicted the position as hopeless, which in view of its information may have been the right thing to have replied in all honesty.

The reply of the oracle to the Athenians was to the effect that all was lost. The Athenian suppliants would not take this for an answer and consulted the oracle again, whereupon the oracle told them that there "was but safety in the 'Wooden Walls' which would not be taken." Some authorities are inclined to the view that Themistokles induced the oracle to give this reply, but it is just as likely that the oracle got to know of his purpose and intention, which it thought sensible and worthy of encouragement.

The Medes and the Persians were now coming down the mainland of Greece, capturing, slaughtering, and enslaving, but Delphi they did not manage to take, for the god himself intervened with a most violent thunderstorm and hurled rocks from above.

In Athens there was argument as to the interpretation of the oracle, and some insisted in barricading themselves on the Acropolis behind a wooden wall, but these were very few. The others listened to Themistokles, who said that the wooden walls referred to their ships. He ordered all men capable of fighting to board the ships; all who were too old, as well as the women and children, were to take what possessions they could and to escape to wherever they might find safety, in the islands, or the Peloponnesos.

When Xerxes reached Attica he found a city completely deserted except for those on the Acropolis, who were soon despatched to the underworld. The Persians did all the damage they possibly could, not only to the city but to the whole of the countryside, while the Greeks in their ships riding at anchor in the bay of Salamis could see the smoke arising from their burning homes and property.

The oracle at Delphi had made, however, one exception to its tales of lamentation, for it pronounced that the winds would blow favourably for the Greeks. It was not wrong, for Boreas, the doughty North Wind, destroyed four hundred of the Persian war vessels while at anchorage and before they had sailed forth to round Cape Sounion. This was a blow which, though in itself not so severe to their great strength, may have been of some consequence. They suffered further losses through encounters with the Greeks and the winds, and Boreas therefore well merited the subsequent temple they erected in his honour.

On board the ships at Salamis a first-rate quarrel was now developing. The Spartan admiral in charge, who was backed by the other Peloponnesians, was all for sailing towards their homes, the better to protect them, a policy which would have been scatterbrained. Themistokles wished to act in accordance with his duty to discipline, but he thoroughly disapproved. If, however, he had decided to withdraw the Athenian ships, the remainder would have been sunk in all senses. The argument became so heated that on one occasion the Spartan admiral made to hit Themistokles, who remained unperturbed and merely said calmly, "Strike! But listen to what I have to say."

Themistokles argued, and as it proved, rightly, that the only chance that the Greek fleet had was to remain in the narrow waters of Salamis Bay, where the heavier and less swift ships of the Persians could not manoeuvre. Herodotos tells that Themistokles was not in the least happy that his plan, which had been temporarily accepted, would prevail. He therefore sent a trusted slave to Xerxes. The slave was to pretend that Themistokles wished well to the Great King on whose side he was, and therefore warned him that the Greeks were preparing to escape and sail away. Xerxes immediately called a council of his subordinate kings, princes, and rulers, of whom there were close on fifty, and who sat around the Great King in order of precedence, and asked their opinions as to whether a sea battle should be risked. All agreed with the exception of Queen Artemissia of Halikarnassos who expressed herself in the most outspoken manner. She told Xerxes that the Greeks were more valiant and better fighters and that he would be badly advised to fight. Xerxes, somewhat unusual for him, and possibly in good spirits at the prospective victory over the trapped Greeks, took no retaliatory action at her boldness. He accepted the decision of the majority and gave order for battle. He spent the day on a specially erected throne overlooking the bay where he saw his ships outmanoeuvred, outfought, and routed, though he reserved his admiration for the valour of Queen Artemissia.

Herodotos, in measured words, sums up by saying that in truth it was Athens that saved Greece, and Herodotos was a native of Halikarnassos, the city of Queen Artemissia, which was Dorian in its roots, and thus, in fact, any partiality of his would have been unfavourable to Athens.

Xerxes had had enough and that very evening made as hasty a departure as he could, but he left Mardonius behind with a vast army of some three hundred thousand to finish off the Greeks. Mardonius accompanied the retreating Persians as far as Thessaly and remained there for the winter because Attica and Boeotia had already been devastated and he would not have been able to feed such a huge army there.

Next year Mardonius marched south and returned to the fray, so that the Athenians once more evacuated their city while the Persians finished off the destruction of everything that had been left standing. Their success was of short duration. They were finished off when they met the Greek forces at Plataea. Mardonius was killed and most of his men perished either then or on the long homeward journey. What was more, at this very same period the Greek fleet inflicted an equally severe defeat on the Persians off the coast of Asia Minor.

The Persian invasions had forced the Greeks into concerted action, even if not to well-cemented unity. The Greeks, had, however, become alive to the need of a close pact to face the danger from the barbarians. Sparta was once more put in charge of organising it, on the same type of basis as that of the North Atlantic Organisation of today. It was realized that importance must be given to the fleet, in priority to the army, but in spite of this the Spartans were still put in charge of the Greek fleet as well as of the army. The Spartan king who was at the head of the Greek fleet, however, did not manage to make himself popular; he was haughty and his impartiality was doubted, and finally he was suspected of being in touch with the Great King. Sufficient evidence was found for the Spartans to recall him, and guilty he no doubt was, for on his arrival at Sparta he took refuge in a building close to the sanctuary of a temple to Athene. There the Spartans built a wall to enclose him therein so that he should die of exposure and starvation, and among the first to help in building the wall was his own mother.

After the expulsion of the Persians, Athens must have been like a modern city devastated by bombing, but worse, for the surrounding lands as well as the city had been destroyed. At first she would lick her wounds, and the citizens would secure any fallen masonry to build or patch up a home. While this was going on, Kimon, the son of Miltiades, was leading the Greek fleet from one victorious exploit to another against the Persian fleet, and, indeed,

THE WAR WITH THE MEDES AND THE PERSIANS

he claimed three resounding victories on one and the same day.

The Athenians faced life with a song in their hearts. With the Persian fleet wiped out of existence and with the rise of the Athenian Empire, the citizens of Athens felt on the top of the world, victorious and glorious, and, as we shall see, they built that beautiful city in the Golden Age of Perikles of which they felt so rightly proud, but perhaps too arrogantly so, for they were finally to fall to ever-jealous Sparta.

CHAPTER X

FROM THE PERSIAN WARS TO ALEXANDER

THE PERIOD we intend covering in this chapter is that from the final defeat of Mardonius in 479 B.C. to the accession of Alexander the Great in 336 B.C., a period about as long as from the battle of Waterloo to the present day. It is a period teeming with historic events and battles. An alternative title to the chapter might have been "The Rise and Fall of the Athenian Empire," but this would not have indicated how, later on, Sparta was in the ascendant, and was then replaced by Thebes. We shall confine ourselves, however, to some of the trends and the political personalities that loom up in this period. It is a period of (1) Spartan jealousy, apprehension, ascendancy, haughtiness and defeat; of (2) Athenian greatness, supremacy, distinction, arrogance, humiliation but resilience.

The struggle of Athens and Sparta somewhat reminds us of that occasion towards the latter part of the nineteenth century when Bismarck, the German Iron Chancellor, was informed that Britain was at war with Russia, and he laughingly remarked that it would be amusing to see a whale fighting an elephant, though on this occasion the comparison of Sparta to a tiger would be more appropriate than to an elephant.

In this period the political map of Greek lands was considerably altered from its composition at the time of Solon, for not only did the cities of the mainland and the Aegean Islands prosper but many of the colonies reached an advanced stage of maturity and strength. The underlying feature of the first eighty years of this period, that is, to the end of the fifth century B.C., is that, whereas the whale is fighting the tiger, and the two can hardly get to grips with each other, all the onlookers are forced to join the fray whether they like it or not. Many of the cities are placed in the invidious position of having to consider their geographically exposed situation and weigh it against their natural sentiments or allegiance, or in the case of the colonies, the ties with their mother cities. The other feature is that whereas Athens rises to a pinnacle of civilisation and culture, it develops into too large and too prosperous a corporation for its constitutional suit of clothing, which no longer fits.

At the beginning of the previous chapter we commented on the institution of "ostracism," which probably had been developed by Kleisthenes. In its early days it may have been a beneficial if somewhat remarkable idea, and might have continued to serve a useful purpose if it had been made to conform with the changed conditions and the development of Athens. With the development of the Athenian Empire, which will be explained later, Athens was prospering commercially and the state was enlarging. The citizens, what is more, were living to a ripe old age, and thus the electoral roll was also increasing from this aspect. In addition, the Persian wars had concentrated the population from the devastated outlying districts into the city itself, and so, with political parties more organised, and by means of canvassing and electioneering, it would not be difficult to whip up six thousand votes for ostracism. Though the exact interpretation of the application of the six thousand votes cannot be certain, it is still true that there were many Athenian statesmen of integrity whose wise counsel was lost to the city through an institution which seems to have become pernicious.

We start the period with the rapid elimination of Themistokles from the political arena. How exactly he came into disfavour we do not know, except that he was jealous and grumbled. Nonetheless we can make a fairly good guess, for both Aristeides and Xanthippos had been ostracised prior to Salamis, but had returned at their city's call of danger, and it would have been the party of Themistokles that would have secured their ostracism. Aristeides himself, however, would certainly have been above any petty intrigue. The year after Salamis we find that Xanthippos has replaced Themistokles as admiral, but we discover the latter in another setting which may well be interpreted as the distant but ominous roll of thunder portending a most catastrophic storm that was brewing, later to break over Hellas.

Under the instigation of Themistokles the city walls around the Piraeus and Athens are being built in such frantic haste that the aged, the women, and the children are working day and night and laying their hands on all useful material available. Why should Themistokles, a man of the most outstanding foresight, be urging this on, since he knew that henceforth there was but one defence against the barbarian invaders, and that was in the strength of the fleet? The Spartans are calling for a meeting of all Greek cities to discuss the demolition of all city fortifications and walls, since there was no longer any need against the outsiders. Themistokles went to Sparta to discuss this, and pretended that he had not the full authority to negotiate any agreement at this "disarmament conference" and that he was but awaiting the other members of the Athenian delegation to arrive. Thus, by one means and another, he kept them sufficiently happy, however suspicious they may have been, until such time as he received word that the walls had been reconstructed, and was able to inform the Spartans that the Athenians who had abandoned and sacrificed their city to the Medes without asking for the permission of Sparta, had also seen to their walls being rebuilt, also without their permission.

No doubt Themistokles knew what he was doing and, being such a good judge of character, he realized the quality of Spartan jealousy and what it might breed. The relationship between Themistokles and the Spartans must have been strained after the incidents prior to the battle of Salamis and his deception regarding the building of the walls of Athens must have incensed them still further. We are not surprised, therefore, when a little later Themistokles was ostracised and went to live in Argos in the Peloponnesos, that he was denounced by the Spartans. He then fled to Persia, where the Great King, now Artaxerxes, made him a provincial satrap, and there he lived in opulence and luxury for several years until his death.

It is interesting to note, in the recent excavations at the Agora of Athens, that several voting ceramic potsherds for the ostracism of Themistokles were found, though in some his name is written as "Themisthokles."

We can now resume where we left off at the end of the last chapter, having noted that the Spartan admiral king had been caught acting treasonably with the Great King, of whom he had asked his daughter in marriage. This act, as well as his lordly and haughty airs, had estranged the Greek cities of Asia Minor, which had managed to regain their independence through the Greek victories. They turned to Athens, which had helped them at the time of their revolt, and which, indeed, had suffered so grievously as a result of it. They were enthusiastic in forming a league, or "Confederation" as it is habitually called, directed against Persia, and with Athens at the head.

Headquarters of the league were established at Delos, the small Aegean island sacred to Apollon. Aristeides was put in charge, with the task of assessor, computing the wealth of the various member states and cities, and their consequent contribution in either ships or the equivalent value in money. The size and strength of the league was very impressive for it included most parts of Greece itself, though Sparta soon abstained. In practice very few cities contributed ships and therefore Athens soon developed a mighty fleet manned by Athenians and financed by the member states, and simultaneously her citizens also obtained much profitable employment in shipbuilding and other directions.

Many years had not gone by when one of the island cities wished to secede from the league, but Athens imposed its will by force and made it a now unwilling participant. Thus it gradually transpired that Athens in reality had accrued an empire, and with it the detestation of the Ionian and other cities, which felt that they were now forced to contribute sums to maintain Athenian imperialistic power, and to fight fellow Greeks rather than the subdued Persians.

Aristeides, who had been known as "the Just" even prior to his assumption of the office of Assessor, unfortunately did not live long, for while he had the treasury in his hands all the members were more than satisfied with his fairness, and there is not even a record of a single complaint. In substantiation of his integrity we can note that when he died he was so poor that his funeral was at the public expense.

After the death of Aristeides, Kimon, the son of Miltiades, took over. He was a doughty old sea dog, with the reputation generally bestowed on seamen ashore, that of loving a carousal and of being a *bon vivant*. We cannot help feeling, however, that just as his naval strategy was brilliant, so, too, was his policy astute, with much to recommend it. Kimon insisted that the future of Athens lay in working in harmony with Sparta, and that whereas Sparta should be the military leader, Athens should be mistress of the seas. Kimon, in spite of severe opposition from the rising young Perikles, the son of Xanthippos, carried his policy through. He went to the help of Sparta when it became involved in trouble through an earthquake which was so severe as to cause serious material damage. It gave the Helots a chance to revolt and take to that same stronghold of Mount Ithome where their Messenian ancestors had resisted three centuries earlier. Inexplicably the Spartans suddenly dismissed Kimon and his four thousand Hoplites who had come to their help. Athens was so angry that it ostracised Kimon, though he returned later and died in harness, with the naval might of Persia completely broken.

After the death of Kimon in 461 B.C., we have fifteen years marked by continuous battles between the Athenians and the revolting cities, with Perikles the guiding figure, but punctuated by a most significant event.

In 454 B.C. Perikles removed the league treasury from Delos and placed it in the safekeeping of the Acropolis at Athens. All the "allies," some voluntarily, but most otherwise, are no longer contributing ships but only funds, used mostly by Athens for her fleet, while Perikles is saying that so long as Athens is defending them from the Persians they have no right to interfere with the finances of the league.

Sparta and her allies finally came to grips with Athens. The fortunes of war are about even during these fifteen years, but at the end (446 B.C.) Athens got the worst of it, and Sparta and her Peloponnesian allies enter Attica. Athens is forced to come to unfavourable terms, though mitigated by a thirty years' peace treaty with Sparta whereby both cities agree not to tamper with each other's allies. This peace treaty endured exactly half its intended period, when the Peloponnesian War, so brilliantly and impartially described by Thucydides, burst on the whole of Hellas.

The Age of Perikles is habitually described as the Golden Age of Athens. The foreign policy of Perikles may have been unwise, and probably his imperial policy was not founded on the strictest morals, for there were others who opposed it on these grounds and wished the activities of the league to be confined to opposition to the Great King. Thus we learn of at least one other wise and honest Athenian who opposed it, following the path of ostracism.

Perikles, apart from his debatable imperial policy, was undoubtedly a great patriot, and although he was in control of the Athenian government, his official position was never other than that of an annually elected general. He was an orator, second only to Demosthenes of a century later, and had a sonorous voice, so that the very earth did quake. Withal he never got excited in his speeches and held the people spellbound, never pandering to their wishes. Unlike most Athenians he did not frequent the Agora, but stayed at home, planning for his beloved city and devising ways to glorify it, so that in fact he did make it the most beautiful city of the ancient world. To the great, everything is permitted, and thus it was accepted that the home of Perikles should not be that of his wife from whom he was estranged, but a home shared by the most famous of Greek hetairae, the Ionian Aspasia.

Perikles has been accused of using the funds of the league to beautify Athens, and it seems that he may have done so, though only to a limited extent, for Athens not only had the wealth of her silver mines and of her commerce but a vast accumulation of rich spoils from the Persian wars. Apart from this, Perikles no doubt felt that it was but just that the other cities of Greece should contribute for the glorification of the Temple of Athena. They had not done so and they had not been called upon to share the sacrifices that Athens had undergone. There was, however, some justification for that public taunt made by Elpinike that, whereas Perikles spends the funds against their brother Greeks, her brother Kimon had spent his life fighting the barbarians. We can sympathize with Elpinike, who was not only the half-sister but also the wife of Kimon, for not only was there a feud between the family of Xanthippos (father of Perikles) and that of Miltiades (father of Kimon), but Perikles had offended her by saying that "the best that could be said of any woman was that nothing was said of her."

Not only did Perikles help to make Athens the most beautiful of cities but, under his patronage, there flourished the fullest and richest period of Greek creative life, and it included the greatest sculptors, the greatest architects, the greatest tragedians of ancient Greece. When, too, Perikles died in 429 B.C., Sokrates, the first of the three great Athenian philosophers, was forty years old, already a power in the Agora, teaching mankind how to think and, what is more, to think of what should be mankind's aims in virtues and ethics. Unlike most of the world's greatest moralists, Sokrates fully practised the precepts that he preached.

The essence of the Golden Age was that of its culture, but we will leave the discussion of this to the second part of the book. Indeed, there were fifteen years, from the Peace of Sparta, in which Athens prospered and arrogantly glorified herself as the teacher of Hellas. We must note, however, that even in the preceding period of Perikles, when fighting was prevalent, the rich intellectual and aesthetic life of the city by no means suffered, nor did it for that matter in the subsequent war, apart, of course, from the tragic two years of the plague.

Then came the Peloponnesian War, caused just as much by Spartan envy, jealousy, and apprehension as by Athenian intransigeance and arrogance. The actual first cause of it was the help given by Athens to Kerkyra, a colony of Corinth, against the latter, her Mother City, with the result that Corinth appealed to Sparta.

When Perikles realized that war with Sparta was inevitable, he planned resistance both logically and well. He knew that Sparta and her allies had not the wealth to maintain a protracted war, and that the Athenian fleet could harry all the exposed Spartan allies. When, therefore, war did come in 431 B.C., he ordered the flocks to be sent to the safety of Euboea, while all the population of Attica was to take refuge within the impregnable city walls. During the summer the Spartans came and laid waste to the whole of the Attic countryside, and returned again the following year with the same objective. Here the first event occurred that Perikles could not have foreseen, for a plague attacked the Piraeus and spread to Athens, so terribly overcrowded, and decimated the population. Thucydides, who was attacked by it, but survived, indicates that between a quarter and a fifth of the population died of it, and even Athenian sailors, fighting afar in Thrace, were smitten as severely by it. Perikles saw all his family die of it, and broke down at the funeral of his son. Finally he himself caught it, when it reappeared again in the following year, and he died from a fever resulting from a relapse.

With a small interlude, when a peace was made which lasted only a few months, war with Sparta went on till 403 B.C. It degenerated into passions and atrocities, with one half of Greece fighting the other, and Sparta cleverly inciting disturbances as far away as possible from herself, not only for her safety but so as to dissipate Athenian strength.

During the years after the death of Perikles to the end of the Peloponnesian War, two demagogues appear on the scene, both vainglorious and both doing extreme harm to Athens. The first was Kleon, a tanner, risen from the people. He is described as unrefined, uncultured, and chauvinistic. The policies he advocated were merciless and imperialistic, and his success in getting them approved only inflamed the detestation of the rest of the Hellenic world. Kleon was a braggart, and on occasion he had to eat his words, but in one instance when he told the mob that if he were on the battlefield he would have secured victory within twenty days, they made him go and try, and he pulled off an unexpected triumph. On the next occasion, however, both Kleon and the Spartan general who opposed him met their deaths in battle. Kleon, however uncultured he may have been, must have been, and was, a good orator.

After Kleon a new leader appeared, and he was as different from Kleon as anyone could possibly be, but he was the greatest factor of all in causing the downfall of Athens. He was Alkibiades. This young man was not only of noble blood but he was a dandy who delighted the Athenian populace. His appearance was that of a matinee idol, and where he went the crowds gazed and admired, for he was a great showman, and his company added lustre to any party. In his way he was just as much a demagogue as Kleon, but he was consumed with vanity and vainglory. Unlike Perikles, who thought only of the glory of the city, he thought of nothing but of how glory could come to crown him. When, for instance, his chariot teams at Olympia carried off most of the events, his conceit and attitude were quite insufferable.

In seeking to find an opportunity to glorify himself, Alkibiades secured a vote of the people to send an expedition to conquer Sicily by telling the mob that, if Athens got the power of Sicily into its hands, it would have such strength, and such control of the seas, that Sparta must inevitably fall. Nikias, one of the generals, opposed the expedition as strongly as he could, but to no avail, and he had to participate in it as one of the three leaders. Thucydides rightly points out that the people of Athens were in no position to know anything of Syracuse, which could be but a name to them. Syracuse was probably the greatest city of the Hellenic world, possibly larger even than Athens.

Alkibiades had let success go too much to his head and respected nobody. He held nothing sacred, so that in merrymaking before the expedition he had committed certain acts which were considered sacrilegious. One of these was a travesty of the Eleusinian Mysteries at a symposium, and another, attributed to him, was that, returning home late one night, he had knocked off the heads of some street "Herm" statues.

When the acts of Alkibiades became known, the Athenians recalled him on his way to Syracuse to fight. Realising what might be in store for him, Alkibiades treasonably went to Sparta, instead of returning, and revealed the Athenian plans. Although the expedition to Syracuse was a foolhardy one, Athens was actually on the verge of success when the Spartans and their allies, warned by Alkibiades, sent their forces to Sicily and foiled their plans. The final defeat of the Athenian forces at Syracuse was complete. All the Athenians were enslaved, so that most of those who had not been slain in battle died in the quarries.

In spite of this defeat Athens would still have been a power with which to reckon, but then came the other factor which Perikles had not foreseen. Sparta demeaned herself by asking the Great King for financial help, and this was given so generously that she was gradually able to build a great fleet in conjunction with her allies. The Athenian fleet was nonetheless still very much the mistress of the seas, but had an unforgivable lapse. The Athenian fleet was taking it leisurely off the coast of Asia Minor, where day by day they would beach their ships and go ashore without a care in the world. The wily Spartan admiral got to know of this, and one day he was able to surprise the whole of the Athenian fleet, thus abandoned, and destroy it completely.

Sparta was now able to dictate terms, with the Great King as arbiter. The first thing Sparta did was to destroy the Athenian city walls, to the sounds of music. Sparta emerged as the savior of Greek liberties against the imperialism of Athens, though liberty was not extended to the Ionian and Aeolian cities which, by agreement, were given back to the suzerainty of the Persians.

The cities of Hellas soon learned, and very quickly at

that, that Athens had been preferable to Sparta. Sparta imposed its own rulers on the Greek cities and filled them with garrisons, so that democratic government existed no longer. Athens was ruled harshly by thirty "tyrants" who were imposed on her. Many Athenians were slain, but many also escaped and, for the most part, found refuge in Thebes.

One of the Athenians who escaped organised a "resistance" movement, with headquarters in the surrounding hills and mountains overlooking Athens, whence he directed telling raids against the Spartan occupiers. Before long he became so strong that he led a raid into the city and slew the Spartan garrison. Sparta did not retaliate, either through the wisdom of their king or because they considered that Athens still had too dangerous a sting. It is pleasant to note that Thrasyboulos, the organiser of this movement, in spite of the hate engendered by the wars, forced the Athenians to forget all feuds and cease all enmity between themselves.

Athens was resilient, though she never again quite returned to her former position to take the lead among the great Greek cities. This lot fell to Thebes, which produced two great men who were, incidentally, very close friends, Pelopidas and Epaminondas. They were not only great strategists but they were wise and liberal, and the Greek cities looked to Thebes for freedom. So long as these two lived the cities of Greece were free, for Thebes overcame Sparta. When these two died, Thebes forgot the lessons of the Greek wars, and she, too, became dominating. Theban liberalism vanished and Thebes behaved as Athens and Sparta had done before her.

Thebes had won her supremacy through the military tactics that her two great sons had evolved. This consisted principally of strengthening one wing of an army to a depth of fifty men, so that it was able to plough its way through any force.

This new military formation was noted by a young lad, a prince of Macedonia, who was being held in Thebes as hostage. This young lad, who later became Philip II of Macedonia, kept his ears and eyes alert to everything else that was going on, and he learned how very disunited were the Greek cities, and of the frailties of each. Philip prided himself that he was a Greek, of ancient lineage, and asserted that he was a descendant of Pheidon, a king of Argos of the eighth century. He was an ardent admirer of Greek culture.

It is difficult to know exactly how the Greeks regarded the Macedonians. In Athens Demosthenes, who is considered the greatest of Greek orators, devoted his life to trying to induce the Athenians and the Greeks to prepare themselves to resist the Macedonians, now under that Macedonian prince who had become that most wily strategist, King Philip, before it was too late. If it were not for the orations of Demosthenes we might not have considered the Macedonians to have been so very much non-Hellenic barbarians, though they had no polish or culture, and were bucolic in the extreme. The Macedonian stock may have been largely Dorian, being of that early invasion that descended upon Greece about 1100 B.C. but had found the Macedonian pasture lands a suitable home, and did not venture farther southwards. This, we may possibly surmise, was their origin, though opinions differ widely.

A fact which may not be unconnected is the manner of the Macedonian intrusion into Greece. Normally they had no connections with the rest of Hellas, but King Philip intervened in its affairs at the invitation of the Pythian Amphictyonic Council of Delphi to settle a dispute with a member. The Delphic Amphictyony was, of course, Dorian.

The military genius of Philip was not only backed by ample strength but also by the wealth of the newly discovered Macedonian gold mines. By extreme mobility he was able to run through Greece, so that after some little resistance it capitulated, including Sparta.

Demosthenes, in Athens, had finally aroused the Athenians and a few other cities to resistance, but not only was it too tardy but luck also went the other way.

Philip owed his success as much to graft and gold as to strategy. Athens he flattered; his admiration being entirely genuine, he sent his young son Alexander, handsome and learned, as an unofficial ambassador, though he also imposed a Macedonian garrison. Philip then called for a representation of all the cities of Greece, to be held close to the city of Corinth, and there he had himself elected as their leader of an expedition to conquer Persia and pay off old scores. This was not only his ambition, but one which also proved a rallying point for the Greek cities.

The Macedonian king did not interfere with the institutions of the Greek cities, and though they were nominally still self-governing, they had in reality become a part of the new Macedonian Empire. Philip, however, was a great statesman, so that the cities hardly realized their yoke. He was not able, nonetheless, to achieve his ambition, for he was soon murdered, at the instigation of his former wife Olympias, soon after she had learned that she had been divorced in favour of the very young Cleopatra (not, of course, the famous Cleopatra of Caesar's time).

The new king, Philip's son Alexander, had the backing of the troops. Though he was barely twenty years old he proved his mettle, notwithstanding that his inclination had been to continue his studies and follow research work under his tutor Aristoteles (Aristotle), then established close to the Macedonian capital.

Alexander the Great started with four great advantages. These were: firstly, the inheritance that his father had left him, other than material, as leader of the Greek cities; secondly, the possession of an army organised on the most up-to-date lines, based on the Theban formation, but improved to form the Macedonian phalanx; thirdly, the advice of trusted and experienced generals; and, fourthly, luck. Alexander had also profited from his devotion to his scrolls, so that he was very quick to learn, and that which he learned above all else, when taking over the actual command, was to make instant decisions when necessary. At first such decisions were erroneous, but his generals and his luck saved him, and before long his training stood him in good stead. However impetuous he might have been, he not only learned to profit from his mistakes but to calculate the details methodically himself.

On his accession the Greek cities revolted, but before they even knew what was happening he had descended upon Thebes, which he impetuously attacked, and, in reality, the promptitude of his generals captured. Thebes was sacked and rased to the ground, and he only allowed the house where Pindar the poet had lived to be saved. Alexander listened to those who had advised that he should show his strength, and so the Thebans were killed or enslaved. Though he seems to have regretted his harshness, it brought Athens and the other cities quickly into line. At a second meeting near Corinth, Alexander was elected, in his father's stead, to be the leader of all the cities of Greece, with the exception of Sparta, who, as a former recipient of Persian gold, was not invited.

His former tutor Aristoteles did not approve of his actions, for he did not consider that the Greek cities should have been coalesced by force, nor did he approve of imperialistic conquests of foreign lands. Man, thought Aristoteles, had the far more important task of finding out for what good purpose did mankind exist. In all fairness it would seem that Alexander would have preferred to join his tutor, but he was finally persuaded that not only was everything prepared for the expedition against Persia but that, unless it was undertaken, Macedonia must later perish, for she had not the strength to resist the gold of Persia.

Alexander set out to conquer Persia, but by the time he died, at the age of thirty-three, he had not managed to return to his native land. Not only had he conquered the known eastern world but also a huge area of the unknown world, advancing far into the Punjab.

Would it be right to say that with the advent of Alexander upon the scene, that Greek art degenerated? No! Its decline had started as a result of the Peloponnesian War. The Greek, and especially the Athenian, who was a citizen-soldier could no longer fight the city's battles and attend to his property or business, and he hired a mercenary to take his place, if he could afford to do so. He was becoming more attracted by luxuries, and he devoted himself more to expanding trade and business. His artistic products were more in demand in many lands and he commercialized them, so that by the time of Alexander that period of Greek art known as Hellenistic was well on its way. Perhaps it was still very great art, but hardly the inspired art of the Golden Age. With the final Roman conquest of all Greece in 146 B.C., the period known as the Greco-Roman began, which no longer could lay claim to any real greatness.

What we may note, however, is that, at the death of Alexander, Greek civilisation had been spread far afield. His mighty empire, however, became divided among his generals. Though the city of Pergamos in Asia Minor shone brilliantly for over another century, and the Isle of Rhodes emerged opulent and powerful for some years, the centre of learning moved to that city of Alexandria, in Egypt, which he had founded. Here, under the Ptolemies, Greek thought went on developing and laying the foundation of almost all modern science.

PART II
GREEK CULTURE AND THOUGHT

CHAPTER I

GREEK CULTURE

WHEN AND WHAT was the height of Greek culture?

The great art, the great philosophy, the great science of the Hellenic world flourished in the spring and summer months of her historic period, but there were also glorious blooms in the autumnal months, even if they were not so redolent.

The poet sings:

> "Oh, to be in England
> Now that April's there!"

That is the time of the early spring flowers, the daffodil and the hyacinth, flowers that are permeated with the freshness of the youthful year. That is the time of the freshness of Greek art and the early vigour of her philosophy.

Then comes summer with the mature beauty of the sophisticated rose. Thoughts are no longer so simple, and the promise of the future is no longer the primary driving force. That is when philosophy in Greece is more theologic and psychic. That is when the great dramatists are inspired by the mysteries of the unknown, and when life has inculcated that stern and inexorable fate which holds the will of the individual but of little account.

Finally comes the autumn, the season of the dahlia and the chrysanthemum, neither sweetly perfumed nor coy with charms, but ready to impose themselves with sedate majesty and a full, satiated life. At this period technical skill in art has already surpassed the vigour of inspiration. Professional wisdom produces erudition, and the thinkers of Alexandria classify and give us Euclid and astronomy, while in the realm of art old age yearns rather for the prettiness of the gullible wench than for the glory of womanhood.

The purpose of the above digression is not so much to give us a simile of the rise of the various forms of Greek art to their zenith and subsequent decline, but rather to indicate the progress of Greek culture as a whole, and that the different phases will bud and blossom and in turn fade and give way to others. Culture, we understand, to be of the spirit, but we need not confine this to art. Art is the doing of things, and the mere knowledge of how to do things is no longer art, and possibly not even culture.

In the autumnal days of the Greeks they could still believe that what was good was beautiful and what was beautiful was good, but inspired art gave way to inspired thought. Even in the summer days the Greek philosophers became less engrossed in scientific enquiry and more absorbed in matters ethical, so that the enquiring mind of Sokrates should lead Platon and Aristoteles to pursue the psychic and ethical aspects of life.

Platon in particular turned thoughts away from pragmatic enquiry and from such matters as of what is the prime substance of terrestial or universal composition, to matters entirely of ideals and the soul. Platon furthered a trend of philosophy which later developed, perhaps on a far less elevated sphere of creative thought, to Neo-Platonism, and that in its turn, when married to a Hebraic background, gave us the teachings of Christianity, a legacy to the world, far, far greater than any scientific progress or technical advancement. Such philosophical precepts of human understanding can be as useful in preventing global wars as technical advancements can be in winning them.

The art and literature of Greece of the age of Perikles has been called a miracle, and a miracle it undoubtedly was, for a miracle is an extraordinary manifestation of nature which astonishes and amazes us, and is beyond our ability to explain. The miracle of Greek art does not differ from any other great national art of any period or of any country in that it had its rise, its zenith, and its decline.

What was the cause of it? The best we can do is to enumerate some of its contributory factors and make our guess.

Greek art passed its zenith and declined with the passing of that implicit and devout faith in the gods. It was a faith that demanded a negation of self. It required that duty to the city, and thus to the gods, should have prior claim. It lifted man into a sublime state beyond his own individuality. There is much truth in this.

Greek art passed its zenith and declined when that pride in the "City" and the glowing achievement of Hellenes against the stupendous might of Persia degenerated into the greedy ambitions of states, and the petty rancours of individual cupidity. Of the significance of this we can be sure.

Greek art passed its zenith and declined when that period passed in which the high ideals of womanhood gave inspiration, and when femininity not only symbolised what was beautiful and good both aesthetically and ethically, but also was appreciated as a creative force in the pride of race. It is certainly true that the bloom of art started to wither at the time when women were being forced into more seclusion and the spirit which revered femininity declined to a mere esteem and thence to scant consideration. Rather, however, than ascribe this as a cause of decline, we might consider it as one of the resultant aspects.

The victories over the Persians caused an elation which stimulated inspiration, while the degradation of the squalid Peloponnesian War caused a depression which damped inspiration. The emergence of Sparta as supreme, elevated the soldier, for the time being, over the artist.

The triumphant joy of victory requires expression so

that it can be magnified by being shared with others, and of such is the creative inspiration of art. The despondency of defeat requires the solitude of thought, and of such is the composition of philosophy.

The repercussion of momentous events upon creative art and thought is even more strikingly correlated by the fact that Athenian creative genius never completely revived with the hegemony of Alexander the Great. Whereas Athens still existed, with its main institutions unimpaired, for a further century and a half before the advent of Rome, we are nonetheless confronted with a lack of outstanding artistic genius. It is of course one of the greatest fallacies of logic to say that because one event follows another that the former is the cause of the latter, but we cannot help feeling that in this instance there is a very close connection.

A point that requires consideration, and to which we do not propose to attempt any definite answer, is that if such external events do affect the creative urge, then how long is the period of gestation before it is expressed in mature art? It depends, of course, on how ripe the soil is already, both aesthetically and in technical skill. The mental intake of the events may be almost immediate, the period of rumination a matter of a few months or years. The reaction in creative urge follows, but that is only the beginning of the artistic impulse that is engendered, and it may take two or three generations to reach maturity, and then only provided the soil is ripe.

At the beginning of this book we dealt first with the nature of Greek lands, and secondly with the origin of the ancient Greeks, and though we did not wish to start with these rather dull subjects, we felt constrained to do so, and described the first as being the soil, and the second the seed, and then we dealt with the historical events, which were the climatic effect on the growing seedlings. The choice of this order was deliberate as these are the "data" upon which we can examine the development of Greek art and try to understand it.

The racial antecedents of each city are as important as any in the quality of the art produced by that city. We continually come across so much to persuade us that the artistic, creative instinct is dependent on the admixture of stock and blood.

A contentious point is that of patronage and we have to acknowledge that all great art seems to have flourished most when patronage in some form existed, be it the Church, the Medici, the Chinese emperors, the kings of France, or the Stuart kings. In Athens the times of pure democracy were punctuated with great interludes of patronage when there was a spurt of creative art, and of such patrons were Peisistratos, Hipparchos, and his brother Hippias, Kleisthenes, and Perikles. Behind and beyond all these the real patrons of the great Greek sculptors were the common people of all non-Dorian Hellas. Surely there never have been communities in which the ordinary citizen has his critical faculties so highly developed for the appreciation of what is beautiful in art.

The first Greek art to emerge is that very one which is most overlooked, and that is poetry. The reason for its comparative neglect is simple, for it cannot be translated without losing its bloom. The English language is a rich one, and lends itself to poetry, and for this it is not inferior to the French, and certainly not as cacophonous as the German, yet it is not as perfect as the Greek for the conveyance of human thought or for expressing it so poetically.

Homer, then, was the father of Greek art, and the grandfather, too. It may be said that you cannot compare the different forms of art, and you cannot compare the greatness of Homer with the greatness of Pheidias the sculptor, or Euripides the tragedian, or Shakespeare the playwright, or Leonardo da Vinci the painter. Perhaps that is so, but not entirely so, and this fact is known to the moderating assessors in the technical schools of art whose care is to find a common level or standard so that diploma or degree should represent equal proficiency and attainment. On this basis we can say that Homer was as great an artist as there ever has been. Throughout Greek history Homer was invariably taught at school, and we must therefore include Homer as one of the continuing, inspiring influences of all Greek art.

The great poets flourished early, before writing was common. In fact, poetry may have flourished because of the absence of writing, for in this form creative art, which could not be perpetuated on paper, and for which there was not the skill to do so in stone, could be perpetuated mnemonically on the mind.

So very much of Greek poetry has unfortunately been lost, including most of the songs of Sappho, who was perhaps the greatest woman artist that the world has ever known. Pindar the Theban was also of the same breed, and we will recollect earlier than he that famous bard Tyrtaeos, who enthused the Spartans and led them to victory over the Messenians.

Of all Greek culture, that which we admire most, and that in which the Greeks attained their greatest heights, is sculpture, and we shall therefore not only give it the bulk of our attention but priority in mention.

CHAPTER II

SCULPTURE

WHAT CAUSED the miracle of Greek sculpture to germinate in the first place? Can we say the institution of the Olympic Games? We would not be so very wrong. The apotheosis of the human figure as a demonstration of piety is certainly an original form of religious ritual.

From the first Olympiad the games were consecrated to the worship and glory of Zeus, but they had been held for decades and decades prior to this. Olympia was also very much an earlier shrine to Hera, as her temple there, the Heraion, attests. Yet more than the Earth Mother or the Father of the Gods, it was Herakles (Hercules) who originally sanctified the site. There is a tradition that here he raced his four brothers and was the victor.

Kings of the Peloponnesian cities were Heraklidae, the apogeny of the demigod Herakles. Glorification of Herakles was not only an act of reverence to the Immortals but an outward sign of loyalty to the ruling families.

Since Herakles was a demigod, which means that one of his parents was an Immortal, he must have been, at the very least in form, in the likeness of the gods. The essence of Herakles was his superlative figure and strength, his prodigious feats of athletic prowess and endurance. The nearer man reached to the demigods in physical form, the more the gods would esteem him as being on a higher level and worthy of their consideration.

Is this putting the cart before the horse? It was the imagination of the Greeks that created Herakles as the all-powerful, infallible super-athlete. Whether the egg came before the chicken does not really matter; what we are concerned with is that at the two most hallowed places of Greece, Olympia and Delphi, as well as Nemea and elsewhere, athletic contests were held in praise of the god. Victory therein was a sign of the god's grace to the fortunate winner, a divine blessing and favour so great that it should not be sullied by any prize, other than a purely symbolic one.

The Greeks tried to express the intangible divine of the god through the most noble form of the human body, and sculpture lends itself to this. The earliest statues were of wood, and statuettes were of burnt clay, that is, terra-cotta, and later of limestone and bronze. These were the more primitive materials, available before the evolution of elaborately and scientifically perfected paints, and their use was one of the reasons why sculpture should evolve before painting.

There is also another and most important reason. The shores of Greece are bathed in the clearest, softest, and most pellucid atmosphere. The air itself is light, ethereal, intoxicating, inspiring, and not the harsh crystalline light of Spain, nor the full-bodied sensuous light of northern Italy. The landscape, the seascape of Greece are of a brilliance of mellow colours in perfect harmony, and they are ever serene. There is not the contrast of northern colours in juxtaposition, sombre and threatening, gay and jubilant, and overpowering the essence of form by their values.

Wherever you are in Greece, the sky line is that of mountains. If you are on the seashore, or on the islands, you will always see mountain ranges jutting out into the seascape or rising ruggedly over the horizon. You will see their sky line silhouetted in the essence of a rhythm, a song of Hellas which is visualised in form. On the land you will find the trees not clustered together, but each separately standing out, humbly perhaps, but consciously proud of showing its own form to its full value. You will see the incredibly twisted and gnarled tree trunk of a venerable olive tree, its foliage singing its silvery ode. Each is proud of its separate existence, independent and self-satisfied.

If we could but interpret the song of the Greek landscape, I think the olive would be chanting in praise to Athene, the heavy-laden fruit trees to Demeter, the asphodel and the anemone to Persephone, the vine and the ivy to Dionysos, the oaks of wild Dodona to Zeus, the ripples of the sea to Aphrodite, the sky line of the mountains to Hera. Yes! And the human form, too, would have its ode, in Olympia to Zeus, in Delphi to Apollon, and around Corinth to Poseidon.

The Greeks tried to catch the hymn of the perfect human body, and they tried to express it in their sculptured statues.

There is an essence in the sculpture of Greece of the best period which lifts it above the great sculpture of other lands and times. When we see these statues of a goddess, in form perfect, or of an Apollon, we, of whichever sex we are, would not think of them as mortals among us, whose perfection might captivate our senses. There is no sensuality, only sensitivity. They are impersonal and above personality. The statues are interpreting that ode to the gods which the Greeks could hear and interpret in stone, marble, and bronze.

In its first form Greek sculpture was purely emblematic, but it always aimed at a higher purpose, which precluded its worship in idolatry. The very first statues, after the intervening dark age following Mycenaean times, were mere emblems, originating in such wooden posts as the Herm, dedicated to the landmark god. Its evolution was to portray the shape of a head, then the indication of arms, still column-like, glued to the figure. When legs next appear, they, too, were in unity, and the column formation was maintained. Later still, seated figures are attempted. There is no sense of motion, but there is a sense of eternity.

At about the beginning of the sixth century sculpture attempts to be other than purely emblematic and takes the form of the archaic. It is genuine statuary, but impressionistic, because the technique and the skill have not yet matured. The sculptor does not try to get out of his depth, beyond his powers, or otherwise he would not be able to express that serenity and majesty which nonetheless he succeeds in conveying. By every reasonable standard these archaic forms are not beautiful, yet they manage to convey so perfectly the awe and the reverence for the gods that they emerge finally as great works of art, and we are contemplating something which is above the commonplace of mortals.

The Archaic is featured by protruding eyes and coarse lips, but the general impressionistic effect subdues them. Before proceeding, however, to statuary in its highest form, we must interpose a little thought which may help us to conceive the perfection to which it attained and the extent of its production.

In the first place it must not be forgotten that the Persians twice entered Athens, and Mardonius was out to avenge the ignominy of his previous defeat. His men were steeped in a sun-worshipping religion which was iconoclastic, and as they wrecked everything that they found before them, they would have destroyed all statuary with added fervour. Of statuary in Athens there must have been a prolific quantity for the two previous generations were those of the patrons of art, the sons of Peisistratos, and Kleisthenes, but we have next to no examples of Athenian statues in the stage of evolution from the Archaic to the Classic.

The best-known examples of Archaic art existing are the twin statues of the "Kouros," one of which is in the Metropolitan Museum of New York and the other holds pride of place in the National Archaeological Museum of Athens. These two statues were discovered in 1932 by smugglers who managed to get them out of the country, though the one duly returned to its native land after visiting Paris.

Among the few that we have are those known as the "Tanten," or "The Aunts," which were unearthed some fifty years ago, and the way that they received their name is rather amusing. A few years before the Persian invasions there had been an occasion when Hippias and his supporters sought refuge on the Acropolis, where they had barricaded themselves. As the defences were not very secure they had taken certain additional measures, including the filling in of a gap. This they had done with all the material that they could lay their hands on, but presumably they would not have been sacrilegious and touched the statues of the gods. Among the rubble there were some statues, all of women and in a similar stance, with an arm extended in which something was held. The meaning of the statues we do not know, but they are of a progressive period covering several decades, and may even have commemorated some order of high priestesses. As these statues were being brought to light the archaeologists were thrilled and excited with the totally unexpected find, and one of their Teutonic members was unable to control himself when a somewhat archaic female statue was lifted from the depths and faced him. He exploded nostalgically with thoughts of the Fatherland from which archaeology had separated him. "Why," he exclaimed, "in truth, it is my Aunt Mathilda!" And for the want of a more accurate description they have been called "The Aunts." Now, however, in Greece they are generally called "Korai," "The Maidens," which is the feminine of "Kouros," "The Youth."

Apart from the paucity of Athenian statues of the period, statuary in its highest expression finds its initial development in the Peloponnesos in the middle of the sixth century B.C., whereas in Athens it is not till a little later, and with the wave of thanksgiving to the gods for the deliverance of the city from the barbaric Medes.

It is in the city of Argos that the classically supreme statues have their birth, and, as we might expect, they appear as the nude male figure. In the Peloponnesos the tradition of the Herakleidae was strong, and so were the Olympic Games. A century and a half earlier, Pheidon, king of Argos, who during his reign had become virtual master of the peninsula, displayed such interest in the games that he took them under his aegis, to the fury of the Spartans who were then unable to interfere. We are not astonished, therefore, that statuary in the Peloponnesos should first be in this form, and should continue to be the basis of the Argive school, with the characteristic of boldness and vigour.

When later the inspiration came to Athens, at a time when skill had matured, the sensitivity of the Athenian expressed itself in all that he held spiritually to be most beautiful and to be reverenced in femininity, in the form of the female draped figure.

The two schools, the Argive and the Ionian, influenced each other, so that when the great masters produced their statues with the parenthood of the wedded inspirations, the vigour of the Argive and the delicacy of the Athenian, the result was superlative.

Not only have we but few examples of the Archaic statues, but it is not sufficiently realized how very few we have of the great masterpieces, descriptions of which exist to some extent through Pausanias.

The British Museum possesses much of the severely damaged pediments of the Parthenon, but we have no real knowledge as to what extent they are the work of Pheidias, or merely executed under his supervision. His two great works, the Zeus of Olympia, and the Athene of the Parthenon, no longer exist. Dismembered or decapitated as the Parthenon pediments are, however, there is to be seen workmanship so delicate and exquisite that there is no hesitation in crediting him with much of it. Practically all the other known works of Pheidias that we possess are but copies, executed in a later, and even possibly Roman, period. All the works of Myron that we possess are copies, and all these copies are clearly inferior to the originals. Of the named statues of the great masters practically the only one that exists is the "Hermes" of Praxiteles, and the craftsmanship and delicacy of this none can exceed. It is, however, of a later period and bereft of the divine inspiration.

In Edwardian times, the "Hermes" of Praxiteles at Olympia and the "Aphrodite" from Milos at the Louvre were admired as the finest statues that we have that Hellas produced. Fashion changes, and although we need not detract from their greatness, there are others to which present-day taste gives pride of place and, for that matter, they were discovered only in comparatively recent times, such as the "Poseidon" at the National Museum of Athens, and the "Charioteer" at Delphi.

Of the very few names that we intend mentioning, beyond the three already given, are Ageladas and Polykleitos, and these two are sculptors who had the greatest influence, for Ageladas was the teacher of Pheidias and of Myron, as well as of Polykleitos. The latter wrote a book, "The Rule" which was the textbook for sculpture for many a long day, and he, like Ageladas, was an Argive.

Ageladas died in the middle of the fifth century, about 455 B.C., and thus reached maturity before the Persian invasions. Pheidias is of the Golden Age and died about 430 B.C., whereas Myron, who was born some ten years before Pheidias, died about 410 B.C., then aged about ninety.

Colour In Sculpture

Colour in sculpture? Yes! The sculpture of Greece was painted. Possibly the whole of it, and that is the present-day conclusion, but it is a subject on which we must not make too positive assertions for our knowledge is rather hazy. That both statues and temples were painted we definitely know from contemporary writings. Broadly, the painting was decorative, and not primarily concerned with making the statue more lifelike. Apart from the inspiration, the beginning and end of the statue was the figure, the form, the style, its delicateness or its vigour, and not the colour.

The Parthenon would be painted, and so, too, would the statues by Pheidias in the pediments (the triangular spaces between the tops of the columns and the angle of the roof, at the front and back of the temple). Most of the decorative design would also be painted, but only the ornate capitals of the columns, all of it in keeping with the colour scheme of the building.

In the statues the draperies might be coloured blue, red, green, pink, or any other colour, and in all likelihood of fairly bright tones. The hair would be brown or golden, or possibly even black, and the eyebrows would match. The lips were painted red. Jewelry such as earrings, and the pins fastening the draperies, would be gilt. In so far as we know the flesh parts of the statues were not painted. There was a process known as "ganosis" which probably was a rubbing of wax, or possibly oil, not unlike our furniture polish. This substance, whatever it was, may have been tinted flesh colour, and may have been superimposed by a hot iron.

We have become used to seeing noncoloured statues—or photographs of them—in museums, so that it may give us a shock to think of them as not only painted but possibly painted with an eye to decorative value rather than to enhance the natural effect. Yet a statue in pure white marble is not only cold and inanimate but it loses the contrasting values which show up form. We must not forget that the ancient statues as we see them today have lost their milky whiteness and are transformed by the patina of age. New pure white marble statues such as may be seen in cemeteries will exemplify the loss of value and distinction of form. The sunlight of Greece must also be taken into account, for it would assimilate such coloured statuary and temples to the scenery and surroundings, more so than in northern climes.

We know that in earlier times such animals as lions were also painted other than their natural colours, and whereas the eyes and even the mane might be naturalistic, the body might be blue or red. The thought may shock us, yet it should do so no more than the hundreds of unnaturally coloured animals calling thirst-quenching attention and decorating the inns of town, hamlet, and village in heraldic splendour.

Bronze and Marble Statues

Bronze statues were usual in Classical times, but not many have survived. Marble buried in earth does not deteriorate, but bronze does. More important, bronze statues, when found by looters, are taken and melted for the metal, and therefore the chance of excavating bronze statues is less than that of finding marble statues. As against this, marble statues are destroyed in sea water very rapidly, unless they sink quickly below the mud of the sea bottom. Bronze statues do not deteriorate at all in sea water. With one or two exceptions, therefore, the finest bronze statues that we have are those found at the bottom of the sea. In Roman times Greece was pillaged of many of her best works of art by the Romans, and in earlier Roman times such statues were sent to Rome, and in later times to Byzantium, renamed Constantinople, capital of the Eastern Roman Empire. The Romans, however, were frequently greedy in their looting and overloaded their ships, with the result that many were wrecked. Some of these statues have been recovered in recent years and are among the very finest that we now possess. Among them are two statues of youths, and the statue of Poseidon, though some believe it to be of Zeus Keraunobolos, Hurler of Thunderbolts, all three being at the Athens Museum.

A bronze statue found about fifty years ago, but not under the sea, is that of the "Charioteer" of Delphi, erected to celebrate a chariot race winner of Syracuse at the games. This statue, one of the finest that exist, has eyes of onyx.

Bronze was used extensively by the Argive school, and was well adapted to their boldness of conception and execution.

We have mentioned the pediments of the Parthenon by Pheidias, and that we do not know precisely what is his own work or what is that of his assistants. Not only does Pheidias make the contrary qualities of grandiose and of delicacy harmonize but he gives such perfect rhythm to the cavalcade of the frieze that you can see the horsemen advancing forwards, and if you listen carefully enough you will assuredly hear the pounding of the hoofs.

There were two other statues on the Acropolis which were of the genius of Pheidias, one of which certainly was purely of his own craftsmanship. The first of these two statues, the "Athene Promachos," stood before the Parthenon about halfway from the entrance gates, the Propylaea. It stood erect, sixty-six feet high, the spear and the helmet being either bronze or gold. The travel-weary sailor, journeying home from afar, would first see the reflected Attic sunlight blazing from Athene's helmet, and would know that he was nearing the end of his travels and being welcomed to his city by his goddess.

More famous was the statue of Athene within the sanctuary of the Parthenon, the "Athene Parthenos." It was of ivory and gold and was thirty-eight feet high. The draperies were of gold but the face and other parts of the body were of ivory. This statue, together with a somewhat similar one of Almighty Zeus at Olympia, were the most famed of ancient Greece, but they have disappeared, for it is believed that they were later taken to Byzantium by the Eastern Roman emperors.

Of other statues by Pheidias we have just a few copies, but contemporary literature tells of their fame. Principally they were of draped goddesses.

Of Myron's statues we have but poor Roman copies, yet two of them are famous. The one is the "Diskobolos," the thrower of the discus, well known to almost all. Of this statue there are two copies extant, and the first of these to be found had its head broken off and was reconstructed, unfortunately with its head obviously in the wrong position. Though we could hardly have expected the learned statuary plastic surgeons to have been discus throwers themselves, they should have known better. The head should be bent downwards and looking back rather than forwards, yet copies are still seen without the fault being rectified.

The other famous statue of Myron is that of the satyr Marsyas, "Athena and Marsyas," and this depicts one of those very many legends of Arcadian myth regarding the gods, goddesses, nymphs and satyrs, which were of the genius of Greek fairylike phantasy, and of which so far we have not had occasion to narrate. The statue already shows the change in the evolution of Greek sculpture, for we are passing from the pure expression of the divine to the feeling of incident. Here Athena has been playing the pipes, and she was enraptured with the enchanting music which her divine artistry could command, but she happened to pass by a humble stream which fitted well to the strains of her inspiration, and there she halted for a while. Of a sudden she caught sight of her reflection in the peaceful waters, and horror-struck at the sight of her puffed-out cheeks, so unbecoming to a goddess such as she, she hurled the pipes away in disgust. Close by among the reeds lay Marsyas, a satyr, enchanted by the divine notes. When unexpectedly he saw the pipes flying through the air and landing not far away, he avidly went to pick them up. As he looked, he saw the goddess and was taken aback at the apparition, for no mortal may pry upon the gods unbid, and yet live. Myron shows us Marsyas in the act of sudden recoil as he realizes that he is in the divine presence.

Of Praxiteles we have the famous Hermes holding a child in his left arm, while his right is extended but with the hand missing, so that we do not know what he held, and Pausanias who saw, noted, and admired the statue, does not tell us. This is among the first of the statues that show composition and more than one figure. It is a state of wonderful craftsmanship and exquisite delicateness, but it was executed at a time when statuary had become more personal and even emotional. No more is there the feeling that the sculptor is searching to express the serenity and divine eternity of the gods. He was no longer giving himself selflessly and inviting you to join him in feeling something spiritual and above your own individuality, but appealing to your passions or your sentiments. From such statuary it was not such a long step for art to rejoice even in sentimentality.

Of other statues of Praxiteles we have the Vatican copy of the statue of Aphrodite, which was bought by the city of Knidos (Cnidus), and truly it is exquisitely beautiful, but it is no longer the chaste draped figure of the goddess, but a nude female figure. From the copy we can assert again that it is truly beautiful, for it is the figure of a lady whom every great dress designer would like to have model for him, and one whom every young man, as well as every old man about town, would be in ecstasy to take out to dinner. It is of a lady we would today call a goddess, but not possessed of divinity.

In conclusion we will mention the two famous winged Victories, both of which must rank as of the greatest statues in the world. We cannot understand how marble can be imbued with the lightness of thistledown, beyond which we will neither describe them nor give their history.

CHAPTER III

ARCHITECTURE

THOUGH it is normal that the buildings of interest in any great city should be the national and municipal edifices, and even more so the places of religious worship, yet in most capital cities there is also some palace, or the great and magnificent houses of the nobility. In Classical Greece we have no record of such luxurious residences of the wealthy, though there must have been some in the Greek cities of Ionia. Our survey, however, must be confined to what we know of the planned centres and the temples, of which there are many in a fair state of preservation. Many cities, of course, just grew, yet however much they did so, there would always be certain parts which would be very carefully planned. The two foremost of such parts would be the Acropolis, which we might call the Citadel, and which wherever possible was on raised ground, and the Agora. Both of these would be designed symmetrically and rhythmically so as to conform to the logical requirements of their purposes.

When Athens started to prosper and trade expanded, it was the port of the Piraeus which was first affected. Here Themistokles was inspired to build a dockyard, the need being more of a naval nature. Perikles followed by having a Commercial Exhibition Hall built, the use of which explained itself by its name, "The Deigma," that is, "The Sample," and to which all merchants could bring and exhibit samples of the goods they had imported or offered for export. Perikles also had the city of the Piraeus extended and replanned, and the town planner was Hippodamos, an Ionian who gets the credit of being the originator of the present-day American system, for the town was laid out in rectangular blocks.

The most important architectural planning was the Civic Centre, the Agora. Here were concentrated all the booths, stalls, fashionable shops, bankers' tables, and also the civic buildings, including the parliamentary offices, the Senate (which in the case of Athens was a circular building), and here, too, were police and magistrates' offices, as well as close-by taverns and other places of diversion. Normally the Agora of Greek cities was not paved, and, indeed, few Greek streets or squares were. Although most Greeks wore sandals or shoes, it was by no means invariable—Sokrates being an example of one who did not—and for that matter horses were not shod—but the reason would not have been only for greater softness, but to avoid the heat. You can have a thermometer reading of 90°, 100°, or a little over during the summer months in Greece, but the sun reading can be in the 130's, which you would soon know if you trod barefoot on a stone or marble slab. Stone slabs and stone or marble building surfaces absorb the sun's heat during the day and release it at sundown, when the citizens might hope to enjoy the cool of the evening. This fact affected the construction of Greek dwellings. Trees were planted in the Agora, and these would normally be plane trees, where water was obtainable as in the case of Athens, and the whole centre would be beautified with colonnaded porchways and porticoes. In Athens the most famous of these porchways was the Poikile Stoa, the "Painted Arcade," in which we know that Polygnotos, the greatest artist of his day, depicted three scenes of the battle of Marathon. In the Agora of each city there would also be innumerable statues, many of which would have been of Olympic winners.

Other planned areas were the Gymnasia, the physical-exercise centres (of which Athens had three), on a grand scale. The focal point would be the wrestling arena, on each side of which would be changing rooms, bathrooms, and amusement lounges. They would extend beyond—normally on the farther side facing the entrance—to running tracks and to javelin-throwing and archery-practice fields. The two main sides would probably be colonnaded, and we know this to have been the case in some instances.

Our interest in Greek architecture is, however, centred around the temples, if only from the fact that there are so many in a fair state of preservation. They conform to the nature of the belief of the ancient Greeks, and we can better understand this if we compare their purpose to the religious edifices of the Christian era.

Old Saxon churches had the utilitarian purpose of a beacon tower, but the Gothic cathedrals aimed at a mighty spire, rising to the heavens to pierce them and pave a channel for prayers to ascend to the Immortal Mansions. Gothic cathedrals are the very contradiction of Greek temples, and aim at impressing the devout by a multitude of chapels and ornate excrescences, so that the whole cathedral becomes a building of luxuriant architecture and an agglomeration of disconnected details that often do not even make an entity.

Let us now consider Byzantine architecture in relation to that of the ancient Greeks, in order better to understand the latter. Although Byzantium was refounded as the capital of the Eastern Roman Empire under the name of Constantinople, it very quickly became entirely Greek in character and carried on the traditions of the Greeks, although, of course, these had evolved during several centuries. It is worth interposing that the present inhabitants of Greece, who still have many of the traditions and beliefs, as well as many of the characteristic traits of the Classical inhabitants, look to Byzantium for their traditions, and not to the Classical period, just as the British might look to the great days of Elizabethan England, and not to the earlier Roman or Saxon times. This is all the more the case as few religions, due to historic causes, can be so interwoven with patriotic sentiment as is the case of the Greek Orthodox Church. The point of the above is this—that the Byzantine churches, which have incorporated the Roman arch, have a balanced and symmetrical plan in the old tradition. The roof, which is a cupola, is meant to represent the heavens, and is supposed to rest on the supporting walls, and not to be built on them, and so that if one could imagine an airship passing by, and trailing an anchor which might be hitched onto the surmounting cross, the roof should be lifted off as if it were a saucepan lid. In theory the heavens are thus brought down to earth to the worshippers, and this feeling basically emanates from that of the Greek temples. Here also we may note with interest that the great Greek cathedral of Saint Sophia of the Orthodox Church at Constantinople, is that of the "Holy Wisdom," which, after all, is the maintenance of the attribute of the great ancient goddess Athene. We could also cite many present-day Greek churches which are dedicated to saints whose attributes have been taken from temples erected to gods of a similar character. There are churches dedicated to St. Dionysios, for instance, where once there were temples to the god Dionysos, or churches dedicated to St. Demetrios where there had been temples to Demeter. Where there had been a temple to the god Poseidon, we may today find a church dedicated to St. Nicholas, or St. Spyridon, the saint of mariners.

This aspect of Greek churches may help us to understand what the ancient Greek architects aimed at when they planned their temples. We will understand it even better when we realize that the Greeks did not kneel or make obeisance when they prayed, but stood erect, for they were like unto the gods, and some even prided themselves on descent from them. The god would descend to earth, if so inclined, when his priest made burnt offerings at his altar, which was sanctified ground and out of doors. The temple was therefore built just for those requirements of the altar, and for the glorification of the god or goddess, so that the people might express their reverence, but it was not built to engender a feeling of reverence. The temple, therefore, was the glorified house of a deity, who, however, did not reside there, and required neither bedroom nor eating rooms. The temple only served as a background to the altar and as a room to keep the treasures, the general construction being that of the portico of a house. The temple was therefore an idea, untrammeled with fussy details, and like all Greek art had to express a self-contained ideal. The temples were in harmony with the site, and sought to blend with the seascape and landscape. They were of one conception, on the proportions of which depended the majesty or elegance, the austerity or benevolence. The temple was flat and long, thus merging with the scenery as part of the landscape, even if in a prominent position.

The height and thickness of the columns varied considerably, but in general the length of the temple was about double the breadth, and the number of the columns at the sides was normally about one more than double the number on the façades. In the early pre-Classical period the columns were of wood, and both in Minoan and Geometric times the more slender part of the trunk rested on the ground with the larger part supporting the roof. In Classical times the temple was almost invariably of marble, of which there were two main sources, that from the island of Paros, and that from the quarries of Mount Pentelicon close to Athens. The Parian marble was of pure gleaming whiteness, but the Pentelic was more creamy, and also had certain mineral contents, which with the patina of age gave a slightly rusty tint. Mount Hymettos, even closer to Athens, has marble of a bluish tint.

Temples

Temples were of three architectural orders. The main feature of these was the shape and decoration of the columns, and with which the frieze would be in keeping, though this was not strictly adhered to. We shall not describe the orders in detail, for not only is it beyond the scope of the book but an illustration can do so more effectively. The orders were: Doric, Ionic, and Corinthian; but the first one was the more extensively used in Greece itself.

The main feature of the Doric column is that it has

no base; it is slightly tapering, with an imperceptible bulge in the middle, and is surmounted by a rounded moulding, over which there is a fairly thick square slab; the column has sharp-edged, broad flutings. The Doric column has a more solid and majestic appearance than the others, and it was of this order that columns were chosen for the Parthenon.

The Ionic columns are more slender than the others and give a more elegant appearance, originating rather in Ionia, of Asia Minor, than in Athens. On the Acropolis there are Ionic columns in the small temple of the Erechtheion. Some temples had exterior Doric columns with a parallel row of Ionic columns within the aisles. The flutings of these columns are narrower, and there is a base to them. Their main feature is the capital which consists of two pairs of parallel spirals.

The Corinthian column was a late-comer to the temples, and only after the time of Perikles. As might be expected from its name it has more of the luxuriance of the mercantile city, its feature being a capital of thistle (or acanthus) leaves, but it is nonetheless not overornate, imparting grace as well as opulence to the column. The temple of Olympian Zeus in Athens is one of the best-known examples.

Of Greek temples of which remains are still standing, there are several in Sicily and southern Italy. Among the best preserved temples is that one known as the Theseion, not far from the base of the Acropolis in Athens. Until some years ago it was believed to have been the temple where the bones of Theseus were reinterred, but after recent excavations over a large part of old Athens the archaeologists have come to the conclusion that it is really a temple to Hephaistos, the God of the Forge. It has been definitely established that its site is in the centre of what was, and incidentally still is, the smithies' neighbourhood. It is an imposing temple but has not the inspiring majesty of some of the others, its columns being like those of the Parthenon, of the Doric order.

One of the most ambitious temples, and of which there are still several columns standing, was that dedicated to Olympian Zeus, which is situated to the east of the Acropolis in Athens. Though started by Peisistratos, no doubt originally with Doric columns, it was not finished till the time of the Emperor Hadrian at the beginning of the Christian era. Its columns were nearly sixty feet tall and of the Corinthian order; there were a hundred of them, the full length of the temple being just over 350 feet. There were similar temples, too, in Asia Minor, those to Artemis in Ephessos, and to Apollon at Didyma, being also about 350 feet long and having over a hundred columns.

In Corinth itself there are some columns of a temple to Apollon, and these are also of the Doric order. In the Peloponnesos there is a temple designed by Iktinos at Phigalia, not so very far from Olympia, in a fairly good state of preservation. In a fair state also is the Temple of Aphaea on the isle of Aegina. Both Delphi and Olympia have interesting remains, for the Persians never reached them. Present-day visitors to Greece, however, are more frequently attracted to visit the few columns left standing at Cape Sounion, from a temple sacred to Poseidon. It was built of local Sounion marble, the quality of which is similar to that of the Parian, and still looks as gleaming white as the day it was quarried. Its position, perched on the commanding height at the edge of the most southeasterly promontory in Attica, is so imposing, and so scenic in its setting of variegated inlets, seascape, and mountains, that it creates a far more lasting memory than many a finer temple. An interesting fact about the temple of Sounion is that imaginery lines joining the temples of the Parthenon, of Aphaea in Aegina, and of Sounion, form a perfect isosceles triangle.

Though we shall conclude this chapter with a short description of the Acropolis of Athens and its temples, we should first mention some of the other architectural features, of which the athletic stadia and the theatres are the most important. In both cases sites were normally chosen so that the slope of the land could serve as part of the construction and help to cup the seats and give the tiers a good incline so that the spectators could have a clear, unimpaired view. In the case of the theatres one can guess that deliberate choice of site was made so that the spectators could have the background of a distant vista over and beyond the stage, for the theatres were open-air. The most famous of these theatres is that of Dionysos, which nestles in the southern foothold of the Acropolis. It was here that first were performed many of the great dramas and undying comedies of the Athenian genius. The most imposing and best preserved is the theatre at the shrine of the Health God, Asklepios, in Epidauros of the Peloponnesos. The impression of these theatres is deceptive, for whereas they look intimate, they can, in fact, seat many thousands. The theatre of Epidauros, where ancient dramas are at present staged in summer, holds 17,000. There are also large theatres in many other places, including ones at Megalopolis (which held 20,000), Argos, Delphi, Dodona, and elsewhere.

We also have records of many civic buildings and halls in other parts of Greece and Ionia, as well as in Athens, and the feature of these is the amount of interior columns that were needed to support the roof. Some were quite large, such as the Leonidaeon at Olympia, which covered an area of about 250 feet square, and had an outer colonnade of 135 Ionic columns, with 44 roof-supporting columns in the interior. Among other such large buildings were the Concert Hall of Athens, built by Perikles and known as the Odeion, but replaced by a later structure in Greco-Roman times, and also the Hall of Ceremonies for the mysteries at Eleusis.

The Acropolis of Athens

Modern Athens is dominated by a miniature mountain and by a table-shaped rock. The former is Mount Lykabettos and it presents a cone-shaped formation to the northeast of the city of Theseus. It did not feature in the ancient city, being outside its precincts. The table-shaped rock was transformed into the Acropolis.

The city itself is under four miles from the sea, and the intervening ground rises in gently undulating slopes so that Athens is about three hundred feet above sea level. Mount Lykabettos rises a further three hundred feet, and its pinnacle is but an odd mile from the Acropolis.

The rock of the Acropolis is a rectangular oblong lying almost in an east-west direction. The eastern façade is entirely precipitous. The southern façade, except at the top, has a steep slope which becomes gentle at the bottom where nestle the Theatre of Dionysos and the Concert Hall of the Odeion. The northern side is precipitous for the top half, then radiates out, descending steeply to the Agora and the main body of ancient, inhabited Athens some two hundred feet below. The western façade is steep only at the top, the remainder of the slope being but a gentle rise, and it was from this side that the only entrance to the temples at the top was reasonably possible. It was at the foothold of this western approach that meetings were held, and here, among others, the Apostle Paul preached about the new and hitherto unknown God.

The summit of the rock of the Acropolis is fairly flat, except for an incline on the western side, and the Parthenon was built a little to the south and on the top of the incline, so that it had the most commanding position.

Except from the very footholds of the rock, most of the Parthenon can be seen from the city level, and somehow, though Mount Lykabettos towers above it not so far away, the Parthenon manages to impose its majestic, serene, and permeating benevolence over the whole of the Attic plain. Thus the Athenians, who by Hellenic instinct were community conscious, would have the feeling of being in the fold of the eternal overlooking presence, and that both the Parthenon and they were of the city, part of the city, and of its very constitution, just as members and organs of the human body constitute the body itself.

From the shade of the northern side, immediately below, we cannot see the Parthenon, but we see part of the Ionic portico of the Erechtheion peeping over the top, and this tripartite temple is the repository of the most sanctified ground of Athenian veneration. Herein grows the olive tree where Athena struck the ground with her spear, and here, too, is the gash where Poseidon smote the rock with his trident, and here, too, was lodged the sacred serpent. As the Ionic portico peeps over the top gazing at the busy life of the Agora below, it spells that elegance and youthful gaiety which was the essence of the Athenian, and it also whispers of those things that he held most sacred. When, however, we are on the summit of the Acropolis itself, we are rather astonished to find an exception to the prime instinct of the Greek which insists on equipoise and balanced proportions. The configuration of the ground, which at the Erechtheion is of two, if not three levels, imposed the need for reason to overrule symmetry, and to the aid of reason came the veneration which demanded that the older and most venerable precincts should not be disturbed. The Erechtheion, however, does not jar, but it looks a little amorphous. Perhaps when the Acropolis was at the height of its glory, populated with statues, it may have fitted into the picture without any feeling of segregation, and in true Hellenic harmony.

Noteworthy in the Erechtheion group is the little part-temple which juts out facing the Parthenon, and in which the columns take the form of graceful maidens supporting the capitals. Of these maidens, known as Caryatids, there were six, but one of them was abducted by Lord Elgin, and she is now in the seclusion of the British Museum. A terra-cotta replica has replaced her. This little part-temple porch is very remarkable in its grace, for although the Caryatids bear the weight of the roof upon their heads, they do it with the ease of supporting a feather.

The Parthenon was begun about 447 B.C. and the architects were Iktinos and Kallikrates, the former being the designer and the latter the builder. The Propylaea was started some ten years later and the architect was Mnesikles. The Acropolis was entered by a small gateway from the southwest by a zigzag path which led upward to the main entrance of the Propylaea at the top. The Propylaea is, or rather are, in principle a marble wall, through which are five tall gateways flanked by Doric porticoes, with Ionic columns supporting the roofs of the porticoes. On each side there were to have been magnificent colonnaded halls, but it was only on the north side, overlooking the Agora, that the hall was completed, for on the other side there is a temple to Athene, "Athene, Bringer of Victory." The temple is generally called "Nike

Apteros," or "Wingless Victory," on the unsupported belief that the temple had been dedicated to Victory, of whom the Athenians had traditionally amputated the wings so that, perforce, she should be obliged to remain with them. Mnesikles never got his way, and was unable to complete the Propylaea to plan. Possibly the temple may have pre-existed, or more likely the site had been already dedicated to Athena Nike, and respect for it would have been too strong for demolition or desecration. More probably still, the calamities of the Peloponnesian War which befell Athens postponed the costly plan. This diminutive temple is but twenty-seven feet long and has only four Ionic columns at each end. The frieze, part of which is in the British Museum, is of exquisite delicacy, especially in the carved draperies, and the whole effect of the temple is that of extreme daintiness.

The Parthenon itself impresses as the most beautiful and imposing building of antiquity. Its proportions are 228 by 101 feet, and there are 17 columns on each side, with 8 each in the façades, the height of the columns being 35 feet. The precision, care, and thought in its construction are such that we can confidently use the phrase, "it passes all understanding."

It is believed that Pheidias so planned and executed the continuous Ionic frieze and outer sculptured work so that it should appear at its perfection when viewed from the ground level.

Iktinos made such minute calculations that its appearance should be as perfect as human ingenuity could make it. It is generally asserted that these most minute calculations were elaborated to counteract the defects of the human eye, but whether this was so or not, it is certain that they were deliberate and minutely calculated deviations. It is said that the deviations, or refinements, as they have been called, were first discovered when a replica was planned in the United States on the exact proportions, yet the result achieved fell far short of the beauty of the original. On investigation, as a result of this, it was discovered that the whole base of the temple was not flat but deliberately rounded, but so very imperceptibly that this cannot immediately be seen merely by looking at it. In viewing any building, perspective makes the ends seem to curl slightly upwards, and it is not impossible that the purpose was to cure such an illusion created by the imperfection of the human eye. In its length the centre of the basis is four inches higher than the ends, whereas in the façades the difference is less than three inches. Visitors to the Parthenon who are inclined to discredit this, often make a test by placing a hat on the steps at one end, and looking at it with the eye on the ground level from the other end, when the intervening central bulge will either hide the hat or allow only its top to be seen. All the pillars have an imperceptible slant inwards, and the corner pillars slant inwards in both directions. The pillars themselves, like those of most Greek temples, are slightly tapering and have a very slightly larger diameter at the centre.

Within the Parthenon, the main room was to the east, that is, at the back, and was a hundred feet long with a double tier of Doric columns, and within this hall was the gigantic statue of the goddess in gold and ivory, executed by Pheidias. Between the Propylaea and the Parthenon stood, proudly erect, the other statue of Athena, with golden helmet and spear reflecting the Attic sun, heliographing the glory of the goddess throughout her realms.

Since Classic times the Parthenon has undergone many vicissitudes, and at one time it was used as a Christian chapel, remains of the painted icons still being visible in the interior. It had remained in almost perfect condition until two centuries ago, when the Turkish garrison had established itself therein and made its arsenal. When the Venetians tried to dislodge them by firing a gun from a hillock opposite and got a direct hit on the Parthenon, the arsenal exploded and did serious havoc. Part has been reconstructed with the original pieces, and yet even in its ruined state the Parthenon is able fearlessly to challenge any building in the world for beauty, majesty, and, above all, serenity.

CHAPTER IV

THE THEATRE AND OTHER ART

IN DRAMA and comedy we have another example where the supreme genius of Greek art fits into the same pattern and ideal, and we might well say that Greek artistic genius, when wedded to the goddess Athena, begat as children Sculpture, Architecture, Ceramic Painting, Philosophy, Drama, and Comedy, and that all bear the family imprint.

Though its perfection was attained in Athens, it was the Greek race as a whole that brought this supreme art into being, and so, too, with the theatre, for drama had its root in Dorian Peloponnesos, while comedy had its antecedents in Sicilian Megara. Drama and comedy resemble other Greek arts in most of their characteristics, for first of all they started with a purely religious significance. The first inspiration of drama had the same feeling as that of archaic statuary in its deep awe of the divine and, like it, passed to the stage of humanistic and well-balanced perfection and then declined to an expression of human frailties. Just as is the case of the other Greek arts, the wealth that survives is but a minute fraction of that which was produced.

The drama originated from entirely religious rites in the worship of Dionysos, whom we have hitherto described as principally the Wine God, but who, in fact, like the

Photo by Spyros Meletzis The Parthenon crowns the Acropolis, here viewed from the southwest

Plate XVII

Photo by Alison Frantz
Ionian columns of the Erechtheion on the Acropolis

Photo by Alison Frantz
Corinthian columns of the temple to Olympian Zeus

Late black-figured lekythos, circa 510–500 B.C. Apollon with lyre leads, followed by Athena, and Herakles comes last. Introducing Herakles to Zeus on throne. Hermes.

Plate XIX

The theatre at Epidauros held seventeen thousand. Ancient drama and comedy are revived here every summer

The temple of Athena Nike on the Acropolis

Photo by N. Stournaras
Bas-relief of Bacchos on proscenium of the theatre of Dionysos, south slope of the Acropolis.

Plate XXI

Acropolis. The Caryatids of the Erechtheion

Photo by N. Stournaras

The Erechtheion from the west

The Hermes of Praxiteles at the Olympia Museum

Plate XXIII

Photo by Alison Frantz
The site of the ancient Agora with the Hephaistion on the left, the Stoa of Attalos in the center, and the Acropolis at the right

Sides of two rectangular bases for archaic Kouros

All eight sides have sporting scenes from the palaestra

On some there is still the pink background paint

Plate XXV

Courtesy American School of Classical Studies
A model of the civic centre of the Athens Agora

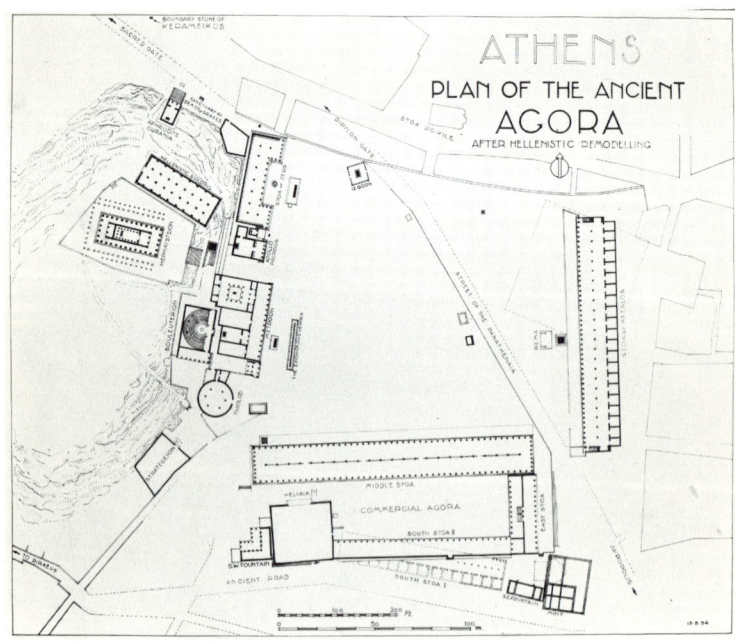

Courtesy American School of Classical Studies
Plan of the ancient Agora in Hellenistic times

Plate XXVI

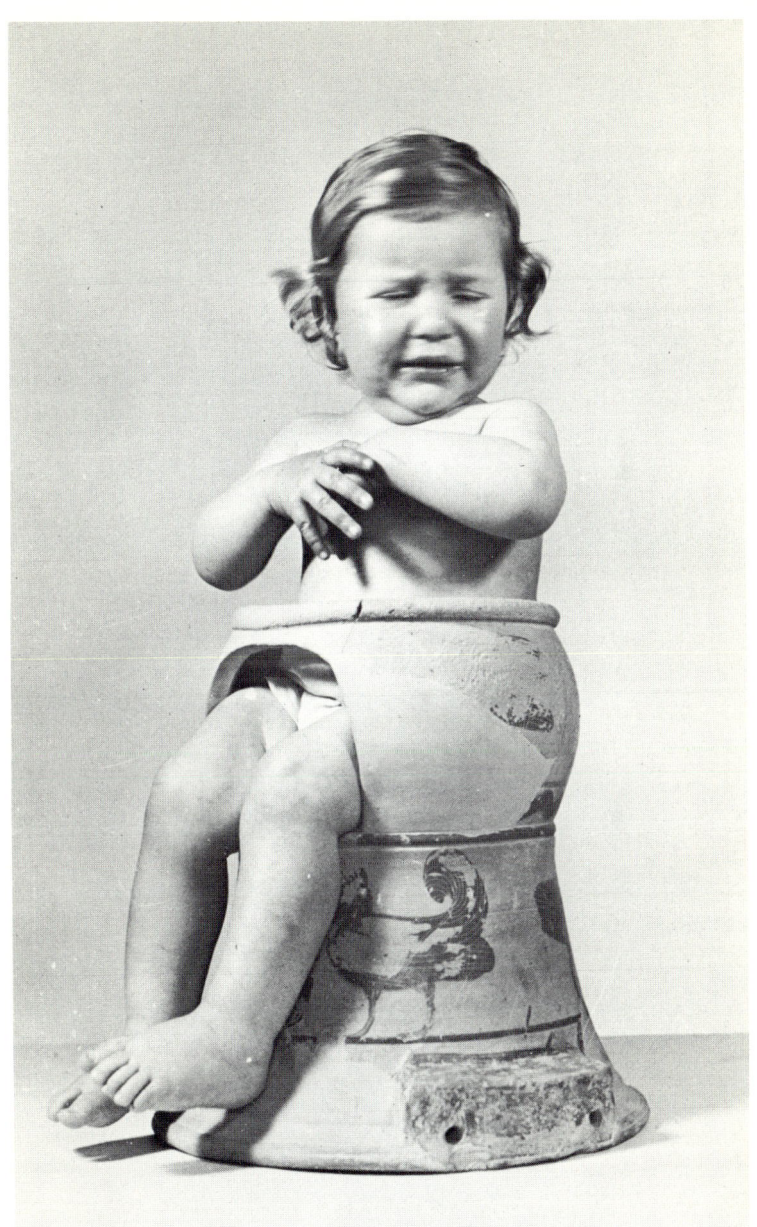

The use of this nursery utensil could not be understood until a similar pottery drawing was found. Agora Museum.

Plate XXVII

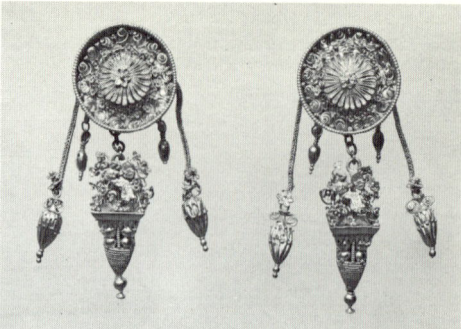

Gold earrings of the fourth century B.C. Benaki Museum, Athens

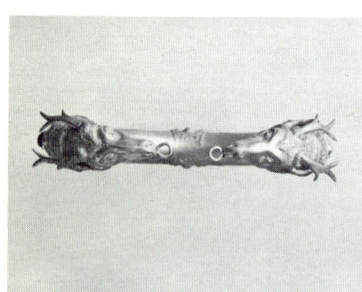
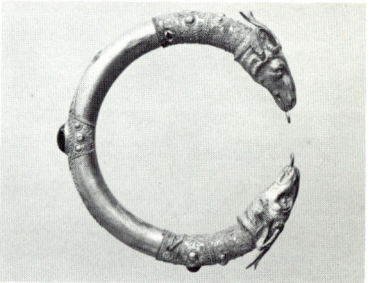

Gold bracelet of the third century B.C. Benaki Museum, Athens

Above, gold forehead ribbon from Kos, seventh century B.C. Below, gold belt of the first century B.C.

Victory loosening her sandal. From the temple of Athena Nike * * * on the Acropolis. Now in the Acropolis Museum.

Plate XXIX

The head of Hygeia, believed to be by Scopas, from the temple of Athena Aleia at Tegaea. Now in the National Archaeological Museum.

Plate XXX

Lindos, on the Isle of Rhodes. Temples on the Acropolis.

Plate XXXI

STELE INSCRIPTION

PREAMBLE

In the archonship of Phrynichos, when the tribe Leontis held the presidency of the Council, in the ninth term for which Chairestratos, son of Ameinias of the township of Acharnai, was secretary; of the presiding officers Menestratos of Aixone put the matter to the vote; Eukrates, son of Aristotimos of Peiraeus, made the following motion: with good fortune to the People of Athens, it was resolved by the Committee on the Revision of Laws:

TEXT OF THE LAW

If anyone should rise against the people of Athens with a view to establishing a dictatorship, or if anyone should set up a dictatorship or should suppress the People of Athens or the democratic government in Athens, any man who kills the person who has done any of these things shall be guiltless.

Should the People of Athens or the democratic government in Athens be suppressed, the members of the Council of the Areopagus are forbidden to go up to the Areopagus or to sit in council or to deliberate about a single thing. But if at a time when the People of Athens and the democratic government at Athens have been suppressed, any member of the Council of the Areopagus should go up to the Areopagus or sit in council or deliberate about anything, he is to be deprived of civil rights, both he and his descendants, and his property is to go to the state, one tenth being for the goddess.

PUBLICATION OF THE LAW

The Secretary of the Council is to have this law inscribed on two stone tablets, one of which he is to place at the entrance of the Areopagus as one goes in to the Council House and the other in the meeting place of the General Assembly, and for the inscribing of the tablets the Treasurer of the People is to provide 20 drachmai out of the authorized expense account for public purposes.

The Democracy Stele, 337/6 B.C., at the Agora Museum. Inscription at left.

Plate XXXII

goddess Demeter, was a nature deity and a god of productivity. These two deities were Olympians, and both have some quite different characteristics from the other gods. This can be seen in the nature of their worship, for quite likely they were the resurgence of older beliefs of pre-Homeric times. Both these deities presided over mysteries to which the votaries required initiation, and while in the case of the goddess the initiates were men, those in the case of the god were women. Dionysos, being a nature god, is associated with the labour pains of spring and the birth of nature, with the struggles of growth and survival, with the decadence of autumn and the obliteration of winter. The worshippers of Dionysos associated themselves with his sufferings and his struggles of change with the passing of the seasons, so that his worship had different aspects which might appear contradictory. He was surrounded by the curious creature forms of fawns and satyrs, which are expressions of the inexplicable mysteries of genesis. The plants sacred to him are the vine and the ivy, and most of his festivities were celebrated with wine which the worshippers felt it incumbent on them to drink copiously and even to excess so that they might share with the god not only his sufferings but also identify themselves with his intoxications.

If the vine was one symbol of the productivity of nature, the worship of Dionysos was even more associated with the phallus, and emblems thereof were always carried in the processions held in his honour. This was also the case, it would appear, in that procession which went to Eleusis for initiation into the mysteries of Demeter, to the shouts of "Iacchos! Iacchos!" the other name of Dionysos, which, when adopted by the Romans, became "Bacchus."

Originally it would be the rustic folk who were closest to nature that would have the worship of Dionysos most to heart, and who celebrated it by folk dances. Though perhaps these were very crude and conspicuous by liberal vinous merriment, the dances to Dionysos were accompanied by phallic songs of a particular measure and type known as dithyrambs, and in their spontaneity they must have had the same nature as the Caribbean calypsos.

By dancing, or *choros,* we must understand something far more comprehensive than our present-day notion of the word, for in Greek it refers principally to male dancing, and formed one of the principle elements of the curriculum of a boy's education. It included almost what we might call gymnastics, though always to the accompaniment of music, and was particularly favoured in Dorian lands: Sparta, Corinth, and Crete. Dancing to the dithyrambs may have started in early Sparta, but its inception is ascribed to Corinth in the seventh century. It was certainly danced in Attica in the sixth century, when the countryfolk, in imitation of the fawns and satyrs that surrounded Dionysos, donned goatskins. The Greek word for a male goat is *tragos* and the dance was known as a *tragōidia* ("goat-song").

Peisistratos, when he was at the head of the Athenian state, revived these dances and held special festivities for them in Athens during the celebrations which became known as the Great Dionysia. For these a theatre was constructed on the slopes of the Acropolis, though for several generations it was only a timber erection constructed each year for the occasion, and it was not till well over a century later that the permanent marble and stone theatre was completed, the remains of which still exist in a fair state of preservation. Peisistratos put Thespis in charge and he first produced these "tragedies" in 535 B.C. At first the stage itself was nothing more than a central altar, and the chorus sang and danced around it. Thespis is said to have added an innovation to the rustic dances which were to give birth to drama, for as well as the dancers he included himself as a masked actor, separate from the chorus, so that no longer did the chorus improvise, or divide into sections, but it now held dialogue with the central figure. The actor had various set masks and disguises, but the point is that it now became necessary to prepare the dialogues, and this brought authorship and dramatists into being.

The "tragic" chorus-dialogues only gradually reached the stage of classic tragedies, for at first there never was more than one actor on the stage at the same time. When Aeschylos added a second masked actor on the stage, and the dialogues thus became independent of the chorus, everything was set for the development of drama. This was especially so when a third actor was later added, though during the whole period of the Classic dramatists there does not seem to have ever been more than four.

It appears strange to us that the actors should always wear masks. It becomes more understandable when we consider the other manifestations of Greek art, for first of all the dramatists themselves had the same higher singleness of purpose of expressing the divine order of existence and not the poignancy or pathos of mere individuals. From a practical point of view, too, the theatres were of a great size, holding many thousands, and those perched on the distant and upper tiers would have missed any subtlety of facial expression. The fact that the theatres were large and in the open air, however, would not have required a louder voice, owing to the genius of the architects in acoustics and the clarity of the air and the consequent resonance.

Although originally the whole production was around an altar, during the time of Aeschylos stage pieces were introduced, though these were always more symbolic than scenic. These were such as trees, rocks, temples, or statues, and also such stage devices as doors, rolling platforms, and even machinery for the ascent or descent of the deities, though the full development of this was not until a generation after the death of Aeschylos. It became the practice to have central and side doors for the actors' entrance, and only the actors impersonating the major parts would enter and depart by the central door. There were different masks for the dramas and for the comedies. The masks were in more or less recognized categories: for fair or dark; for young, middle-aged, or freemen or freewomen; for male or female slaves. Characters or professions were even recognizable by the colour of the garb, which became stereotyped.

The tragedies had a quite different basic concept from our present-day dramas. They put over some great exposition of the hard facts of life, some deeper feeling wherein man is but a pawn that counts for next to nothing before that Necessity to which even the almighty gods must bow. The actual play was but a channel to illustrate this higher concept. Details of incident and background were unimportant, and such details as we might add in order to emphasize and bring a present-day drama to life would merely have brought down the Classical drama from its celestial ideology to mundane earth. The early drama appealed in clear terms to the intellectual faculties of the audience and made an attempt to create reaction to the misfortunes and predicaments of the characters.

Not only was the theatre religious in its roots but it was under the complete control of the State and under the appropriate archon of the year. It had exactly the same element of competitive structure as the Olympic Games, for the rules were of the greatest strictness, so that the Greek passion for fairness would be assured, and the competing dramatists have an equal chance. The production was paid for by one of the "leiturgies," that is to say, each entrant for the prize-winner's crown was allocated a producer by lot, chosen from one of the citizens whose capital wealth assessment made him liable to be chosen. This would be his tax due for the year, and would pay for the production of one play. The producer would have to pay not only for the actors but also for the maintenance of the chorus during training, which included such food "as would be conducive for a good voice." The attendance fee for the public was two obols, but Perikles arranged that those who could not well afford even this small fee should have the tickets at the expense of the State, and finally he saw to it that every member of the audience should receive a free ticket, the entrance money being devoted to the maintenance of the theatre. The plays started early in the morning, well before the heat, and the people went to take their seats "from dawn onwards."

There has been much controversy as to whether freewomen went to the theatre, but Platon distinctly says that the audience consisted of men, women, and children, of slaves and free people. It is believed that they did attend, but that the women sat separately from the men, though of the freewomen it must have been only the matrons. It is unlikely that they went to the comedies, which could be, and sometimes were, coarse. That the "other women," the hetairae, attended, is considered certain.

The audience was quite an excitable one, ever ready for sympathy and to respond to the power of the tragedy with tears, or to indulge in uproarious laughter at the sallies of the comedies. It would show its disapproval of incompetent acting by clucking or loud whistling, and it would honour such actors as merited their admiration.

It is clear that if there were several entries each year, and even if we reckon only the period from Salamis to Philip of Macedon (480-350 B.C.), there must have been many dramatists and hundreds of plays, but of the dramatists we are here only concerned with the three outstanding names. These are: Aeschylos, 525-456 B.C.; Sophokles 495-406 B.C.; and Euripides 480-406 B.C. We know that between them they produced over three hundred plays. Of these only seven each have survived from the first two, and eighteen from Euripides. Of many others whose works were worthy of being crowned we have nothing at all. Aeschylos, for instance, first entered for the prize in 499 B.C., but it was only in 484 B.C. that first he won it, and in 468 B.C. he was beaten by Sophokles. Almost all the tragedies, with very few exceptions in so far as we know, had as their theme one of the old historic legends of Homeric stories, and this would have had the advantage that the elements of the story were already known to the audience.

In the time of Aeschylos the tragedies were immersed in the awe in which the creed of Dionysos was founded. It is the awe of the unknown and the fearful imaginings of mankind; it is the tragedy of inexorable fate, the tragedy of "Woe! Woe! The worst is yet to come!" It is the tragedy of the higher intellectual concept, which is the very antithesis of Shakespearean drama regarding the foibles of human nature. Sophokles, however, was of the age of Pheidias, and we therefore can expect a more cultural polish to his tragedies, though at the same time there may be some loss of dynamic and majestic intensity. The art of Euripides is more approaching the time of Praxiteles, and more akin to it in expression. The art of Euripides approaches more to the Shakespearean outlook, for the Peloponnesian War had started before he had attained his maturity of production. The passions that the war engendered had dragged down the Athenian genius from the height of its idealist outlook.

Perhaps these three great dramatists, and the period they represent, can be summarised by ascribing to Aeschylos the plays of the divine order of things; to Sophokles, of men as they ought to be; and to Euripides, of men as they were and still are.

The evolution of the drama from the time of Thespis was, however, not of a single track in one direction, and there was some reaction against too sharp a departure by Thespis from the satyric element. Immediate successors produced satyrical drama in great profusion, for one of them is even said to have written a hundred and fifty plays, and that as a consequence of this the production of "tetralogies," became necessary that is, three tragedies followed by a satyrical drama. Later, Sophokles lengthened the plays, and the tragedies were followed by a comedy. The satyrical dramas did not give way entirely to comedy, however, for in "The Cyclops" we have such a play by Euripides, which has survived.

Before considering comedy, a few words on the role of the chorus is indicated, for even when the development has been reached when three actors are on the stage, the chorus still has considerable importance. On the stage the role of the additional actors was largely to make the meaning of the principal character more precise by expressions of sympathy or criticism and opposition. The chorus, however, finally became in the nature of an interval of the play, and expresses comments on what is going on, and to a large extent the morals that are to be drawn, that is, the conclusions that the dramatist expects right-minded people to draw.

The origin of comedy does not differ much from that of the tragedies, except that instead of its source being found in the rustic dances it was rather in the vintage festivals to Dionysos, when Phallophori gave vent to exuberant merriment and expressed their humour at the expense of passers-by. In these processions there were two types, the one which wore masks of drunken persons, while the other, the phallus bearers, who did not wear masks, but wore chaplets of wild flowers, principally of violets, or of myrtle, thistle, ivy, or thyme; and wore skins of goats or leopards. They would sing a hymn to Dionysos and follow it up with ribaldry, and in general behave in a somewhat drunken carnival spirit. The gradual formation of comedy was among the Dorians and the Megarians, but it had such elements of unrestrained coarseness that at first it went against the grain of the Athenians, and thus comedy did not find root in Athens till a later date, that is, till two years after Marathon, in 488 B.C. The original Athenian comedy, known as the Old Comedy, was in essence a caricature of all social and political matters. It attained its greatness under the broad-minded tolerance and administration of Perikles, yet with all its lampooning and wit it had a salutary effect, for it criticised and made fun of anything which did not meet with the approval of the citizens' ideology.

We possess very few works of the comedy poets, and though we have the names of over a hundred, there is very little indeed that has been saved except eleven of the comedies of Aristophanes, which was about a quarter of his production. From his contemporary reputation, however, we feel confident that Aristophanes, whose dates are about 445-380 B.C., was the greatest of them.

Aristophanes satyrised all manner of habits and customs of which he disapproved, and at first made very direct attacks on some of the prominent Athenian citizens, and in particular on Kleon, whom he portrayed as a brutish demagogue. Kleon brought an action against Aristophanes, and although he did not win it, it blunted the edge of any future personal attacks. Although immense latitude was given to the comic poets, there were still certain matters which would have been considered *lèse majesté* of the Demos, and would have been indictable, such as improper allusion to sacred religious matters or to the mysteries.

From the plays of Aristophanes we have some of our most valuable information as to the conditions and habits of the Athenians, though they must be taken most judiciously, just as to-day we would have to be careful in assessing the behaviour of the average mother-in-law from the music-hall jokes. Among the pet aversions of Aristophanes were the jurymen who neglected home and duty out of the entertainment they derived from the court cases. "The Wasps" deals mainly with the way they swarmed to the courts, for he was also just as averse to the inordinate amount of litigation practiced. Neither did he like the demagogic orators, or the Sophists and their education, including even that of Sokrates.

Aristophanes was against the megalomania of the empire builders, which of course included Kleon, and it would seem that he deplored the expedition to Sicily. In his "Plutus" (the God of Wealth, and not Pluton, the God of the Underworld) he had his apt comments on the inequality of incomes, while in his "Ecclesiazusae" and his "Lysistrata" we see suffragettes as the main topic. In the "Thesmophoriazusae," which deals with women attending a certain festival which was limited to them, they plot for revenge on Euripides who was well known as a misogynist, but find a man disguised as a woman in their presence. Aristophanes shows some disapproval of the oversecluded life of women. Perhaps among the most interesting of his comedies to read is "The Frogs," of which there is an excellent translation by Gilbert Murray, for it also gives some feeling of the high quality of the poetry and language of Aristophanes.

The comedies from the beginning of the fourth century to the time of Philip of Macedon are known as the Middle Comedies, and the main characteristic of them is that they no longer lampoon individuals. The later comedies, known as the New Comedies, lasted about another eighty years, down to about 260 B.C., and of these comic poets the best known is Menander.

Poetry

We shall have but comparatively little to say of poetry, though it was the earliest form of Greek genius, and apart from its greatness had a supreme influence on general culture. Our appreciation of Greek poetry must neces-

sarily suffer as it is that one art which, unless we know
Greek, must lose through translation. The early philosophers, and even legislators, invariably used verse, and ascribed great importance to it. The poetry used by the
early scientist-philosophers of Ionia, or by such legislators
as Solon, has very great intrinsic value as such. We should
add here, too, that the works of great dramatists, and even
comedy writers, should more correctly be described as the
works of the dramatic and comedy poets, and those of
the former should rank very high in poetry. The word
"drama" itself means "something that has been done" or
"is being done," though some would translate it as "action."

The significance attached to poetry by the Greeks can
be judged in that the Greek meaning of this word is "creation," and therefore has something of the same meaning
as the Latin "art." Among the Greeks it was reserved
for this form only of art, and "poesis" to them was at
the very root and very essence of education. The Greek
poets were many and great, though of most of them we
have only a few fragments. Fortunately, however, we
have in their entirety the whole of the two great epics of
Homer, the greatest of all poets, though it is probably
the case that the dialect in which we now have them underwent some small change in the seventh or sixth century,
though not necessarily to their detriment.

Possibly contemporaneous with Homer, or just a little
later, was Hesiod, who lived on the Boeotian slopes of
Mount Helikon, not so very far from Athens. He was
not of the stature of Homer, but his importance could
easily be underestimated owing to the fact that one of
his great works, the "Theogonia," which attempts to tell
of the birth of gods and men, is somewhat a failure in
its concept. The poet was not really Olympian-minded,
but the "Theogonia" contains much of great poetic beauty.

Hesiod was, however, in many ways the father of our
present-day notion of the Poetic Muse, and incidentally,
it is the Muses that he imagines as coming to visit him
at his country estate to introduce us to the "Theogonia."
Though he has been called a rustic, he is really a deep and
poetic lover of nature. Perhaps his poetry is occasionally
marred by his discontent with the lot that fate has in store

for him, for he considered that the judges had been corrupted by his brother in the apportioning of his just paternal inheritance. He is nonetheless full of wisdom, though mingled with the superstitions of pre-Olympian beliefs. His grudge inspired him to plead for more justice on earth, and this is one of his main themes which make him a humanitarian. Whereas he recognizes that it is love that makes the world go round, he himself is afraid to get caught in its gyrations, for such dizziness may be a snare and a delusion. The dialect of Hesiod which has many Aeolian traces, supports the belief that his family may have migrated from northern Asia Minor, though he states that his father came southwards from Thessaly. Possibly the importance of Hesiod is that he is a true poet in our sense. Whereas he has not the martial note or the epos of Homer, he finds his inspiration in the beauties of nature, other than feminine charms which are left to the sublime genius of Sappho.

In poetry we have the one and only Greek art in which women distinguished themselves, for in lyric poetry Sappho was superlative, and the fact that we only possess a few surviving lines of hers is one of the very greatest losses sustained by Greek art. Her love songs are unequalled and exquisite, though through these, her native isle of Mytilene, better known through its city of Lesbos, has been associated with feminine homosexuality. Undue prominence has been given to their eroticism, especially since Lord Byron refers to the isles of Greece, "Where burning Sappho loved and sung."

In the time of Sappho, towards the end of the seventh and the beginning of the sixth century, and in the isle of Mytilene, women must have had far more freedom than in Athens, anyhow of a later date, and in the house of Sappho, which she called the House of the Muses, was a centre where other feminine poets foregathered. Though Sappho did write ecstatic verse dedicated to some of her beautiful feminine friends, telling of her love for them, there would seem no corroboration for the sensualities ascribed to her as the mainspring of her character. Anyhow, this does not affect the aethereal quality of her poetry, of which the deep beauty is not that of the impermanence of passion, but of the elevation which only great music can inspire.

Though there are many other poets, and again not forgetting the great dramatists, the only other one we shall refer to is Pindar, the Theban who, however, went to Athens as a boy, and was there educated. He was born at about the same time as Aeschylos, though he lived to a riper old age, and was therefore also of the time of Perikles and Pheidias. Pindar was much travelled, and for a time, like Aeschylos, was a protégé of Syracuse. He was a most prolific writer and his works filled many scrolls. He is especially known for his many odes in praise of the mighty and the distinguished, including winners at the Olympic Games. In later times he was much admired by the Romans, and Horace, it would seem, pays him the sincerest form of flattery. Pindar was a supporter of established religion, and his Athenian education influenced him to be opposed to the Persians during the invasions, unlike most of his Theban fellow citizens. Perhaps it was because of this as well as the genuine admiration of Alexander the Great that the latter ordered that the house of Pindar should be spared when the rest of Thebes was rased to the ground. It is said that his inclusion of traditional mythology in his works was at the instigation of a Theban poetess, Korinna, who influenced him and inspired him when still a youth. This is of interest as it shows that at the beginning of the fifth century there were still women in many parts of Greece, if not in Athens, who were of education and of many parts.

We will conclude this section with reference to a writer whose name will surely always live, a writer who came along at the time of Sappho and who was a slave, for it is not known whether Aesopos (Aesop) first wrote the *Fables* in verse form or not, though they have survived only in prose. So wise are these *Fables* that in France La Fontaine achieved immortal fame by doing little more than translating them into French verse. Aesop is also of interest to us as it gives us an example of the Greeks' love of nature, a quality that has often been queried as it is so little expressed in the writings that have survived.

Other Art

There are still many subjects with which we should deal in this chapter and these include painting, ceramics, terra-cotta figures, choreography and dancing, gold and silver ware (including such trinkets as earrings and mirrors), and coinage.

In approaching these many subjects we must be careful not to let the chapter become a catalogue of Hellenic art, or let it absorb space that is required for dealing with philosophy and thought, for there is still much ground to be covered. What might interest one reader could prove laborious to another.

Painting

Next to nothing remains from the painting of Classical times, not even enough for us to make any reliable assessment of its quality. We assume that it had not the superlative technique of the sculpture, but that, in fact, its qualities were sculpturesque. From contemporary records we can judge that its standards must have been high, and of this we can be sure by judging from the deftness of the pottery decorations and illustration. What we do not know is the extent to which artists were inspired by that singleness of purpose and expression invariably present in the other forms of art. We do not know whether it was too disinterested to include background and episode, which mean so much to painting as we understand it today, or at least as we did until quite recently. We are fairly certain that in the Classical Period painting for home decoration was almost nonexistent, but there would have been a fair amount for civic buildings, porches, and porticoes. We have several names of great painters who enjoyed a reputation in their time, yet we shall mention but two, firstly, Polygnotos, who was the great master of the days of Perikles, and Apelles, whom Alexander the Great favoured as his portrait painter.

Polygnotos not only painted the scenes of the battle of Marathon for the Poikile Stoa, the painted portico of the

Agora, but also the compositions for the halls of the Propylaea on the Acropolis.

It can be but a personal opinion, but there may have been more incidental background in painting than in other forms of art. Though in some cases artists only used four main colours, expert authorities consider that the Greeks possessed a range of colours at their disposal which has been described as equal to those used by the great Italian masters of the sixteenth century, and we know the raw materials from which they produced each of their colours. Of the qualities of their paintings we might judge from one story, and we know that the Greeks were neither prone to exaggerated self-praise or to undue boasting any more than they were to false modesty. According to the story, Apelles considered that the greatest flattery he had ever received was that when he had painted a bunch of grapes, a bird was deluded to the extent of trying to snip one. His ire, however, was kindled, according to another story, when he exposed a painting for the passers-by to see, while he hid to overhear the comments of those master critics, the Greek public. Among the first was a cobbler who turned to his companion and indicated that the painting depicted shoes which were improperly made, whereupon Apelles emerged from his hiding place and bade the cobbler to confine himself to his cobbling and not to criticise works of art about which he knew nothing. Thus, too, we would be well advised not to delve too deeply into this form of Greek art, which largely would be conjecture on our part.

Pottery

Although ceramic pottery is so fragile, more of it has been preserved than the remains of most of the other arts, and among the reasons for this is that so much of it was made to serve three different purposes. The first was for domestic use, another was for the export trade, and yet another was for the oil jars and other food containers for burials. Of the domestic ware the commonest form is the "Amphora" which by its name means that it has handles on both sides of the neck. The amphora had a narrow neck as it was mostly used for such liquids that required preservation, and generally a pointed bottom so that it could be fixed in a hole in the ground or into a stand. Wine was generally contained in an amphora, which might also be of a particular size, in the same way as we have the pint or gallon bottle. As a wine container, however, it would neither be of such fine substance or be decorated as a work of art. The amphora was also used for the unguents and perfumes of my lady's chamber, as also of that of my lord's, and with the exception, perhaps, of some silver caskets and other trinkets, would be the only works of art in the household bedchambers.

Beyond this there would be little else in the rest of the house except the statuary, the couches, the little tables, and the oil-wick lamps. There being no windows, in our sense, there would be very little in the way of curtains, though they might be hung over an open doorway. Carpets do not seem to have been used. Colour, perhaps, was thus not used in pottery as it would have been out of keeping in the house, yet we must note that a thousand years before the Classical Athenian times, the Minoans not only had pottery of an almost porcelain substance, but decorated it with illustrations and designs of artistic, mellow, and sometimes bright colouring.

Glass was known, but hardly used, and therefore drinking vessels were also of ceramic substance. An important piece was the central mixing bowl in which the wine was mixed with water and ladled out. This was called a krater and it was made in cuplike shapes of very diverse character.

The great expansion of the export trade probably took place immediately after the Persian invasions, and pottery was then very largely an Athenian trade. The reasons for this were that the countryfolk who were forced to take shelter in Athens, after their vineyards and orchards had been destroyed, found employment in this industry. What is more, the city must have encouraged it, for it always was essential for Athens to import corn which is not too happy in the dry Attic soil. With the destruction of the olive groves by the Persians, ceramics had to replace the main commercial export, which previously had been oil. At a later stage, under Perikles, when the confederated cities were linked to Athens, the production requirements must have been enormous, and ceramics were exported to many lands.

A great source of finds of Athenian pottery of the best period has been among the lands of the Tyrseni, who probably first learned of Greek pottery from Megale Hellas and then became keen collectors from the master potters of Athens. Some three generations ago, when this pottery was being discovered in Etruscan districts, it was much admired and wonder expressed at the advanced art of the Etruscans in ceramics, who were, however, artists of note in other forms of art. It was gradually confirmed that much of it was not Etruscan pottery at all but Athenian. It is nonetheless curious that so much should have been found in this part of Italy. The guess is that it was used for burials, and that when Etruscan power collapsed, the graves were either respected, or neglected as of little interest, and we might incidentally also add—outside the path of the Crusaders.

Of burial ceramics there was one especial form, and that known as the "lekythos," which was a burial oil jar, somewhat bottle-shaped, of which the neck is enlarged at the top and there is a single handle on one side. Its lower part is narrowed, and then at the very bottom spread into a circular stand. The characteristic of the lekythos is that it has very delicately delineated figures, and some design, on a white background. Some amphorae may also have been used as funeral urns for the ashes.

Early ceramic vases were decorated with black silhouettes on the natural red-brown of the terra-cotta, with certain details of the figures being shown by eliminating the black paint in thin lines. There was some variation also of the thickness or the opaqueness of the black pigment, while some application of white paint was used for certain objects. Most of the vases decorated in this style are of the period before the Persian invasions, or, to be precise, before Marathon, after which there was a sudden innovation in that the figures were left uncoloured on pottery which is more reddish than before, while the background is painted in with black. This new style was accompanied by far greater skill, and this method lends itself to more delicate work, not only in outline but also by the addition of the apposite lines on the figures themselves.

Perhaps Greek ceramics may not appeal so much to many of us because, subconsciously, we might think of the pieces as *objets d'art* for our reception rooms and would plead for something more colourful to harmonize with the decorative scheme. If viewed more in the light of a museum piece, we can appreciate that the vase painting of the best Athenian period is of the most delicate and exquisite art that Athenian skill produced.

The quantity of Greek ceramics that we possess is very great when compared with the other forms of art, and the information that we are able to obtain from these pieces regarding habits, dress, customs, and life is immense. They are, of course, more instructive in many respects than descriptions given by the written word. As one example alone, the modern vogue for Greek dancing has been built up almost entirely from vase paintings, and one exponent of this form of dancing told me that every pose and every figure of classic Greek dancing could be gleaned therefrom.

Coins

Coinage did not come in till the beginning of the seventh century B.C. Greek money was mostly of silver, though smaller denominations were of copper. Gold was rarely used. In Asia Minor there was an alloy known as *ēlektron* which was also employed. The idea was that the official stamping should be a guarantee of full weight. Each city, of course, had its own coinage, and some had greater repute than others for accuracy. The emblems used were very much the same as those which have survived till today, though the heads of kings did not come in till after the time of Alexander the Great, when monarchies took the place of democracies. Special occasions and victories might be commemorated, but generally the design would be connected with the deity or some well-known legend of the city. Some of the finest coins, and those of the greatest beauty, are from Syracuse and southern Italy.

In Athens we have no coins worthy of note, for the reputation of Athenian coinage was so high that it was decided not to change the design from the original archaic one. Of the Athenian coinage the one side bore the head of Athena, of archaic design, in profile but with the eye looking full face, whereas on the obverse was her emblem of the Owl and a twig of olive branch, and the initials of the archon eponymos who gave his name to the Athenian year.

Sparta differed from all the other cities of Greece for, since the earliest times of coinage, its money was of iron, and apparently it continued to be so during the whole of its history. From what we know, and from what we are told by Thucydides, the character of the Spartan was sufficiently venal for it to be a good thing that the temptations of gold and silver should be removed from him.

Jewelry

Greek women wore bracelets and some jewelry, but they disliked overostentation and were sparing in its use. Among the more enchanting ornaments were the earrings, of which the National Museum in Athens has samples which would make many ladies of today quite envious. Pins, or "agraffes" for dresses were in great use, and all free men wore signet rings for seals, which took the place of present-day signatures.

There are also many beautiful mirrors of polished metal, mostly circular, with or without handles, and the backs of which had raised metal figures. Many fine specimens have survived.

CHAPTER V

PHILOSOPHY AND THOUGHT

UNDER THE heading of philosophy we propose giving a very short account of the subject which the Greeks understood by this word. It is much broader than the use of the word implies today, for it means the "love of Wisdom," and that includes all knowledge which requires constructive thought or any matter to which reason has been applied. Reasoning is of two kinds and is either based on hypothesis, theory, and the principles of logic, which is deductive reasoning, or on comparison, trial and error, which is inductive reasoning. The mere collation of facts almost automatically requires inductive reasoning, unless, of course, they are just jumbled down without any connection or relationship, such as in the enumeration of property. Tabulation means that each fact has been considered as to whether it may have the qualification for inclusion in the compiled list. An example of such tabulation is the case of one of the later Greek philosopher-scientists who drew up a list of six hundred species of vegetation, and then examined their beneficial or nocuous properties with respect to human consumption. To the Greeks, therefore, philosophy was the realm of all knowledge, and would even include the knowledge of how to do a thing, for art is the doing thereof, not the knowledge required. Today the meaning of the word is confined to the study of those subjects which are incapable of test and proof by their very nature.

Almost all departments of knowledge have Greek names, for the Greeks laid the foundation for their study. Some few new realms of study have been added since their time, such as psychiatry, aerodynamics, or telephony, and these, too, have been given Greek names to be in keeping. Let us consider the main faculties of learning which they initiated and advanced well on the road to their present attainment, so that we can gather how vast was their scope: Anthropology, Astronomy, Botany, Chronology, Ethics, Geometry, Grammar, Logic, Mathematics, Metallurgy, Metaphysics, Physics, Politics, Philosophy, Theology, Therapeutics, Zoology, and we might add History and many more. For all these sciences we owe an immense debt to the Greek philosophers. Of recent years more interest has been shown in the civilisations anterior to the Greek, so that there has been a tendency to detract from our debt to the Greek philosophers and even to suggest that other civilisations might have given them foundations which were merely re-echoed, or that they amplified previous knowledge which was possessed by the Chaldeans, Babylonians, Phoenecians, Egyptians, and others.

Undoubtedly the Greeks were in contact with other civilisations, and profited from them, but nonetheless they laid the whole solid floor on which the edifice of all science and all philosophy has since been erected, and they themselves went very far in building this immense pile of knowledge. It may be true that in laying that floor they used building material obtained elsewhere, but it is certainly true that they discovered the method of assembly and construction. Further, of all these studies and sciences, the only apparent ones in which they may have utilized the foundations of others were astronomy and geometry, the former from the Chaldeans and Babylonians, and the latter from the Egyptians.

Greek philosophy was born in Ionia, and this very fact gives weight to those who might argue that it owes much to non-Hellenic influence, for these Greeks would be more in contact with the other and possibly prior civilisations of the Middle East.

There were other reasons why Greek philosophy should find its birth in Ionia. The culture of the Asia Minor Greeks was in advance of that of Hellas in the seventh century B.C., for whereas they had taken it with them from Greece and nurtured it, their brethren who had been left behind on the mainland had been living for many decades under the shadow of Dorian danger and repression. Another secondary and possible explanation was that Ionia was the homeland of Homer, and the land where the bard sung his epics, and thus where the capricious escapades of the gods came under the most frequent reminder, notice, and analysis. When thought and reason were applied to the Olympians, their Homeric attributes were bound to evanesce, or at least leave much inexplicable, and something had to be found to fill the void. Thus it was in the nature of these enquiring Greeks to supplant by reason what was being lost in faith.

Before we proceed any further it would be appropriate to consider a subject which is of the very highest significance in judging Greek civilisation as a whole, and more so still in examining Greek thought, a subject which may not always be given sufficient prominence in this context, and that is the Greek language. Only short mention of it was made with regard to poetry. It is generally accepted that the Achaeans were the Greek-speaking people and that they brought their language with them. In substantiation of this it is acknowledged that the Greek language is Indo-European in its glossary.

Vocabulary is not the most important part of a language, and it is certainly not the part which has earned for the Greek language the praise of being "the most perfect channel for the conveyance of human thought yet devised." We believe it is well deserving of this praise but how the language thus came about, we have no notion.

First of all there is a question that we cannot answer, and academically it is of greatest interest. Was it the supremacy of the Greek clarity of mind that imparted to the Greek vocabulary the addition of its perfection of syntax, or was it the perfection of Greek syntax that gave the Greeks their unique clarity of thought? We cannot help feeling that it was the Greek-Achaean clarity of thought that gave the Greek language its perfection. The one fact that we know is that, with the difference of idiom, the Doric Spartans spoke the same language as the Achaeans, and on the whole it is unlikely that when each invaded Greece they spoke the identical language (though they may have had similar deities). From this fact, however, no positive deduction can yet be made.

Let us leave this discussion, however interesting it may be, and glance at that language which our forefathers, and even fathers, appreciated sufficiently to realize that the young scholar must learn it, should he hope to train his mind culturally the better to speak his own language with elegance and clarity.

The Greek language gives the possibility of constructing sentences not unduly long, by the use of gender, conjugation, declension, case, inflection, and accent. It is served by the addition of those little words and half words indicating the value of each sentence in its proper relationship to the whole meaning, and in such a way that the whole thought flows smoothly and progressively without any suspension or reservation. Each sentence in Greek immediately lets you know its value and quality the very moment you come across it. If, for instance, it is a negative sentence, then it is shown by a negative sign, if necessary divided into two parts with the second part attached to the very word where the force of the negative is desired.

Greek scientific thought was born in Ionia, had its student days in Sicily and Megale Hellas, and matured in Athens, where it later shared its erudition and sagacity of old age with Alexandria, which ultimately became its home. We have next to nothing directly from the teaching of the first two stages, Ionia and Megale Hellas, but the Athenian and Alexandrian thinkers have preserved representative thought, either by their dissertation and comment, as in the case of the Athenian philosophers, or by tabulation, as in the case of the Alexandrian professors.

Nearly all, and possibly all the early thinkers of the first two periods propounded their wisdom and science through the medium of verse. Why? We cannot be entirely sure. Probably it was because writing was only in its infancy of rebirth, and books, that is to say, scrolls, would have been extremely rare. Poetry also is the finest of mnemonics, not only more easily retained, but less easily alterable by repetition from mouth to mouth. From the little we possess we can see that these early philosophers had even the right to rank in the world of fame by virtue of their poetic merit. Somehow, though, we have a feeling that the mnemonic reason is not the full explanation, for the very word "poetry" gives us this feeling, as it means creation. God, for instance "poeted" the world. Did the early Greek thinkers believe that through poetry they could better impart their thought so that there should be keener perception and responsive insight? How else can we explain the statement by Aristoteles that poetry is more worthy of serious study than history, though he may have considered history as only the raw material of a science, or sciences. Indeed, Aristoteles' book on politics epitomises all that there is to learn of wisdom in the study of constitutional and unconstitutional government.

If we were to list the names of all the world's great original thinkers, those of the Greeks would form a very high percentage. Indeed, the textbook of one of the sciences is actually called by the name of the Greek originator, Euclid. We even habitually refer to the outlook or teleology of any philosophy by classifying it under one of the Greek schools of thought, such as Stoic, Cynic, Platonic, Hedonistic, or even scholastic and academic.

It was around 600 B.C. that Greek scientific philosophy was born, and the first of the great names that we know is Thales of Mileto. Even if his conclusions were not correct, he was the first to disregard completely all questions of ascribing the creation of the world to divine origin. Thales was a physicist who set out to discover what was the prime matter which constituted the universe. There must be, he thought, some substance which took different forms under different conditions, and his reasoning led him to believe that this something must be water.

Others followed and applied their scientific reasoning in the channels to which Thales had directed them. Thales is also known because there was an eclipse at the time when the Lydians were fighting the Medes in one of those battles which might have changed the history of civilisation, but the eclipse so overawed them that they ceased fighting and made peace. This was on May 28, 585 B.C., and Thales had predicted it accurately. We can feel assured that his ability to do this was an example of the indebtedness of the Greeks in matters of astronomy or geometry to the science of other races.

The others that followed after Thales had their own explanations as to the substance of the prime matter, believing it to be such as "fire" or "indeterminate matter in a state of flux." All these thinkers based their conclusions on the observation of nature and life. Shortly after Thales we get an Ionian philosopher who rather anticipated Darwin's theory of the "origin of species," for he indicates that the fish of the sea must have been an earlier form of life than the animals of the land, and therefore of man. Yet another of the early philosophers gives us a picture of the evolution of man from even before his early cave days, and this tallies completely with our own ideas upon the subject.

Demokritos is also a name that we should record, for he believed that the universe was constituted of atoms which were of the same substance but which were arranged in different composition. According to him the quality of things was not intrinsic in itself, but existed in the manner that our organs of sense reacted to them and could apprehend them, which is also a philosophy which has found favour in the twentieth century.

From the islands inhabited by Ionians, off the coast of Asia Minor, came equally great scientists, and we must record the name of Hippokrates and his school, for they gave their attention to medicine. They are accepted as the fathers of this science but, unfortunately, only a little of their work survives, and only from records preserved three or four centuries later at the great library of Alexandria.

From Ionia, too, we get pure philosophy and theology as well as physical and scientific thought, and of these philosophers we should record the name of Xenophanes of Kolophon who denounces the immaturity of thought which conceives of the Deity as having human form. He explains that black men conceive of God as being a black man, and if animals could express themselves they would think of God as magnified and ennobled in their own image. The philosophy of the Ionians must have met with considerable opposition by religious thought of the day, but first of all there was no organized professional priesthood to oppose it, and secondly the background in Ionia was sufficiently ripe for it to survive. Under similar conditions persecution would have been meted out by the Inquisitors in Spain some two thousand years later, and there would also have been opposition, though many might not realize it, in the countries of the Western World today.

Not so long after the Ionians of Asia Minor, we get philosophic science flourishing in Megale Hellas, though in a sense this is but an extension of Ionic thought, which was being curtailed in its homeland and had migrated owing to the threatening ascendancy of the Medes and Persians.

The greatest name of Megale Hellas is that of Pythagoras, known to all of us through his famous theorem of geometry, and he, though born around 570 B.C. in the Isle of Samos, migrated to the Greek city of Kroton in southern Italy when he was about forty. Few men can have had as much influence on human thought as Pythagoras, for not only was he a great scientist and mathematician, but much of the substance of present European religion is founded on his belief and teachings, for it was followed by Sokrates, adopted and adapted by Platon, whence it went to Alexandria, and there was married to an Hebraic background to produce the tenets of Christianity.

As a scientist Pythagoras considered that everything depended on the relationship of numbers, of which the number ten had special significance. He it was that discovered that the tonal vibration of strings depended on the length of the chord for the note. This relationship of numbers he believed to be universal and even had its application in astronomy, in which science he also advanced thought. He believed that the planets (which should be ten in number) revolved around a centre, though he included the sun among the revolving orbs. Curiously we get the word "tonic" from Pythagorean philosophy, for he followed up his theory of numeric relationship by be-

PHILOSOPHY AND THOUGHT

lieving that when a man was indisposed the condition was caused by the various tensions of the nerves being out of harmony, and that the remedy was to get the tone right by a "tonic."

The import of Pythagoras, however, is as a mystic, for he believed that there was something more in life than the human frame, and he therefore not only believed in the immortality of the soul but, also, in the transmigration of souls, in consequence of which he is said to have been a vegetarian. Unlike some great thinkers whose original thought only received recognition after many generations, Pythagoras himself made his widespread, for he founded a powerful secret brotherhood, membership in which required a previous strict scrutiny of the life and worthiness of each applicant. On election each brother was enjoined to dedicate a period each day to meditation.

The school of Pythagoras produced many great thinkers, many of them practical scientists, for it included the pursuit of scientific investigation through the dissection of animals. We shall, however, not pursue their evolution but will turn, instead, to consider the three outstanding philosophers of Athens, who, a century later, flourished for a period covering about a hundred years. These (with the latinized form of their names) are: Sokrates (Socrates) 469-399 B.C.; Platon (Plato) 427-367 B.C.; and Aristoteles (Aristotle) 384-322 B.C.

Sokrates

Sokrates was a teacher who never wrote a word, and was a man of such character that today we would have called him holy, for he practised the precepts that he taught. Sokrates, the satyric-looking snub-nosed and hardy philosopher, was no sedentary professor, for he earned his living as a stonemason and sometime sculptor. As an Athenian citizen he participated in such wars as were waged in his day and had his full share of fighting, where he distinguished himself not only by his valour but by his remarkable uncomplaining endurance and hardihood. Although he wore the same shaggy clothes winter and summer and was anything but elegant in appearance, he he was a welcome guest at parties of the great. He was in touch with matters of everyday life, if only through his wife who maintained a high reputation as a nagging shrew. Sokrates could scarcely have put in any overtime to earning any of the extra material comforts of life, as he was forever in the Agora, questioning and thus teaching.

Sokrates called himself "The Gadfly," for his pertinent questions must have stung the vanity of many of his listeners. As far as we know his questions were never directed with the purpose of catching anyone in order to score a point, but he always showed the greatest humility in so far as knowledge and learning were concerned, and he was completely sincere when he would say, "I know but one thing, that I know nothing." Yet his questions were directed to people in order that he could elicit a reply which would be the subject of a further question, until he had reached a point where the unfortunate person realized that he was contradicting the untenable basis of an earlier answer. In this there was no objective of showing his own superiority, but of himself learning, which is not normally possible from anyone who agrees with you.

Sokrates always had a following of young men of the Athenian intelligentsia around him, including many from the aristocratic families. It must be understood, however, that, unlike the teachers known as the Sophists, he never asked for, or would he have accepted, an obol for tuition. We might interpose here that it was fashionable to decry these Sophists and consider them in the nature of what we might call quacks, yet some of them seem to have been of great learning and erudition. The real objection to them was only that they amassed fortunes by their lectures, a fact which Sokrates considered as prostituting philosophy.

Sokrates originated a new approach to enquiry, making it scientific in its analysis and thoroughness. He did not, for instance, deny the existence of the Olympian gods, but probably only because there could not be any proof that they did not exist. Of such was his humble approach to all matters, yet he made it clear that many of the legends and attributes of the gods could not have been compatible with the essence of being a Deity, thereby indicating nothing more than that some of the beliefs about them required reconsidering.

Sokrates, as all free citizens were bound to do, took his turns in civic and parliamentary duties, and we know that at least on one occasion when it was his turn to be chairman of the committee of the Senate of that day, which would correspond to the office of the president of the republic, he then refused to forward a question for discussion and vote. His reason was that he thought it unjust and out of order, and this in spite of all the yelling, insistence, and threats of the convocated assembly. There were other occasions, too, when he showed that nothing would induce him to move his ground when he thought that to do so would be perpetrating an injustice or committing an act against the constitution or the established procedure of the courts.

Even if Sokrates did not teach, but only interrogated in his search for knowledge, it would nonetheless be equivalent to propagating dogmas, or even creating a school of thought. In these questions, therefore, what Sokrates did was to bring to Athens a new outlook to philosophy, for he made their chief enquiry a subject which had already interested Pythagoras. That subject centred around Man, and not as a corporeal being, but as a psychological entity, that is to say, as a soul which had an existence separate from the body.

Among the very many that sought the company of Sokrates and crowded around him were some whose names later became the most outstanding and distinguished of Athens. Of these we will mention but three: Xenophon, Alkibiades, and Platon, the last of whom founded the *Akadēmeia* ("The Academy") and presented much of his philosophical work in the form of books in which there are dialogues with Sokrates as the questioner. We do not know to what extent these dialogues represent the actual questions asked by Sokrates, or whether they are really Platon's philosophy, yet we are confident that whichever they are, they are based on the principles and methods of Sokrates. They must be of the essence of his teachings, for otherwise there would have been remonstrances from many of the other friends of Sokrates.

Xenophon is well known to all who have had a classical education, for he is the first Greek writer that we meet at school, just as Julius Caesar is the first Latin commentator. Xenophon's best-known work, the *Anabasis*, is about the expedition of ten thousand Greeks as mercenaries of Cyrus the Younger into the interior of Asia Minor, of how Cyrus was killed and the generals slain, and of how Xenophon led them back across the wild and unknown country till they reached the Black Sea. It is a remarkable book of adventure and shows how the Greeks survived through their self-discipline. Like his other works, it is characterised by the simplicity and clarity of his style.

Xenophon also wrote a book on household management, the *Oekonomika* (or, if you anglicize the title, *The Economics*), in which Sokrates also figures as the questioner. The reason we bring Xenophon into the picture here is that he was an officer and a country gentleman of Athenian origin who was most pious and God-fearing, devoutly fulfilling all his religious obligations towards the gods. The fact, therefore, that Xenophon so admires Sokrates, attests that the latter could not have taught in a way that was either sacrilegious or could cause offence. Xenophon, however, was also an admirer of the Spartan virtues, as we might expect a soldier to be, and a close personal friend of Agesilaos, the king of Sparta, who was a brilliant strategist and who died on the return journey from a military expedition to Egypt which he had led at the ripe age of eighty-two. It is believed that there was something connected with this friendship that caused Xenophon to be ostracised by the Athenians.

Of Alkibiades, the vainglorious aristocratic rake and sacrilegious traitor we have already heard, but in his heyday he esteemed the company of Sokrates and sought him as an honoured guest at his banquets. It may well be that the Athenian public considered that the sacrilegious acts of Alkibiades were influenced by the teachings of Sokrates, and also they would have looked with disfavour on the friendship of Sokrates with Xenophon and others. It may well be that when, therefore, Sokrates was indicted for corrupting the youth, and brought to trial, that some of the superstitious ascribed the very recent calamity of Athenian defeat by Sparta to the behaviour of these friends of his, and the consequent wrath of the gods. Athens was then at the lowest ebb she had ever been.

In order to understand a little more as to how Sokrates was condemned to death, and to gather a little more about the Greek way of life, mentality, and tolerance, it is necessary that we should give some general explanation of the system of Athenian trial, so that we can also see that there was no necessity for such a sentence if Sokrates had willed to resist. First, however, let us point out that the imputation often made that this accusation of "corrupting the youth" referred to pederasty was most certainly not the case, for whether Sokrates was thus addicted or not is quite immaterial from the point of view of the trial, as this was no offence against the penal code.

Trial in Athens was by jury, which jury also acted as judge in determining the sentence, whether the case was public or civil. The jury was always a large one, and in the case of the trial of Sokrates was one panel, of which the normal full strength would have been six hundred. It was habitual in such trials for the accused to secure the services of a lawyer who would prepare the speech for the defence, which, however, was learnt and delivered by the defendant himself in answer to the oration by the prosecution. After evidence had been heard and the speeches on both sides had been given, the verdict was then pronounced. If the defendant were found guilty, the prosecution then suggested the penalty, while the accused countered with his proposal, and it was up to the jury to decide which of the two would hold good.

In the trial of Sokrates the prosecution demanded the death sentence, which Sokrates could have countered by a proposal of banishment for a short period. We feel quite sure that this would have been accepted and confirmed, but Sokrates did not consider that he had sinned to any extent or transgressed against the laws of the city, and he proposed a trivial fine, as he thought that it was right and just, so he refused any alternative suggestion which would have saved him. Sokrates had already refused the use of a brief prepared for him by his friends, and, once the sentence had been confirmed, he also refused all offers to help him escape, which his friends could certainly have managed with the approving blind eye of the authorities, and would have none of it. The Athenians soon regretted the act which had brought about the death of this saintly man, for the sentence had only been by a narrow majority. Had Sokrates not so antagonized the jury it is doubtful whether the verdict and the sentence would have been carried. As it was, Sokrates accepted and drank the allotted potion of hemlock with the same calm imperturbability as if it were a glass of wine, and he remained philosophical to the end.

CHAPTER VI

THE ACADEMY, THE LYCEUM, THE MUSEUM

PLATON brought the philosophy of Pythagoras, in both its aspects, to a fuller bloom through the intermediary of Sokrates, his master. Platon summed up the subject matter of philosophy as revealing "How to die, and be dead," and followed Sokrates in diverting it from the teaching of physicist enquiry to that of Man and his Ethics. Of Man, it was the soul that interested him, the body being but a means of contact and communication with matters of the material world during such time as the soul was in its transitory, mundane existence. He differentiates between the eye of the body and the eye of the soul, and it is the latter that counted, so that the basis of his philosophy follows from this, in that its aim is to attain near to excellency in everything. Platon's philosophy conceives that for everything there is a perfection in the existence of a divinely inspired shape or pattern, which, however, only exists in the Idea thereof, which was, is, and ever will be. The nearer things on earth approach this Idea, the better they will be. The concept of the universe is a universal totality of these Ideas, for which everything, including the soul, must strive, and the objective therefore is the Ideal, whence we get the use of the word Ideals in its present-day meaning.

The above is the primary aspect, but, as we have said,

the new Sokratic-Platonic interest in philosophy now centres around Man, so that Platon was greatly absorbed in elaborating the closest approach to human conception of the Ideal Man. There is invariably a pronounced natural tendency in treatises written on politics, and still more so in those on its sister science, economics, that the writer cannot see the wood for the trees and is dominated by the conditions that are prevalent throughout the world in his time. Platon was no exception to this, for he correlated his idea of men to the Athenian of his day, who still regarded himself as of far greater import in existence as a member of the Polis, the City, than as an individual. Platon's main book on Man therefore takes the form of an exposition on the prototype of the Ideal State, which is planned in the book we know as *The Republic*, as also supplemented by *The Laws*. Platon thus became the first of the great writers who have conceived of an ideal Utopia.

In Platon's book it is clear that he can no longer approve of pure democracy, which gives governance into the hands of the lowest educated level. He thus moves towards the later Aristotelian idea that perfect governance of a State should be ideally through one man, the all-wise sage and philosopher. Possibly Platon felt this all the more strongly since democracy had made it possible by its institutions for his dearly beloved master to be removed prematurely from the world. Indeed, on one occasion we learn of Platon visiting Syracuse at the invitation of its tyrant who is seeking advice on government, and of Platon no doubt hoping thus to be able to put his ideas on the subject into execution, only, however, to be disappointed that the young tyrant is not even wise, let alone all-wise. Of the contents of the *Republic* it is not our purpose to be concerned, yet it is interesting to note that he takes the institution of slavery for granted, and allows its continued existence in the Ideal State. Platon, however, is not satisfied with the status of women in Athenian society, and would give them more rights and consequence, yet withal considering them as by nature inferior to men. This was, of course, in his time a natural inference, for by the circumstances forced on them by their seclusion, and above all by their entire deprivation of education, they had barely a chance to appear otherwise.

Another reason which should make the name of Platon eminently famous is that he founded a school of philosophy, which it would be more correct if we called a School of Science. This was not merely in the sense of being the founder of a school of thought or outlook, such as the Hippokratic or the Pythagorean, but an actual establishment which became the first real step towards the formation of a university. This school was situated in the olive grove of the *Akadēmeia*, whence we get our present-day word in its anglicized form, the "Academy." Over its portals were written the words—and be it noted that it required but three Greek words—"Let no man enter here who is not proficient in the Science of Mathematics," the exact translation being "None ungeometricised let-enter."

The traditions of Pythagoras were taught in the Academy, and later, on the death of Platon, mathematics took even more prominence. Perhaps it is from this teaching of the Academy that we now apply the word mathematics to arithmetic (the science of numbers) whereas the former merely means "learning."

We may mention here that for the numerals the Greeks used the letters of the alphabet, followed by an apostrophe above the line to show that it was a numeral and not a letter. There were three extra signs, as otherwise there would not have been sufficient letters, and of these number six utilized one, and thus the ninth letter becomes ten, the tenth letter becomes twenty, the eleventh letter becomes thirty, and so on, so that, compared with the use of present-day numerals, it must have been cumbersome, especially for the most profound higher mathematics achieved later by such men as Archimedes.

Of Platon we can also say that he was a man who lived as he taught, with a deep ethical code, but above all a man whose philosophy is one of hope for mankind. Platon believed in man's innate goodness, from which man deviates through temptation, a temptation caused by a precursor of the equivalent of the Devil of the Christian world, whom Platon created—or shall we say anticipated.

It was left to the most outstanding of the students of the Academy to organize a university on modern lines, with divisions into the various branches of learning and an expert professor as the dean of each faculty. It was backed by the requisite paraphernalia, libraries, laboratories, and other facilities. Aristoteles, the son of a Macedonian court doctor, was born in Stagyros, on the Chalkidike Peninsula. He had entered the Academy when very young, that is, equivalent to the present undergraduate age, and at first carried on the philosophy of Platon and amplified it. Gradually, however, he diverged more and more from it, not only in its theoretical and philosophical aspect but also in its excessive stress on mathematics, which limited the general scope of enquiry as well as the scientific yet theoretic approach to problems. Aristoteles had an urge to a more concrete and practical method and sphere of investigation.

Finally Aristoteles left the Academy after about twenty years, and later formed his university at the *Lykeion* (latinized into English as the "Lyceum") and there turned his mind to almost every conceivable branch of knowledge, for each of which he wrote a textbook. In each case he either founded that particular science or carried the advance of knowledge in it on new lines and very much further forward. Not only did he do this, but he also wrote a textbook on logic which is valid today, and which sets out the requisite method for scientific thinking and argument, and upon which all science, whether conscious of it or not, has since been built. The *Logic* of Aristoteles is not only invaluable for constructive thought but is even more valuable in its negative aspect, that of avoiding fallacious argumentation.

The books of Aristoteles were written mostly as notes for his university and, unlike those of Platon, which were destined for normal publication, have not the latter's beautiful, sonorous, and symmetrical style. In the case of Platon the style made his work rank among the finest literary prose achievements of the Greek language, having the perfect proportions which always characterize Greek art and architecture.

THE ACADEMY, THE LYCEUM, THE MUSEUM

Aristoteles was the first great real scientist. When we consider the paucity of books, or scrolls as we really should call them, and the difficulties of communication and transport which might serve in amassing facts and knowledge, we must consider his assembly of the facts alone as veritably superhuman, apart from the scientific analysis and research which he devoted to them. It is really simpler not to try to enumerate them, and merely to say that they embraced all sciences, without any important one being omitted. Perhaps it was in astronomy that he made the least advance, though he did understand the nature and the vastness of the heavens better than his predecessors.

The works of Aristoteles ranged from his treatise on poetics to his books on botany and animals. In these latter he not only made an exhaustive study of their lives but on the manner and periods of their gestation and procreation, and he himself dissected a vast number of different animals. An even greater number were dissected under his instructions by his collaborators and students. His works also included books on ethics and politics, and of the latter it can be said that in the realm of political ideas he has said all that there is to be said, and that anything further which may be added can only be a repetition in a different form. His contribution to chemistry was also of the greatest value, for his was the idea of amassing as many materials as possible and subjecting them to various processes, such as heat, dampness, stress, pressure, etc., and recording their reactions, such as pliability, fragibility, solubility, decomposition, emanation of gases, and the rest.

Both the Academy and the Lyceum continued for many years—indeed, in each case, for almost a thousand years—but the Lyceum soon became the more important, and at its height in the later days of Aristoteles it is said to have had up to two thousand registered students. It did not last, however, so very long in its greatest glory, for its foundation was at the time of the Macedonian conquests by Alexander the Great, of whom Aristoteles was the tutor, and Athens did not survive for long as the one great supreme centre of the Hellenic world. In this it was supplanted for two or three generations in civic lustre by Pergamos in Asia Minor, and still more so as a seat of learning by Alexandria in Egypt, which became, and remained for several centuries, the world's centre of Hellenic thought and learning.

After Alexander's death, his empire, through lack of succession, became divided among his generals. Of these generals the only successful one was Ptolemy, to whom fell the lot of Egypt, and there in the city of Alexandria, founded by Alexander, Ptolemy established himself and soon proclaimed himself Pharaoh or king. Ptolemy and his successors were patrons, but unlike other patrons who aimed at making their courts the centre of art and culture, they aimed at making their capital the seat of learning. The Ptolemies valued learning not only for its own merit but because they appreciated the fact that learning and science, if diverted into the proper channels, could be of inestimable value in promoting the prosperity of the State in every sphere of its activity. This applied in industry, commerce, building, agriculture, irrigation, health, administration, defense, or, in short, in what we would call the sphere of competence of every ministry. Ptolemy I, in consequence founded a university on the Aristotelian model, but on an even more sumptuous scale than the Lyceum. He spared neither effort nor money in attracting the best brains of the Hellenic world to his state-subsidized institution, called the Museum. It had at its disposal a collection of all previous obtainable knowledge in a library (Bibliotheke) containing some half million scrolls. The Lyceum, as also perhaps to a lesser extent the Academy, continued to do in Athens work of the utmost scientific importance. The facilities offered by the Museum, however, and the inducement of higher emoluments offered by the Ptolemies gradually attracted the greatest scientists so that the Museum soon became the chief repository of knowledge and seat of learning of the ancient world.

Mechanics, a subject on which Aristoteles had already written a practical textbook, was carefully studied at the Museum and there was a great advance, including the production of mechanical instruments and devices of value to geology, navigation, and chronometry. We soon hear of Eratosthenes who, by calculation, measured the circumference of the earth and, to all intents and purposes, was accurate. Euklides created geometry as we know it, and he was followed, but in Syracuse, by Archimedes, who lived from just after the beginning of the third century B.C. till nearly its end. He can be called the greatest mathematician, if not of all times, at least of antiquity, of which he was also the greatest engineer.

Among the many contributions of Archimedes to science was the discovery of the laws of specific gravity. He also produced a number of mechanical devices for the defence of Syracuse, the most famous of which was known as the "Liquid Fire" which wrought great damage to the enemy, but which was destroyed at the fall of the city. It is thought to have been in the nature of a magnification and concentration of mirrored rays which were directed on the attacking vessels. Of Archimedes, the true scientist and philosopher, it is said that when finally the Romans captured the city, he was caught by a soldier who found him making calculation figures in the sand, and to whom Archimedes said in Greek, which the soldier did not understand: "Do not disturb my circles!"—among the most famous of last words.

At this period, too, both in Athens and in Alexandria, scientists discovered that the planets revolved around the sun, and that the earth revolved on its own axis, though the validity of these discoveries was not properly appreciated, or possibly it was deliberately not understood, for the planets were still identified with the gods and goddesses whose names they bore and still bear. Medicine, too, was greatly advanced in this period, and so was botany. Chronology, as a dependent of the solar system, was thoroughly studied, and the modern calendar was later worked out (by instructions of Julius Caesar). Also, diverse subjects such as optics and grammar were brought into scientific form.

What the Lyceum, the Museum, and the Greek philosophers of the early Hellenistic period taught remained valid without any contribution of substance being added to these sciences for almost two thousand years—that is, till the eighteenth century, at which period two new factors come to the aid of man, the dynamic powers of which magnified the work of the Greeks in terms of practical utility. The first of these factors was printing, which, of course, had come in earlier than the eighteenth century, though it was only at about that period that books became available to most people. The second was coal (and later on other forms of fuel and power), which existed neither in Greece nor in Alexandria.

It is beyond the writer's province to comment but it is obvious that, on the basis of charcoal, which was scarce at that, for fuel, modern plants could not be erected, or such constructions as foundries. Gas could not have existed without coal, or without coal could communications have progressed. These last remarks are not to explain why the Greeks did not attain anything like the level of our present material advancement but they are to serve as a contrary opinion to such who might assert that Greek culture and art, as well as science, depended on the leisure that they had through the institution of slavery. As a matter of fact during the period of the last few generations paid service has given far more efficient labour and the possibility of more leisure than slavery ever did. The present service which is given to man through fuel and power and machinery reduce the comparable value of slavery to almost microscopic proportions. This is so in so far as getting others, or other means, to do the work, allowing the capitalist, be his possessions in cash, services, machinery, shares or slaves, to have leisure to create artistically.

PART III
EVERYDAY LIFE

CHAPTER I

POPULATION, ORGANIZATION, AND JUSTICE

Population

THOUGH you have been invited to meet the ancient Greeks, you will find that at times, especially in this part, we might have substituted the word Athenians for Greeks for, in truth, it is the Athenians who interest us most. We ought, nonetheless, to bear in mind that even if nearly all the lustre came from Athens, it only represented a small proportion of the Hellenic population.

Athens was possibly not the largest of the Hellenic cities, for that distinction could probably have been claimed by Syracuse, or even by some of the prosperous Greek cities of Asia Minor. These had, however, an interrupted history, due mainly to the interference of the Great King, the King of the Medes and the Persians, just before the beginning of the fifth century B.C. From about 300 B.C., and for the next fifty years, it was Pergamos and Rhodes which were the brightest cities in the Greek world.

In Greece itself dominant supremacy was held only by three cities, in their turn: Athens, Sparta, and Thebes; but we must not overlook other cities of no mean stature. Among these we remember Corinth, which rivaled Athens for wealth and no doubt exceeded it in opulence, as did also the cities of Asia Minor. We must remember, too, Argos, which had its own artistic inspiration. There were, as well, other cities such as Megara and Aegina, both close to Athens, and Sikyon, in the Gulf of Corinth, as well as Aegion, which in later years became the head of the very powerful and peace-loving Achaean League. Close to Olympia there was Elis, of which we have a description of the vast Agora, as given by Pausanias. In the Peloponnesos there was also the city of Megalopolis, sponsored by Thebes for the Messenians whom they had liberated, and which had one of the largest assembly halls of Greek cities. Nemea and Tegea were cities famous for their athletic contests, and of course there were the more ancient cities of Mycenae and Tiryns, as well as Troezen. Farther afield in the islands were cities such as Lesbos, Samos, and Paros, and in the colonies other great cities, not only in Sicily and Megale Hellas but also in such places as Cyrene in North Africa. This last city is of interest if only due to the fact that here women were not secluded and had many liberties. Still farther afield there were Byzantium on the Golden Horn, Trapezous on the Black Sea (the modern Trebizond), and Massilia in the south of France.

All these cities naturally evolved. Perhaps it is in the nature of every living body and institution to have its growth and decline, and it can be of interest to note the cause of these changes. In the case of the Greek cities the decline of their spiritual ascendancy is bound up with their overgrowth. They would have succumbed anyhow to the rising might of Macedon, and later to Rome, both of whom were able to develop a national outlook rather than remain bound by a civic and parochial mentality.

Since the Greek considered himself to exist primarily as a member of his city, just as much as an arm or leg is part of the whole body, we must consider these cities and examine their proportions. Platon, in his proposals for the Ideal City, indicates that Athens already had become too big for its purpose, and we might add for its boots, for Platon thinks that a city should not grow to a size where all citizens can no longer know each other, at

POPULATION, ORGANIZATION, AND JUSTICE

least by sight. This notion of Platon's is illuminating on Greek outlook.

Athens differed from most Greek cities in that it was more of a region as it really embraced most of Attica. According to legend it was Theseus who, as king of Athens, centralized the governance of all the little townlets and hamlets into the city of Athens. There, each local king sat in council, a noble or a prince in his own right, with the king of Athens hardly more than the first among equals. When, however, the kingship was dissolved, it became almost automatic that complete control should pass into the centralized unit. In the time of Solon the Athenian was, for the most part, a country gentleman who preferred a life attending to the business of his rural estates to that of being in a city residence. No doubt, too, at that time the prosperity of the city depended on the produce of the land, supported by the export trade, which was of agricultural produce and which was essential in order to trade for corn. The Persian invasions must have had a rapid and profound change on the constituent nature of the dual cities of Athens and its port of the Piraeus. The size of the cities' urban population must have increased enormously within a generation, though this does not mean that the population of Attica or the number of free Athenian citizens would have necessarily increased.

When the rural population of Attica was forced to take refuge in the city of Athens, it would have started some new business as a means of livelihood, as we mentioned in the case of pottery. When the emergencies were over, not only would they have wished to remain in the new businesses they had created, but they could not, in every case, return to their devastated farms, even had they desired to do so. Athens, it must be remembered, produced plentiful wine for its own needs, but not so much for export, for which purpose the prime agricultural produce was olive oil. The olive groves were destroyed by Mardonius and his hordes, and the olive tree is of a venerable growth. It requires many years to bear fruit, and almost decades to reach its fullest fruition. Something for export had to be produced in the meantime, and thus handicrafts in the city had to replace rural labour.

Regarding the size of Athens, we know that when the cities of Asia Minor asked Athens for aid at the beginning of the fifth century, before Marathon, the voting strength was about thirty thousand. There is no evidence that it had much increased since those days, though the number of foreign residents had undoubtedly grown larger with the development of trade.

The above figure seems the best on which to work out the calculation which will give us the probable population.

Although the Athenian enjoyed a long life, we should hardly expect the average expectation of life to be above sixty, and therefore 30,000 would represent about two thirds of the male population, that is, those aged from twenty and over. If, on this basis there were 45,000 free males, the total population of free Athenian citizens would be about 90,000 men, women, and children, reckoning that the number of women approximated that of the men. The foreign residents were said to number some 12,000, and on the same basis this would give us about 36,000 foreign men, women, and children, and Athens would thus have something like 125,000 non-slave population, especially if we add the freed men and women, who would not have been included in the first two classes.

The slave population is much more problematical. Various authorities estimate it at the lowest at not much more than 100,000, and up to some 450,000. Let us make a guess and choose the middle course, though there are good reasons for estimating a higher level. Let us then say that the total population in the state of Athens was somewhere below half a million.

If we compare Syracuse in the days of its greatness we find that the perimeter of the city walls was about fifteen miles, and the estimated population was about half a million. Sparta was very much smaller, for there was a time when the military population did not exceed 8,000 which would have meant only some 25,000 free men, women, and children, and no foreign residents, though the size of the surrounding artisan class of "Perioeki," as well as the Helots, would have been very considerable indeed. The isle of Aegina, as well as the city of Mitylene, were both reckoned to have more slaves than Athens, and we can therefore say that they must have been of a respectable size, while the mercantile and opulent city of Corinth can be judged by the fact that, of the women of the oldest profession there, one thousand alone were registered in the service of the Temple of Aphrodite.

Administration

In the time of Perikles Athens and the Piraeus were run on ancient lines and traditions, yet the government was still a democracy, administered by the people for the people. A professional civil service hardly existed at all, and every free male had, at some time in his career, to undertake onerous civic duties. By the time of Perikles, however, there had been one innovation. As a result of the empire created by the confederacy of Delos, there were not enough free men for the military requirements. Mercenaries from other states had been enrolled. This fact later became most injurious, as the Athenian slipped into the habit of enjoying his leisure while he paid for others to do his fighting. It is safe to say, however, that no one who reached mature age could have escaped either being a member of parliament for a year, or at least a member of a jury, and almost certainly both.

The members of parliament were five hundred, fifty from each of the ten tribes, elected for one year, and each tribe doing duty for thirty-six days. Thus, within sixty years, every free man would have been elected at least once, and could not have escaped if he attained the age of eighty. With regard to the law courts, jury service could not have been escaped, for each tribe elected six hundred members of the jury annually, a total of six thousand, on which figures a citizen would have had to serve every six years. Each six hundred became one jury and was designated by an alphabetical number. It was then allocated during that year as a unit to any particular court and case as and when required. In some major cases more than one unit might be called to serve. How a member had to serve we do not know, but it is evident that it would have taken up all his time during the case, and that most of the jurors enjoyed the experience.

The high officers of state were also elected, some by lot and some by vote, and yet others by capital ownership qualification. The lower offices such as those of the scribes, and the duties of policemen, were entrusted to public slaves, the number of whom had increased at the time of Perikles to about 1,200. The policemen were mostly Scythians, for it was not fit and proper to impose the exercise of such duties on fellow citizens. Besides this, military service was from the age of eighteen to twenty, after which the citizen went on the reserve to the age of sixty. Thus in the history of Athens, from the time of the Persian invasions, and almost to the time of the conquest by Philip of Macedon, every citizen would have spent many long months fighting away from his home and city. He had to provide his own arms and armour, being in the cavalry only if he were well to do, in the heavy armed hoplites if he could afford it, and in the light armed infantry or with the slingers if he were poor.

Taxation of the rich in Athens was of an unusual nature, for there were many duties, called "leiturgies" (the liturgy used in our ecclesiastical language), which were imposed on those of a certain higher taxable wealth or income. One of these leiturgies was financing the production of a drama or comedy, when an individual had to pay for the chorus, its upkeep and training, as well as for the actors. Yet another was to provide a war vessel, fully manned, for one year, and of which, if he chose, he could be the captain. It was always considered contemptible to provide the mere essential funds and not to carry out the allotted task with good will and a show of munificence. In later years many dissipated their fortunes in their zeal to obtain the approval of their fellow citizens.

Other tasks allotted to the citizens included the financial management of the various civic functions, which would sometimes correspond to our ministries. The accountants would be called in at the end of the year to check up and see that everything was in order, before anyone was relieved of his duties and could hand over.

The Athenian therefore not only had his say in the convocation of the people, where his weekly vote had almost the same value as that of a member of parliament, but he also took active part in the management of the city during some part of his life. When we come to deal with the Agora we will see that life centred here to such an extent that a parochial feeling, as opposed to civic consciousness, could hardly have existed.

Thus, the Athenian, and in somewhat similar fashion the citizens of other Greek cities, felt themselves much more a part of the city than a part of the family, for in a sense the family was part of their civic responsibility that it should produce fit and respectable citizens and mothers of citizens. The family was not an institution where solace and pride might be found in the home circle.

The organization of the cities of Greece differed in many ways, with Sparta and Athens at the extremes, but there were also the Greek cities of southern Italy and Sicily, where tyrants alternated with democracy, and the great cities of Asia Minor under tyrants and satraps. Of the latter some had courts, which, however, were always limited in power by the innate democratic outlook of the citizens. Should the tyrant neglect to respect this sufficiently the tyranny would soon find itself without legs to stand on, and learn that the supreme ruler of the State was the Law, to which they, too, in some measure, must bow.

Military Training and Defence

In so far as we know, the Greeks were the first to appreciate the value of training in the formation of military forces, and the whole history of the Classical Period shows how a small force of trained Greeks was more than equal to the armies of the barbarians which were vastly greater in size. The kings and contending usurpers of Persia and Egypt soon found that it was essential to have trained Greek forces at their disposal in any military operation. Some cities made military training the beginning and end of the citizens' objective, but this was largely confined to the Dorians, who for some reason did not mingle with the populations that they captured, but subjugated them, using the farmers as artisans and serfs, and the others as slaves.

Of the Dorians who lived in this way we have so far only mentioned the Spartans, because it was only the Spartans who played a major part in Greek history, but there were also other Dorians in other parts whose habits and constitutions were very similar, and of these the Dorians of Crete are the most interesting. Crete is a comparatively large island and there were many Dorian communities that became established there. Their problems and dangers through the subjugated races were not so acute as those of Sparta, and their regulations were therefore not quite so "Spartan." They had the same system of "Syssitia," or communal feeding halls, and the Cretans, like the Spartans, were principally absorbed with defence. They, too, thus gave more latitude and home affairs management to their womenfolk.

In the Cretan communal feeding halls we can discern an element which no doubt also applied to Sparta, for the common messes had the purpose of inculcating sectional pride and brotherhood, in some way similar to the present-day colleges and fraternities of universities, or the "houses" of schools. The military units would be identified with the messes, so that in military operations there would be an *esprit de corps* and a desire not to let the side down, for otherwise no one would ever dare meet his brethren of the mess again without the deepest shame. Thus the opinion and esteem of the fellow messmates would carry more valid sanction than the force of the law could hope to do. The indications are that the messes represented about three hundred families, but of course differed according to communities.

It is likely that the women had separate messes of their own, for they certainly did not participate with the males, though the management of the male messes was under the supervision of a capable free woman who had men as her assistants. The serving was undertaken by youths. Strangers were honoured at the Cretan messes, and were served even before the chairman (the archon), but this can be explained by the fact that visitors would be mostly from other Dorian communities of the island, and as masters of subjugated races they would have to hang together; yet apart from that the Dorians always respected strangers, even if the Spartans could not tolerate them in their city, and Dorians always showed respect to old age.

The syssitia were paid for in different ways, sometimes directly out of the city's revenues, but sometimes by direct taxation on the members' income, which in some instances we know to have been one tenth of the produce of their estates. Attendance was compulsory, and absence was only excused on some valid reason, and should this be "hunting," then it was expected that a good share of the "bag" would follow. The fare, however, was mainly plain and though provision of diluted wine was universal, intemperance was strictly prohibited by law. These communal halls also served an educational purpose, for postprandial conversation would be political, or of elevating intent. Tales would be recounted of the noble deeds of yore for the benefit, perhaps, of the youths who sat separately under the supervision of an officer. Perhaps they found that additional appetizing food was required while the moralizing was going on, for dishes such as game might be served at this later stage of the proceedings, and community singing would be included.

There were other communities in Greek lands which depended on vassal races, but there is no clear indication whether community feeding was only a Dorian custom among the Greeks, though it was also a practice among other nations such as the Carthaginians. We know that it was practised at Megara, though Corinth, which was Dorian, gave it up at an early stage as it was found to promote aristocratic tendencies. Of the cities or states that depended on vassal races, which were treated not unlike the Helots, were Thessaly, Syracuse, Byzantium, and Herkleia on the Black Sea.

Of the military training itself we have seen how thorough it was at Sparta, and we have mentioned how a boy's education included Homer and music. By music we must understand the arts that were under the patronage of the Muses, for that art which we have nowadays reserved the name of music was designated as "harmonics." Whereas a youth would begin his two years of military training at the age of eighteen, in Athens anyhow, the previous two or three years were largely devoted to mental and physical training which would be preparatory to his period of national service. The Greeks were firm believers that a healthy body was necessary for a healthy mind, and if only for this reason alone prescribed moderation in intemperance. Thus wine was always mixed with water in ratios varying between three of water to one of wine up to equal amounts of each, and was never taken neat except by a doctor's prescription. The attitude of the Athenian, anyhow, was not bigoted to the extent that he considered intoxication a sin, but only its excess or frequency, and we have seen that on the festival of the Great Dionysia vinous merriment came not amiss. Part of the later years of schooling would also be spent in gymnasia, and to this we might ascribe one of the reasons why the Greeks lived to a ripe old age. As well as athletic prowess and health, the youths were taught fair play and good sportsmanship at the gymnasia and wrestling rings.

We have also seen the importance attached to dancing to music, and of the dances there was an infinite repertoire. While in Athens its cultural import was valued, it was its military value that was esteemed in Dorian lands. In Crete in particular there were many variations performed in armour, as well as spear or sword dances, the music being provided mostly by flutes. The cithara (or lyre) was considered more appropriate for the bard and for feminine dancing at the symposia.

Law and Justice

Of the elements of good government we have so far

touched on matters pertaining to defence, education, and health, and we must now deal with that of justice. Because we have become used to the term "Roman law," which was codified some five hundred years after the beginning of the Christian era under the orders of the Emperor Justinian (and we must not forget that one of the chief compilers was a Greek, Theodosius), it is not generally realized that the foundation of Roman law was entirely inspired by the Greeks. In fact, when the Romans promulgated their early laws in twelve tables, it was a Greek of Asia Minor who was called in to assist in setting them up.

In Athens, where litigation was far too frequent, there was an appropriate form of legal action for almost every conceivable contingency. The very idea of liberty to the Greek was that of living under the aegis of the law, for, as Pindar says: "Law is the Universal King." Whereas the equality of the law was essential, there was, perhaps, a little more latitude in its application than there is today, for the present principle of justice is that "Jus quod jussus (est)" that is, that the law, and in consequence justice, is that which has been legislated.

In practice among the Greeks there was more latitude for equity, and though the law was very precise, it depended on the enormous jury, and thus the human element rather than the written ordinance would have more say. Appeals were allowed, but only on certain occasions, which would be more those of fact than on technical legal points. The convicted person would accept the verdict with good grace. He would be more prone to a feeling that he was unlucky than that he had been unjustly treated, for the verdict would be under a system in which he could count himself as part legislator.

One of the unusual practices of the Athenian law courts was that, unless it were a special case, the speeches for the prosecution and the defence, and especially the latter, were limited as to time. In the courts there was always a klepsydra, which word literally means a "water stealer." This was one of the normal forms of timekeepers, on the principle of the sand glass, but on the basis that water trickled through a small hole in a container so that it took a given time to empty. We might add that the Greeks knew of its inaccuracy in that it might vary a fraction according to the heat of the season and water. If, during the speech there were an interruption for any cause, even such as the production of evidence, the klepsydra was turned off, and only resumed when the speech was continued. The rules of evidence were prescribed, and an avowed friend or enemy could not be produced in evidence.

Women officially had no rights before the law, but that only means that they could not themselves plead or defend, but of this we will speak later. Suffice it to say that nowadays it is extremely rare that anyone should personally plead or defend except through a lawyer. Slaves could be called as witnesses, but their evidence was held to be of no value unless taken under torment, or even torture, when it was held to be of greater value even than the evidence of free men. While one side could demand that a slave of an opponent should be produced to give evidence, the master of the slave could refuse to do so, and might do so for humanitarian reasons, but he might well be afraid to refuse producing him lest it might be considered a possible admission of guilt.

There was a different law for slaves, for there were acts forbidden to slaves, or which could only arise through being a slave, such as attempting to escape. Generally the law was not so different for them as was the punishment, for where a free man might be punished for a certain offence by a fine, the slave would receive corporal punishment. This no doubt would be largely because it was thought a more fitting punishment for them, but also because, just as in our own law courts there is the option of a fine or so many days or months, the slave would not be likely to have the wherewithal for the option of a fine. We can reckon that severity or leniency of the punishments for infringements were not dissimilar to those of the present day, and that, whereas, in the early days of Drakon's legislation they were more harsh—as they were with us two or three centuries ago—they became more humanitarian later on. They did not have the savagery that British law courts had even two centuries ago, when children could be, and were, condemned to death for stealing a lump of coal of the value of five shillings or more.

Respect for law and justice was of the very essence of Greek civilisation, especially in the Classical times. Though the position of both women and slaves would seem to have been most iniquitous, it did not seem to work out so unjustly, and we even have the case of a son reporting his father to the courts for neglecting the upkeep of an elderly slave. This, it would appear, he reported neither out of animosity to his father, not out of pity for the slave, but out of feeling that here was an infringement of duty which it was incumbent on the son to report.

We may think that the system of such an immense jury was impracticable, but if we think it over, and consider that the citizen was so very much a part of the city, there would be an enormous amount of intimate knowledge between the accused and the members of the jury. If the jury were but a small one there would be a danger of undue influence. Although we have no indication that the reason for their large size was to avoid such a danger, we can, nonetheless, assume that this was part of the reason, though the prosecution, the defendant, and the jury were on oath to speak the truth.

A further point in connection with the law was that foreigners in Athens were not allowed to hold property, and thus they had to rent their residences. They had to be sponsored by patrons, and therefore would require continual assistance at law, for the patrons were responsible to the State for all the transactions of aliens.

The position of foreigners in a city stresses the aspect of the Greek as being a citizen to the exclusion of having purely individual natural rights. It applied to almost all non-Dorian cities, though in Athens the non-Athenian resident had more privileges than foreigners had in most cities. Trade was very largely in his hands, in consequence of which he was more of the port of the Piraeus than of Athens itself. The city gave him good protection in trade, and if he were a permanent resident, expected also that he would undertake duties, which included service with the forces and the performance of some of the leiturgies, as well as pay a small residence tax. Trade was regarded in a somewhat similar light to that in which it was regarded two or three generations ago, that is to say, it was looked down upon. If you were big enough and successful enough, it might be another matter, and both Solon, and a century later Platon, indulged in trade on occasion. Retail trade was a very different matter.

Transport

Very little is known about land transport in ancient Greece. Transport was, of course, mainly by sea. It could hardly have been otherwise, for of the famous cities of Classical Greece, only Sparta and Thebes were not on the seacoast, while Athens and Argos are within an hour's walk.

When the populations of cities increased, they did not expand into outer suburbs, and in consequence construction of roads was hardly a normal result. Colonies would be founded, and these colonies were almost invariably on the seacoast. It is interesting to note that, in the fourth century B.C., the population of Greek cities was on the wane.

There is a fair amount of information about the ships of ancient Greece, both regarding their size and the men that manned them, and how many tiers of rowers they had. The most common man-o-war was the trireme, but precisely how the rowers were placed is not clear. In Hellenistic times vessels of more than three tiers were constructed, even of five or six or over. The position thus becomes confused. Some contend that the amount of tiers simply means that there were so many rowers to each oar, while others believe that there were so many inner platform levels for the rowers. If we consider a six-tier vessel, then the top tier would have required unduly long oars, while if there were six men to each oar, the furthest away from the sea would have quite a walk to and fro between the dip and the take out. We also read of a vessel which, in Hellenistic times, was manned by six hundred men and was of five thousand tons, though this was exceptionally large.

We suppose that these large vessels were the galleons of their time with an auxiliary motive power of rowers needed for manoeuvreing in battle array.

There were all types of vessels, especially for war purposes, the "cruisers" being faster than the heavier sea transports. The normal triremes had a total complement of two hundred, of whom 170 were rowers and the rest marines or land soldiers. In addition there might be a few special soldiers whose job was to defend the vessel.

The matter becomes complicated when at a later stage we hear of vessels of as many as forty ranks of rowers, and it becomes hard to imagine so many tiers. Even if the one rower was not immediately above the other, as seems to be the case, but at an elevated position behind the other, it still requires an impossible stretch of the imagination and also of the oar handle. In spite of this we know that the lower-rank rowers had shorter oars than those above, and that they were paid less. The great vessel of Ptolemaeus Philopater had four thousand rowers!

In Classical times the vessels, which all had female names, were drawn ashore when sojourning on any beach. Vessels were also drawn across the odd four miles of the Isthmus of Corinth, between the Saronic and Corinthian gulfs, and very recently the slipway route along which they were drawn has been unearthed.

Apart from Sparta, no city of any consequence lay at any difficult or lengthy journey away from the sea. There was no bulky machinery or other types of goods requiring heavy vehicles with the exception of large slabs of marble. The two main sources of marble were that on the isle of Paros, from which only sea transport was required, and that from Mount Pentelicon in Attica, whence marble brought to Athens could be worked downhill the whole way. Timber was mainly required for naval construction at the seaports and could be brought thither by sea.

Pack animals were mainly used for journeys, and rather for carrying the luggage than for riding. Four-wheeled carts there were, as those used by the wine vendors, but these would have been drawn by oxen. The deduction is that there could not have been much in the way of roads, or, anyhow, of interurban roads. Horses were not shod, and we feel certain that whatever roads there were, were not hard-surfaced.

It has been said that no invention in transport took place between Classical times and the era of Napoleon. This, however, is not correct. An invention of major importance took place sometime during the Middle Ages which must have revolutionized transport, although from our point of view it is difficult to realize what immense significance it must have had. This invention was the ordinary horse collar. Without means of harnessing the horses to heavy wagons, traffic must have been very different and the call for roads relatively less.

We must not get a wrong impression through the popularity of chariot racing at the games. These chariots were hardly more than trotting carriages with only precarious standing footroom for the reinholder and one passenger.

The city planning of Hippodamos, who laid out the Piraeus in rectangular blocks, shows that the city had regular streets, and that there were also roads joining Athens to its port. We also know of the processions of initiates that moved along the Sacred Way to the mysteries at Eleusis, some fifteen miles distant, and that the citizens of Athens would await at the bridge beyond the Academy olive grove for the returning processions which they hailed with lewd jokes. Roads therefore there were, and cities constructed bridges where necessary.

The costings of the building of a temple at Eleusis in 328 B.C. have been preserved and are illuminating. Marble, which had to be transported twenty-five miles, cost 342 drachmae for transport, which worked out at 3 drachmae per ton-mile (for just over four tons). Sea transport of marble is reckoned at between a quarter to a half a drachma per ton-mile—that is, a sixth to a twelfth of land transport.

Alexander the Great believed in the construction of roads and relied on them for control of his empire, but it is interesting to note that relay posts for changing of horses in Persia were about twenty miles apart, and that seems to have been reckoned a normal day's journey.

CHAPTER II

CHARACTER AND CHARACTERISTICS

OF COURSE there were differing characteristics of the Greeks from city to city, with extremes between the Dorian Spartans and the Ionian Athenians. These Thucydides stressed so that we can the better understand the history of the Peloponnesian War. There were differences, just as there are differences between the Northerner and the Southerner, or between the American from the Middle West and the one from the Pacific Coast. When, however, we might wish to compare the American or the Englishman to the Frenchman or the German we would see that there is a greater similarity between the various Englishmen or the various Americans than there are differences. There is a certain mental approach common to each nationality, and this was also the case with the Hellenes.

Thus, the Greek, however much he differed from city to city, still had the characteristics of his race, and we have seen how the most prominent trait was that of regarding himself primarily as a citizen. His other attributes were exemplified by the maxims of the sages which were inscribed at the temple of the Pythian Apollon at Delphi: "Be not excessive," "Excellency is only to be found in Moderation," and "Know Thyself."

At the beginning of this book we dealt with the involved

question of the Greeks' antecedents, and gave it to be understood that, although we have many clues, we do not know exactly what the proportion and admixture of the stock was that constituted the Greeks of Classical times. With the exception of the Dorians, they were an admixture of a Mediterranean race which we can assume would have been excitable, passionate, artistic, and feminine, and of a Northern race which would have been stolid, rational, persevering, and masculine. Whatever the admixture was, we also have to deal with that most controversial of all subjects, the extent to which environment affects character and brains. It is, of course, at the root of political arguments, and this we want to avoid, but it is also a matter in which the medical profession is interested, and raises such questions as to whether the adopted child will be more influenced by its real parentage or by the habits and circumstances of the family in which it is reared. Opinions must vary, but it cannot be denied that the stock must have an important say, for, as a friend once told me, she would never back a horse in a race which had been sired by a cart horse. Over a long period conditions of environment must also have profound influence on a race, and probably the formation of habits is influenced by climatic and geographic food-producing conditions.

We have already dealt with the fact that the Greek religion was a dynamic force so that the Greek considered himself a *politis,* that is, a citizen, rather than an *idiotis,* that is, an individual, and this made of the Athenian a man always seeking company and the companionship of his fellow citizens. It left the Spartan, who was obliged to participate in communal meals, far more taciturn and "laconic."

Did the Greek practice that restraint that he considered the precept of a good citizen? Or did he live in moderation because it was either the essence of his physiological nature or because it had become his second nature? Some would tell us that he was very much of a Mediterranean, and sexually hot-blooded. These people would try, in a similar manner, to explain the fact that the Athenian was a small eater because of climatic conditions, but that would be absurd, for in those same climes, centuries later, the Byzantines became the greediest eaters of stupendous meals of a size probably never exceeded. The point of this latter remark is that too much import should not be given to the fact that the Greeks, as Mediterraneans, would have had the characteristics of Mediterraneans of today.

It is our guess that the Greek was not excessive, and that this had become second nature as well as being instinctive. In Classical times he did not like luxury, though in the Greek cities of Asia Minor luxury was sought to a far greater extent, either because of the example of the neighbouring races or because there was a goodly admixture of native Carian and Lydian blood, as there must surely have been.

The way it might be figured out is as follows: Man's activities are prompted in order to satisfy human desires, some of which are for immediate or bodily needs and some of which are for the future. It is in these desires of the Greeks that we are therefore interested. Just as the Greek had learned the value of training in physical sports, so that the muscles became stronger through exercise, so, too, he realized that the faculties of the brain react in precisely a similar manner to such use. In his desire for mental pleasures he found delight in all opportunities for exercising his brain. His personal acquisitive instinct had been subordinated to his pride of citizenship, and his desire to accumulate possessions in his home could not have been strong, nor did he care whether his neighbour's roses were more beautiful than his own.

The Greek was a sparse eater; he rose from the table with his appetite hardly satiated after having partaken of food that would be considered by our standards to be of the very plainest. No such things as the Roman spectacles were demanded by him, and the theatres—in Athens—were open but twice a year. He was far, far more interested in the intellectual conversation of the Agora, or at the symposia after the evening meal, when games of skill were played, riddles set, and, occasionally, a short "floor show" performance put on. It will be noted that at these banquets there was no administering by female slaves and, whereas hetairae were sometimes present, it seems to have been more the exception than the rule. Sensualities, though not necessarily excluded, would have been rare.

In the taverns, around the Agora, cockfights and quail fights were staged, but there was no outcry against them. Whereas their purpose was for betting, it was in moderation and they were not really considered of a dangerous nature which might dissipate a young man's fortune. Luxuries on which money could be spent were few, and those mentioned are fish and prostitutes. It is our summing up that, just as he did not indulge in luxuries in eating because his desires were attuned to other and more intellectual concerns, so, too, he did not indulge unduly in sexual intercourse, for his desires were more absorbed in other matters.

The above may explain to some small extent why the womenfolk of the Greeks, and especially of the Athenians, had such a poor time of it, for if the attractions that counted most with him were not feminine, then woman's position could not be very much in the ascendant.

The Status of Women

There are many reasons why the status of women was so low, one of which is that the city imposed marriage as a duty, and in some cities there was even legislation to that effect. The Greek got married with but one objective, that of doing his duty to the city by producing healthy and healthy-minded children. As this was the free woman's lot, her education became completely neglected and her life became a vicious circle. The Greek man, other than the Dorian, had little use for company which was not educated and intellectual.

There is invariably a tendency to imagine the ancient Greeks as living much as the ancient Romans, but in truth their habits and character were immensely different. In Classical times female slaves were never used for pleasure, and at meals they did not even serve the tables where the men ate. Nor, for that matter, did the Greek expect the unquestioning servility from the slave that the Romans did.

Another reason which might explain woman's status in Athens is that peculiarity of the sexes which has only been stressed by the medical profession in comparatively recent years, which is to say that the human male and female have all the organs that each other possesses, but some are far more accentuated according to the sex. The Greek, therefore, and more particularly the Ionian Greek, had very much of that which was feminine in his own composition, and that is perhaps the clue to his genius in art. Woman may dissipate her creative nature in procreation and the upbringing of a child. Even the pre-Achaeans imagined their productive deities as feminine. The Greek of Classical times did not look to woman for his creative inspiration.

The Athenian genius is to be found in the dynamic virility of their masculine nature, but embellished by the delicacy and elegance of their feminine attributes. This very nature of their art may incline us to support the opinion that they were not sexually overindulgent, and that for the most part, by Classical times, love did not play such a commanding role in man's life as to make woman so frequently his mistress with the full meaning of the word.

It is not astonishing, therefore, that in Athens pederasty was not considered so offensive and was to some extent practised. There certainly was some objection to it and it was guarded against, but possibly more as detrimental to health than to morals. Precautions were therefore taken that such practice should be discouraged at the palaestra —the wrestling institutions—and parents might be averse to letting their boys participate in the choruses. This fact, whatever its extent may have been, though we can trust that as in everything else it was only in moderation, is nonetheless a factor supporting the view that feminine attraction did not signify so very much, and that women did not get their due admiration. There is often the view, or rather the misconception, that the other woman, the hetaira, played an important role as the mistress of the ancient Greeks, and habitually graced their banquets, but this seems to have been far from the actual case.

There were several divisions in the status of women. There were, first of all, the free women, the wives and daughters of citizens. In Athens the maidens were very secluded and the matrons had scarcely more latitude. In Doric lands it was the other way round—the maidens had a fair latitude which was somewhat curtailed after marriage. The sole role in life for the free woman among the Athenians was to give birth to, and bring up, children sound in health and morals. In this the men had full confidence in the integrity and chastity of their wives, for they gave them little chance or opportunity to be otherwise. Though they were given full confidence to manage the household, the shopping was nonetheless left to the man, or to the supervision of a slave.

The next class of women were the *pallake* who were not slaves, but were employed to administer to the bodily requirements of the man. In a sense they were a type of domestic, but their position is much confused with that of the hetaira, who administered to the pleasures and entertainments. Generally the hetaira might have the profession of a dancer or kithar player, but the very fact that she practised such a profession let it be assumed that she was also to be classed in a not very different position from women of the streets. The *pallake,* or *pallakis,* and the hetaira could very rarely be the daughters of free citizens; each could be an alien or foreigner, or a freed woman, and each was subject, in Athens at least, to the small tax on foreigners. The position is not entirely clear, for there was this tax on foreigners in employment or trade, and there was also the tax on prostitutes, and whether the former paid the foreigner's tax, and the latter the prostitute's, or both, is not entirely evident. It is clear, however, that the employer of the *pallake* had his rights protected by law, so that if he caught her in *flagrante delicto* and slew the paramour, he had the same protection as if the offense had been committed by his legal wife.

Below these were the common prostitutes who came

under the surveillance of the market superintendent (the *agoranomos*). They might even be slaves bought for the purpose, and hired out as such. Lastly came the slave women of the household, and they were almost entirely confined to the duties of the female section of the household, though they might well be employed in the feminine handicrafts, not merely for the needs of the household but for the wholesale and export trade.

We find so many contradictions in examining the status of women, and therefore so many different opinions, that a little reflection on the subject might not be amiss. Most of these contradictions arise from the fact that we are apt to forget how very quickly customs and fashions can change, and we should always therefore be sure, when we weigh up the evidence for or against an opinion, that we are comparing similar dates and places. Even if we are comparing the time of Perikles for or against an opinion, or the time of Aristophanes, or that of Demosthenes, it still gives latitude for immense change. If we but consider our own times we would remember that at the beginning of the century a woman bathing in the sea would require a special enclosure, and be dressed in such ugly and amorphous garb that the delineation of her figure must be out of the question. Only a few years ago, however, she would be expected to wear when bathing, if in line with the fashion, such bikinaceous paucity that Platon no doubt would have described it as being of a nature that if liable to shrink, then it would be no garb at all. At the turn of this century "maidens" could not venture out unchaperoned, and would have been horrified if their dress so much as allowed their ankles to appear, but at that very period dames and matrons went to the theatre of an evening showing so much of their bosoms that today we would consider it outrageous.

To understand the position of women in Athens at the Golden Age we must try to get their actual standing and not their legal one. In this we might be helped if we consider what the Athenians of that time might garner of present-day customs and practice, if the Pythian Oracle had enabled them to visualise forward as we are attempting to visualise backward. The Athenian would find that in our times women were compelled by the vows of marriage to obey their husbands, and that the husbands are responsible for their debts. The Athenian might even come to the conclusion, erroneously of course, that women in his time were better off, for the law did then give them certain protection which does not exist today.

The law gave Greek women complete right to their marriage dowry, so that if divorce took place the former husband had to pay at the rate of 18 per cent per month until the dowry was forthcoming, as well as provide for the woman's maintenance in the meantime. The dowry was a feature of the utmost importance for it was the most concrete of all evidence of marriage having taken place. A marriage without a dowry might bring the woman into the position of concubinage if the husband were to die and there was no evidence of one.

On divorce, or death of the husband, the wife returned to her father's guardianship, or to the nearest of kin, or to some other legal guardian who took care of the dowry. The husband, however, could allot his wife by will to whomsoever he thought fit and proper and, in theory anyhow, without her approval and consent. The men, after marriage, could maintain any liaison or mistress, and this was not considered either unusual or improper, and only became so if the husband carried on to the neglect of his legitimate wife and home.

In Athens there were undoubtedly many hetairae who sometimes lived on their own, and sometimes in groups, these locations constituting congenial meeting places for young men. The hetairae took the greatest care to make themselves attractive, which, as we have already seen from the character of the Athenian, would not only mean personal physical attraction but even more so to educate themselves and cultivate their minds. It is rather difficult to understand whence the ranks of these women were drawn, for there could hardly have been more than a very small proportion, indeed, deriving from the ranks of the free citizens, and they, therefore, must have been, and were from among the foreigners.

Cohabitation with foreign women was expressly forbidden, and we must assume that this only meant that relationship with them must not exclude the proper maintenance of the legal wife. Perikles nonetheless had been estranged from his legal wife and cohabited with Aspasia, who is understood to have had her origin in an Ionian city, but Aspasia was a very exceptional woman whom Perikles consulted and whose advice he valued. Aspasia would discourse with Sokrates and could well hold her own with him. She was even sought by Athenian matrons who took their daughters to her that she might impart the lustre to them of a finishing school. There were other hetairae, too, who held great influence over other prominent men in different cities, but disorderly life, with perhaps the exception of Corinth, does not seem to have been the rule until a far later period, a period after the hegemony of Macedon, when even the stoic Spartans favoured luxuries of food and comforts.

The Athenian

From what has so far been written we might possibly assume that the Athenian was effeminate. He might well have been but for his devotion to athletics, and the training which prevented him from being so; his sturdiness and valour in fighting cannot be questioned. Yet he had feminine traits, for he was most punctilious as to the good care of his beard and hair, and was a frequent visitor to the barber, not only for a trim, but also for unguents and the refreshment of perfumes. It would seem that, on occasion, he did not disdain pomades for the face, and an Athenian has even been mentioned who toned the colour of his cheeks to his raiment. While he was at the barber, our Athenian would avail himself of the opportunity for a pleasant spot of gossip.

We are accustomed to seeing the statues of the ancients, especially the Romans, and sometimes in semblance thereof the great men of Victorian days crowned with wreaths of laurel and myrtle as signs of excellence or prize winning. Let us not therefore think it so strange that the evening dress of the ancient Athenians consisted not only in the selection of a "natty" pair of shoes, but invariably in the wearing of chaplets gay with ribbons and flowers. These were not the leafy crowns of the victors, but of flowers which would vary according to the seasons and would be such as the sweet-smelling Parma violets of Athens, hyacinths, jasmine, and, in summer, the highly perfumed roses of the Mediterranean. No wonder that during the drawing-room games and riddles of the symposia, a winner, or one who had guessed right, might be recompensed by the kiss of a neighbour or the Master of the Symposion. Yet, in spite of this, they were far from being the effeminate type.

The Athenian attributed his quick and scintillating wit to the sparkle of the Athenian air, an air which today most certainly has an invigorating quality; likewise he considered that the dull intellect of the Theban was attributable to the heavy air of the Boeotian pasture land. The Athenian was impressionable and ready to give sympathy, but it was his head that controlled his actions, and not his feelings which did so. He could be hard, though he was rarely of a cruel and sanguine nature. He could be most severe to the enemy, but such severity would be similar to that of a hard-headed business deal to eliminate dangerous rivals. We hardly ever see such practices as crucifixion or similar expressions of vengeance.

The Athenian was easily swayed by oratory, but the orators were of great stature, and it is to be noted that, whereas in modern history successful orators have appealed to the mob by calling upon their instinct of hate, the Greek orator, and especially the Athenian, appealed to the intellect and to action for the good of the city.

The Athenian, however, admitted himself to be fickle, and this could hardly be otherwise in the case of men who were ready to approach all questions with a completely open mind, whereas, of course, the uneducated Spartan had all the stubbornness of ignorance.

In earlier times, before the complete establishment of the Olympian gods, to whom mysterious happenings might be attributed and thus explained, the Greeks had the superstitions of the pagan. This is well discernible in the early poetry of Hesiod, but in Classical times such superstitious fears had greatly been allayed, especially as ventilation could be given by the various rituals of the Eleusinian Mysteries and the Great Dionysia, which gave outlet to the lurking primordial instincts. The Spartan was much more superstitious, as was proved in such extraordinary fashion so many times in the crucial days of the Persian invasions. The Dorians, too, were the guardians, if not the promoters, of the Delphic Oracle, and the Spartan was also the oracle's favourite and most gullible adherent. Curiously, the Spartan, with his strict discipline and precepts, and his hard training and life, was more venal than the Athenian, and though we might think otherwise from the frequent litigation which was a curse of Athens, the Athenian kept his word. In the Agora of Athens great faith was placed in the bankers who sat at their tables, loaning money, or drawing a draft made payable in another land or city.

The Greek Attitude

Much has been made of the readiness of the Greek to turn to the enemy, and it certainly seems to have happened frequently, though its incidence was not so great as might be imagined. Alkibiades was certainly a bad example, yet changing circumstances can easily change an outlook, and whereas on paper ten or twenty years are but a few words or a line, they can have extraordinary effects. We have but to look at modern history to see how Italy pirouetted and gyrated in each of the World Wars, and how Germany allied herself to Russia and then attacked her. Pétain and Laval were ready to show peculiar acrobatic patriotism, while Prime Ministers Lloyd George and Churchill were voted out of office by way of thanks, and President Wilson had a similar experience.

In this chapter we have had the Greeks very seriously under the spotlight, and we have, in a sense, tried to take their make-up off and see what they were like. As every woman will tell you, this is really quite unfair and allowances should be made.

It is still inexplicable how, throughout the period of great Athenian art, in spite of the comparative segregation of woman, feminine *arete* gave inspiration, that word which stands for Greek goodness, goodness of good taste and manners, goodness of noble character, reliability, capability, and demeanour. It was this *arete* which was at the root of the Greek's religion. In the time of Homer it was the goddesses that had the last word, and yet in Classical times woman counted for nought. It is withal puzzling.

In this respect the Greek appears ungallant to his womenfolk, yet in other ways he protected his women, and did not expect undue menial work from them. In many ways he figures as a gentleman, for he was a great host, and a generous one. He did not have the false pride of the parvenu, and was not afraid of work, having a wholesome dislike for the idler and the parasite who was not tolerated by Athenian law. He did, however, disdain such business or trade which could not be efficiently carried out without ungentlemanly conduct. He disdained, for instance, the profession of innkeeper, for to the Greek his house must be at the disposal of his friends and acquaintances from other cities, and to his friends he would gladly proffer board and lodging, whereas to his acquaintances he might offer the shelter of his roof, allowing them to fend for themselves in obtaining food. The innkeepers were nonetheless necessary, for at the great festivals, such as the Great Panathenaea, the concourse of visitors was beyond the possibilities of personal hospitality.

Of those other aspects of the nature of the ancient Greek, in which his outlook was in many ways similar to our own, was that of death, or rather more correctly we should have said that our attitude toward death is much like his. It is largely due to Pythagoras, Sokrates, and Platon that our belief in life after death is founded, as also from such ritual and practice as the baptism of the Eleusinian Mysteries. The mysteries, however, may have been of Egyptian origin, and much of Greek belief in this matter may have had previous antecedents. The Greek has a passionate desire to leave someone behind who would not only attend to sepulchral rites, but continue to perform them.

There would seem to be a curious contradiction in the professed beliefs of the Greeks in this respect, for on death the Greek proceeded to the underworld, where he became a sort of meaningless, colourless flitting shade. It was of the utmost importance to him that he should have a proper burial, or, if his body were not obtainable, a burial service, so that Hermes could conduct him to Charon, the underworld boatman, who was paid by the obol inserted in the dead man's mouth. It was the sacred duty to bury one's relatives, and if one even came upon a corpse, the least one could do would be to throw some earth over it. By way of preparation for burial, the body was first washed and a proper robe put on so that it might not be so cold on the passage to Hades. As well as the lekythos oil jar, a honey cake was added as a sop to Kerberos (Cerberus), the canine guardian of the underworld. At the funeral only the very nearest female relatives were allowed unless the women were over sixty.

Burial was sometimes by interment and sometimes by cremation, after which the ashes and bones would be collected and placed in an urn. This would seem to be a contradiction, as stated above, for it would not seem to fit in with religious beliefs. Those who accept burial by burning normally and anthropologically believe in the survival of the soul, while those who believe in a continued existence require interment. If a journey were first to be undertaken under the patronage of Hermes, it must have been a pretty piecemeal condition if the traveller's ashes were in a jar.

Why the Greek should insist so much on his grave being attended to is also difficult to understand, for before being rowed across the river Styx, he had drunk of Lethe, the river of forgetfulness which disassociated his memory with mundane happenings. Perhaps the Greeks only half believed in the efficacy of Lethe, for when Odysseus visits the underworld, or when the dramatists are visited there in "The Frogs" (the play by Aristophanes), the shades in person are not only met but they possess a memory of the world of the past, and even have some measure of prophetic lore.

Funerals were followed by a banquet, and banquets were also held not only on the anniversary of the death, but also on the birthday of the departed.

After these few comments on some aspects of the Greek character, in some of which we somewhat differ, we should put them again in a more proper perspective by setting out below the Hippokratic Oath. Every apprentice with ambitions to become a practising doctor was bound to take and uphold this oath. It has ever since been the high standard which, with the exception of the duties of the apprentice towards the patron and his family, the medical profession aims at today. We give Greenhill's translation of a hundred years ago. Few vows can have been more elevating, or show a greater sense of duty towards one's fellow creatures:

The Hippokratic Oath

I swear by Apollon the physician, by Asculepius, by Hygeia, and Panacaea, and all the Gods and Goddesses, calling them to witness, that I will fulfil religiously, according to the best of my power and judgment, the solemn promise and the written bond which I now do make. I will honour as my parents, the master who has taught me this art, and endeavour to minister to all his necessities. I will consider his children as my own brothers, and will teach them my profession, should they express a desire to follow it, without remuneration or written bond. I will admit to my lessons, my discourses and all my other methods of teaching, my own sons, and those of my tutor, and those who have been inscribed as pupils and have taken the medical oath; but no one else. I will prescribe such a course of regimen as may be best suited to the condition of the patients, according to the best of my power and judgment, seeking to preserve them from anything that might prove injurious. No inducement shall ever lead me to administer poison, nor will I ever be the author of such advice; neither will I contribute to an abortion. I will maintain religiously the purity and integrity both of my conduct and of my art. I will not cut anyone for the stone, but I will leave that operation to those who cultivate it. Into whatever dwellings I may go, I will enter them with the sole view of succouring the sick, abstaining from all injurious views and corruption, especially from any immodest action, towards women or men, freemen or slaves. If during my attendance, or even unprofessionally in common life, I happen to see or hear of any circumstances which should not be revealed, I will consider them as a profound secret, and observe on the subject a religious silence. May I, if I religiously observe this my oath, and do not break it, enjoy good success in life, and in the practice of my art, and obtain general esteem for ever; should I transgress and become a perjuror, may the reverse be my lot.

Such a vow may seem nothing extraordinary to us who have centuries of precedent and tradition behind us, but when we think that the Greeks of the historic period were the original formulators who moulded the pattern of these things, we cannot help feeling that even if their material development had no comparison with that of our own time, their civilisation, as well as their culture had attained to such a high degree of humanity and ideology that it merits our full and generous admiration.

CHAPTER III

THE AGORA

LET US pick out an ordinary, fairly well-to-do Athenian, and keep an eye on him as he goes to the Agora one day. Let us make certain that it is not the day of some special festival, or one on which the convocation was being called, for there were about four such convocations each month when the Agora was closed.

In Athens the months were of thirty days, and there were twelve months in a year, but as this totalled only three hundred and sixty days, they inserted a month every seventh year to prevent the seasons from getting all mixed up—in fact, the same system we still employ with its variation of leap year. Every city had its own arrangements as to New Year's Day, the names of the months, and their duration. Some cities found it more convenient to follow the lunar months.

The arrangement of rest days varied, and in Athens they found it more to their liking to have their days of rest for the month bunched together, so they nominated the last three days but one of each month as being inappropriate for business, and on those days the Agora would be closed.

On the day, then, that we have chosen, our worthy citizen awoke as usual as soon as the first glimmer of light had appeared in the east, and immediately he recollected that he had matters he wanted to attend to urgently. He had decided to give away his elder daughter in marriage to the son of an old friend, for she had already turned twenty, while the young man had passed his thirtieth year, which was a ripe time for each of them. If the prospective groom agreed, there would be the dowry to be discussed. If the young man were to be caught before he left his house, the matter should not be left till much later than sunrise. He also recollected that on the previous evening he had issued an invitation for a symposion for that very night, and he must get to the Agora to issue the other invitations. It was quite normal that such invitations should be issued personally and on the very day, for they were rarely given more than two or three days beforehand.

He carefully combed his hair and tended his beard, and he took the oblong sheet that he had used as a bedcloth and shook it, and, finding that it was not crumpled, decided to wear it and not to waste time having a fresh cloth brought. As it was likely to be a hot day, he would not need an overgarment. A slave soon came and brought him a sesame cake and a goblet of diluted wine to break his fast, for wine and water were the only drinks he knew. He then sent for the slave who tended to his catering and told him that he would be having seven or eight guests to the evening meal, and possibly double that number to the symposion that was to follow. The slave was a newly acquired one and so the Athenian decided to do most of the shopping himself, as he did not know how much he could rely on the fellow. He told the slave that he himself would engage the cook and buy the fish and certain other requirements. So, having decided what to delegate, he called for three or four slaves to precede him on his walk.

An Athenian might leave the catering to a slave, according to his household arrangements or his mood, but he would never think of letting his wife do the shopping, for it was only those of the most humble circumstances and of acute poverty, who had no slaves, who might let their wives thus demean themselves.

The slave-doorkeeper unbelted and untethered the door, and pushed it outwards for his master to emerge, and our Athenian proceeded to his daughter's prospective groom and arranged everything to his satisfaction. The dowry was fixed, and the marriage would take place in the Athenian month of Gamelion, about January, and so named as it was favoured for marriages. He had also arranged to present his daughter, in due course, to the section of the groom's tribe, and give suitable presents, so that she should be approved as being fully Athenian, legitimate, and suitable. Everything had been all right except that he had been a little annoyed by the inquisitiveness of the young man who had asked about the height of his daughter and the colour of her eyes, and he wondered if this were some new-fangled idea taught by the sophists about eugenics. Perhaps, after all, he meditated, he was merely irritated because he had undertaken to do much of the shopping, as well as to see to the invitations.

But let us get to the Agora, teeming with life, and we will not have to be told the way, for we will see the countryfolk with their carts laden with vegetable produce, drawn by mules or oxen, all making for the magnetic point of the city. When we get to the Agora, we will see so many colonnades, porticoes, municipal buildings, temples, statues, shops, tents, booths, a theatre, carriage ways, and shady plane trees, that we may take some time to get our bearings and realise that method, order, and symmetry reign supreme in sound Hellenic fashion. We might notice that there was a large central space in this the Agora of Athens, as in the Agora of any other city, and also that there was a general scheme of the surrounding arcades, mostly two-tiered. The Civic Centre was easy to discern at once, but it would be necessary for a guide to point out which was the Senate House (The Prytaneion), which in Athens was a circular building, the Treasury, the Residence of the Magistrates of the Year, the Office of the Weights and Measures, the Courts of Justice, the Office of the Archons, and of the Chiefs of Police, and the prison. The various porticoes would be noticed immediately, some of them built with the spoils of victorious wars, as also the statues and the altars. In Athens, too, we would notice the space allocated in the centre for the Scythian police to pitch their tents.

In the Agora the citizen would proceed about his business in much the same way as a shopper in one of the gigantic metropolitan stores of today. Each type of article sold was in its section, either in shops in the colonnaded arcades or, for the most part, in booths of wicker, or with awnings. There would be plenty of noise from the bargaining and the haggling and the vendors shouting in praise of their wares.

Let us then accompany the Athenian to the food sections, and see about the wine, though this section might not be so busy, as the retailers went the round of the city selling their wine, which was piped into amphorae from the barrels in their carts. Next, one of the slaves would be sent to the bread section, for it was not customary to bake the bread at home. Our citizen does not want to go himself as most of the bread sellers are women and they have a most uncivil tongue in their heads. The oil section is an important one, and our citizen would like to make his own choice, though most well-to-do citizens had their own oil from their estates, and had enough in their houses for the year's economy, stored in the great earthenware jars. We can then continue with the citizen to the other food sections, though he is unlikely to buy anything as the slave in charge of the catering has been entrusted with this, unless there was anything he particularly fancied.

We can glance at the fresh cheese portico, the apples and the fresh fruit, the nuts, the onions, the garlic and the spices and herbs. Thence we can go to the frankincense section, as also the unguent and perfume shops. At the ceramic section he may buy a few drinking goblets and saucers, and he will consider whether it was not about time that he bought a few couches from the couch and furniture section.

Before going to any other section we must hasten with him to the section where the female cooks, nearly all foreigners, are waiting to be hired, all ready with their kitchen equipment, and he will engage a cook from Syracuse for the night, for these have a high reputation. The Athenian wanted some slaves, but it was not the day for the slave market, so he went to look at the new and old clothes section, but seeing nothing that attracted him, he decided to go into the barber's for a trim and a chat. Suddenly he remembered that he had undertaken to order the chaplets or garlands for wearing at that evening's symposion, but he did not disturb the barber for there was plenty of time for these, and it was not too late for the fish bell.

For fish the customers had to wait till the fish arrived, and the superintendents saw that it was in order and had given the sign for the bell to be rung. Fish was a much-esteemed luxury and every citizen must be given an equal chance of obtaining it. The superintendent regulated the price, and saw that none of the sellers watered the fish, either to freshen it or increase the weight.

During his shopping tour our Athenian had already seen some of his intended guests for the evening and had invited them. He had also found out where some of the others had last been seen, including a couple who were watching a cockfight at a tavern, and one who was going to a doctor's shop. Two, he was told, had been seen outside a bookshop where Sokrates was holding forth. There was a special guest that he was anxious to find, the father of the bridegroom-to-be, but he knew that he would find him later at that part of the Agora where the bankers sat apart with their tables and their scales for weighing the money. The bankers were men who most highly prized their reputation for integrity.

As the Athenian was proceeding to the bankers' section, he saw a Scythian policeman with a whip in his hand, which was the emblem of his office. Though he was a barbarian slave he had the power to fine citizens in the market for infringements, and actually to apply chastisement to foreigners and slaves; though we can guess that privilege applied in those days as today, and if it were a technical offense caused by some worthy citizen, and not one of the sellers, the matter would be referred to a magistrate or to one of the law courts. The Scythian policeman in question was approaching the section where paints were sold, and he went to a seller and asked for a jug of red paint. Our Athenian put two and two together and asked the Scythian whether a special meeting of the assembly was being called for the next day, and the Scythian nodded assent. When a meeting was being held, normally at the Areios Pagos, below the entrance to the Acropolis, the Scythians painted ropes with fresh red paint, and holding the ends between pairs of them advanced along the Agora, thus forcing the stragglers out of it and towards the convocation. If they were foolish enough or obstinate enough not to budge, their garments would get tinted, and this was prima facie evidence against them and most assuredly they would get fined for nonattendance.

It was now close to the sun's meridian and soon time for the Agora to close for the day, which time we must conclude differed somewhat according to the seasons, but which, anyhow, would be before the normal time for the midday meal.

We should not think of the Agora as merely the market place, for it was the universal club of all citizens, with places of amusement spread around it.

An analogy to the feeling that the Greek had for his Agora could be made to that of a passenger on a luxury liner. The simile of a ship is not inappropriate for Greek orators often referred to the "Ship of State," which required the skill of the helmsman. For the analogy we would like you to think of yourself quartered aboard ship in some luxury cabin or suite. You will get to know the magnificent rooms and lounges, the smoke rooms and bars, the swimming pools and the tennis deck, and the various places of amusement where you will meet and be sociable with others. Aboard ship you may feel that your cabin is but a place to which you resort for the night, or for a change of clothes, while you may develop a certain pride in the qualities of the ship with which you are becoming so intimately associated. Thus the Greek citizen might feel that it was the public part of the ship that counted, like the Agora, but he would feel, additionally, that he was part owner, and that he was partly responsible for the management and the direction of the stupendous engine room. He would take even less interest in his cabin or suite, for whereas you might retire to your cabin to the bosom of your family with which you are bound by ties of closest affection, his home would not even mean so much to him, and not have its comforts and luxuries.

Perhaps, on the completion of his business with his banker, and when he was preparing to make his way back home, our citizen might run into his future son-in-law, who would be in animated conversation with men of his own age, or younger, and our citizen might enquire what was up. It might be that they were members of an excursion club who had decided to go down to the sea in the late afternoon and have an evening meal there. They might have been discussing whether each should bring food and wine in kind, or whether they should contribute so much money and select one of their number to do the catering.

The Agora Excavations

This chapter should not be concluded unless at least some mention is made of the work that has been undertaken in the last thirty years by the American School of Classical Studies in Athens in the excavations of the ancient Agora. An initial munificent donation by John D. Rockefeller in 1931 enabled an agreement to be entered into with the city of Athens whereby buildings covering some thirty acres on the northern slopes of the Acropolis were expropriated, and the whole area excavated. Some seventy-five American universities and colleges have annually contributed for the completion of the work.

The finds in this area have been enormous and include some sixty-five thousand catalogued pieces and two hundred thousand coins. These finds had to be housed, and the school had the inspiration to reconstruct one of the ancient arcades for this purpose. The arcade, or stoa, which was found to have the best preserved remains was that on the eastern flank of the Agora, the Stoa of Attalos

II. That monarch was king of Pergamos in Asia Minor from 159-138 B.C., and had been sent to study in Athens when a young man. When he became king he remembered his "Alma Mater," at which he had graduated, and made the magnificent gift of this stoa in gratitude.

The Stoa of Attalos II has been reconstructed on the actual site, in the precise proportions and colour, and in part using the remains of the old building. In September, 1956, King Paul of Greece performed the inaugural ceremony dedicating the reconstructed stoa as an Agora Museum. The rest of the excavated Agora is being converted into a garden planted with trees and vegetation known to have flourished in ancient Athens.

The excavations have shown that habitation in the district went back to Neolithic times (around 3000 B.C.) and that from the sixteenth century B.C. the area had been used as a burial ground. A leaflet of the school states: "The Agora was thus a focal point of the city and a Civic Center for many centuries. It is only natural that there were continual developments and additions, though the Hephaistion, which stands in almost perfect condition and did not require excavation, being on a higher level, and the administrative buildings below, did not hardly change."

The School of Classical Studies has elaborated the plans of the Agora as it stood at many periods of its history. Though in many ways it is the Golden Age of Perikles that interests us most, it is the plans of later periods that show a more full development, and which also include the Stoa of Attalos II. This we have chosen for illustration so that photograph and plan can be co-ordinated and better visualised.

It can well be imagined how very much has been learned from these vast excavations, not only of topographical and archaeological interest, but also of almost all aspects of life in ancient Athens.

The Democracy Stele (see photograph opposite page 143) is one of the many finds of the excavated Agora.

CHAPTER IV

THE HOME—FOOD AND DRESS

LET US ACCOMPANY our imaginary Athenian back home from the Agora for his midday meal and examine a few facts about his private home life. What we want to find out is something about the house itself, the standing of the women and of the slaves, and about the meals, the dress, and some of the customs. We shall leave the question of the womenfolk and the slaves till the next chapter, but we will now have a little to say on the other matters, though we have already covered some of the ground.

The House

The house itself would be of one or of two floors. The second floor might not be over the whole area of the house; it would be reached by ladders and not stairs, and would be for the guest rooms, though in some houses it might be reserved for the slaves, or the women's quarters, or possibly storerooms. Normally the men's rooms were around the colonnaded "peristyle" courtyard, open to the sky, and this faced the main entrance where the slave-doorkeeper and his dog had their lobby, while at the far end, facing the entrance, would be the door which cut off the women's quarters. Here would be the housewife's section, also with an open courtyard, and it would include the rooms of the female slaves and the storerooms, which came under her management.

Should the doorkeeper slave announce that men were seeking admission, the women of the house would hasten beyond the dividing door and bolt it, and would assuredly blush if they were tardy and had been seen. All the rooms of the house would normally give onto their respective courtyards, for as windows do not seem to have existed, light would have to be obtained through the doorways. Since many of the rooms might not have doors, fabrics would have been used instead for closing out the light. The decor of the house would have been of the simplest. It was not, in fact, till the turn from the fifth to the fourth century B.C. that walls were painted, and this had been an innovation started by the dandy Alkibiades, while the use of mosaics began in the city of Pergamos in Asia Minor in the third century B.C.

Eating and Food

Our Athenian is not fond of eating by himself, especially in the evening, so it is quite likely that he will have brought two or three friends back home with him to keep him company. If he has not done so, his wife is likely to appear. He will then go into the banqueting room and recline on a couch with his left elbow on a cushion. A slave will take his sandals off and bring him water, with the equivalent of soap in the form of sweet-scented fuller's earth or some doughy mixture. As he does not use fork, spoon, or even knife for his meals, it is essential that he should first wash his hands. Then a slave will bring a small table, probably a three-legged one, with a meal set on it, and place it before the couch. It may consist of porridge soaked in wine, and vegetables and cakes, or it may also include game, though this is unlikely, and meat would be still more rare; there will be other small food such as olives, fruit, and fresh cheese, accompanied by diluted wine.

The wife will be seated in a chair beside him, to tend to his needs and answer his questions, and after he has finished and again washed his hands, she will no doubt depart. She will go through the door which separates the women's from the men's quarters, and there have her meal with the children, but they will eat seated on chairs, and not, like her husband, in a reclining position on couches.

Afternoon and Evening

In the afternoon the Athenian might visit one of the three great Gymnasia of the city, but it would depend on the time of the year, for he might find midsummer too hot. Anyhow, he would be likely to return to the house when the gnomon registered some six feet, for it was by this instrument that he approximated the time. The gnomon was a pole in the courtyard which acted as a type of sundial, though not through the angle of the shadow but by its length. The day, as opposed to the night, was divided into twelve sections, and their duration thus varied according to the time of the year. There was also a variation of the gnomon which was less popular. In this the pole was stood in a basin, so that instead of producing long shadows the time was approximated by the height of the shadow on the rim of the basin. At the sixth mark of the gnomon it would be the habitual time for the Athenian to have his evening bath. As he might be expecting guests, he would attend to his toilet and use unguents, and would naturally presume that his guests would respect his invitation by doing likewise.

For the eventide meal the host would allocate guests to their couches, normally two to each couch, and after sandals had been removed and water brought, the slaves would carry in the little tables. The food would be scanty and plain, though there might be two courses, of which the fish would be a luxury. The paucity of the food was not a precept or a restriction, but a habit which had developed, and had not been the case in Homeric times.

It suited them, and what is more, not only was the food of little substance, but the Athenian took comparatively little interest in the niceties and delectation of a meal. The inclusion of meat was almost confined to occasions when sacrifices were made, public or private, or to special occasions for banquets.

Banquets

Banquets would be held for birthdays of members of the family, either alive or departed, or for prominent public figures, and also for funerals. On the occasion of public festivals which included sacrifices, the citizens would receive their share of the meat, as also of bread and wine, while the unfortunate goddess or god must be content to savour the aroma.

At the appointed time the meal would be served, and it was not unseemly to start without waiting for any guest who might be late. Any guest might bring a friend, to whom the host would extend a similar welcome and hospitality as to those whom he had personally invited. Perhaps one of the reasons they did not await all the guests was that they liked some of their dishes to be served hot. Even gloves were sometimes worn to prevent them burning their fingers, otherwise they used the specially prepared bread to cleanse their fingers between courses, which, of course, would compare in our sense to clean knives and forks. The male slaves attended to all that was necessary, and wiped the tables, but it was not till much later, when more luxury and variety crept in, that a bill of fare was first handed to the guests.

Among the foods eaten, sausages were common; so were onions and leeks, but the normal food of the poor and slaves was the wine-soaked porridge of wheat. The food was prepared by the female slaves, unless a female cook was hired for the occasion. In summer, or even on other occasions, the meal might consist of "cold tables" when oyster, shellfish, and raw vegetables and salads would constitute a meal. Tastes differed as to the concluding dishes, some preferring savoury morsels while others liked sweets and cakes, for which, of course, honey and not sugar would be used, but this choice might depend on whether a symposion was to follow. Milk does not seem to have been drunk much, while olive oil took the place of butter in cooking.

When the meal was over the slaves would remove the small tables, sweep the floor free from bones, nut shells, and apple cores, and the host would pour libations on the ground to the various gods, concluding with one to the "Good Genius" who has Health in her care.

The Symposion

The end of the meal would be about the time that the additional guests were expected for the symposion, and the "second tables" would be brought in with the little savoury bits, including olives and spiced fare, all well salted to bring out the flavour of the wine to follow, for wine might not have been served at the meal itself, and also thirst must now be encouraged.

The host would gradually indicate to the guests where to sit, though often the choice was left to the guests themselves, especially as it meant sharing a couch. When the guests, or most of them, had foregathered, chaplets beribboned and colourful with flowers, would be handed round to be worn, and then the master of the ceremonies would be appointed. Whereas it might often be the host, it would seem that more often than not this was not the case, for the archon of the symposion might be appointed by universal assent, by election, by dice, or by some competitive game. Thereafter the company had to submit to his decisions, though if entertainment were being provided by dancers, male or female, jugglers, acrobats, or musicians, this would have been arranged by the host. Sometimes hetairae attended, but as the pleasures of the symposion were primarily intellectual, though permeated with youthful gaiety, it would be the exception. Hetairae, as well as being comely, were expected to brighten the company with their brilliant conversation and scintillating wit.

The first care of the archon would be to make the choice of the available wine, and how it was to be served and mixed with water, and this would be done by a slave, in the proportions of three, two, or evens of water to wine. Wines differed, and Athenian wine was not the most select. Some wines would keep well, even up to fifteen or sixteen years, which was a great recommendation. Some wines required mixing with hot water, while others required cold, or when it was obtainable with snow. Some wines were spiced, some mixed with honey, while the Euboeans mixed their wine with pine resin, as is the custom of the present-day Greeks. The wine was mixed in a central "crater" bowl by a slave, and ladled out into goblets, which at the beginning of the symposion were likely to be two-handled, small goblets, though drinking saucers and even horns were used. The archon would propose the toasts and order the company to drink, and on some toasts he might order no heeltaps, for besides the pleasure of the wine it was his care to see that the proceedings sparkled, for which wine has ever been an exhortation and a mentor.

The archon would also fix the periods for the other diversions, as a change to the conversation. Riddles were always a favourite pastime, for not only did it give opportunities of offering prizes, such as a special chaplet, the right to nominate the next toast or diversion, or even a kiss, but also for amusing penalties or impositions, such as having to drink a large goblet of wine at one quaff, which would be done, perhaps with discomfiture, but always with good grace.

Competitive games were also played, and the favourite was the kottabos, of which there were some variations. Each had a turn, and pouring some wine into a saucer would hurl the wine over a given distance to a saucer floating in a basin, with the object of getting sufficient wine into the floating saucer to make it sink. An alternative was to have the target saucers hanging on a scale, beneath which were metal statuettes, so that if the saucer were well filled it would descend rapidly, registering a metallic "ping" on the head or spear of the figure. This variation was supposed to be of Sicilian origin, and the young men would pretend to divine the fidelity or affection of their mistresses from the quality of the sound and its volume.

Yet another variety to the flying wine, and perhaps saucers, though rare, was to fill the mouth with wine and expectorate it to the saucer, with the same objective.

Other games included one which resembled chess, but we should imagine that this was reserved for the afternoons at the gymnasia and taverns, for withal the Greeks asked for gaiety in their symposia intellectuality. They kept the merriment of youth and joy of life even in riper years, so that the Egyptians commented on the Greeks that "they were always children." There is no indication that these symposia were carousals, or licentious, but on occasion they may have been, and to this there would have been no objection. Possibly, if it were the tendency of a particular archon to give them such character, he might not be elected to the chair so frequently.

It is interesting to note that candles were normally the means of lighting for the poor, while at the symposia lamps with oil wicks were used, some of which were most artistic and decorative, being either on stands, or hung from statuettes, and some with many holes for several wicks. No doubt, on occasion, torches would be used.

As it grows late and time to break up the party, the guests will call their slaves to accompany them home, and if the night be dark, to carry the torches. The host will bid them farewell, and to one of them who is to undertake a distant journey on the morrow, he may wish him Godspeed with a handshake.

Dress and Apparel

The fabrics known to the ancient Greeks were linen, sheep's wool, flax, and probably cotton. The popularity of linen for men's wear gradually gave way to wool, which became universal, and the thickness depended on the season, the winter cloth being shagged on both sides. Silk had been worn in Asiatic lands from early times, but at the end of the Classical Period, at the time of Alexander the Great and Aristoteles, it was still extremely rare in Greece, for the latter tells us how it was made, and that even the cocoons were still imported, and to only one of the islands at that, for processing.

Women also used woolen fabrics for their clothes, but also a cloth made of *byssos* which is presumed to be cotton, but of which there were varieties, for there was one form of which the raw material was produced from a mollusc. Generally *byssos* was of a vegetable origin, and may also have been made of flax as well as cotton. It was white, but a better and more expensive quality was yellowish. The finest cloth which was made for women was of flax, and it was so extremely fine and delicate as to be almost diaphanous.

White was the principle colour, and this as well as yellow was the aristocratic choice, while purple was well favoured, as well as other colours. In the Greek cities of Asia Minor, where silk may have been used by the women, bright colours were liked, but this was never the case in Athens and the rest of Greece, where the working classes and the slaves wore drab or dark-coloured cloth.

Both female and male attire was of great simplicity, and this was not merely because it was suitable for the climate but because it was their natural inclination, just as women were also averse to much jewelry. Earrings were exquisitely delicate, while the bracelets, often curled as snakes, were simple. Sometimes simple jewelry might be included in a headdress bandeau which could be golden, and there were a fair amount of gold agraffes, or pins, for fastening the draped raiment.

Garments were divided into dress and overdress, and the latter would correspond to our use of a coat, but did not differ essentially between the female and male garments, especially in the overdress which could be used equally by the husband or wife. The sole male dress was the "chiton" which was a sort of sleeveless woollen shirt. This the Dorians wore shorter than the Athenians, though by the time of the Golden Age the Athenians had adopted the Doric fashion. The male chiton was of two varieties, and was either of "both armpits" or of a "single armpit," the latter having an aperture for the left arm. This left part of the breast bare, such being the habitual form for manual workers and slaves.

There is some controversy as to whether there was some slight undergarment beneath the chiton, and the opinions are somewhat divided, though it hardly seems likely that the single-armpit chiton would have an undershirt, and further that there would not have been some mention of the fact, or indication in the statuary or vase painting, if this had been normal. The feminine chiton was much the same, and was composed of an oblong piece of cloth fastened over one, or both, shoulders. With it a girdle was worn around the waist. Both feminine and male chitons could have border patterns, and the feminine added, occasionally, fringes or even tassels. There was also an Ionic chiton for the maidens, with ample drapery and folds, falling down to the feet, and also with broad sleeves, which Athena, the goddess, considered suited to her majestic dignity. The Dorian women favoured a chiton which was sewn on one or both sides of the breast, and fastened over the shoulders. The chiton, with but small variations, remained throughout the whole historic period as the universal garb of both women and men.

The overgarment was the himation, also an oblong cloth, which was thrown over the left shoulder, wrapping the back, and drawn forward under, or above, the right arm and over it, and then once more pulled over the left shoulder, or possibly the left arm, being in the nature of what we would probably call a draped shawl. The cavalry wore a cloak, the chlamys, and it was often worn by youths when they had reached the age of military service at eighteen.

The women were not averse to beauty aids, but only in far as colour and skin treatment were concerned, and we can conjecture that owing to the confined life, with little exercise, which they led indoors, it would not come amiss. They would disdain any aids that might impair the noble beauty of the form feminine, though the hetairae, who were not ignorant of the many possibilities of adjusting, rectifying, or improving the figure, might not turn up their erudite noses at them.

Leather was frequently used, and the military might be likely to wear a leather chiton, which was possibly a little heavy, but the heavy-armed soldier took body servants with him to shoulder the shields and armour when not in battle. His armour consisted not only of the twenty-pound shield, but a cuirass of studded leather or of metal, a leather kilt over a linen or leather chiton, a helmet with horsehair plumage, bronze greaves, a short sword at the waist, a six-foot spear, while the shield might have a dangling leather flap to give additional protection to the legs.

Footwear was generally not worn indoors, and many even abstained from wearing it outdoors, though it would appear that the niceties of evening dress required its use, if one were to be in fashion. The footwear varied from slippers and sandals tied with leather thongs to almost a boot. They were of leather; they were likely to be white when worn with a white chiton, but were often coloured for evening wear. Cork was also used, especially for women, Boeotian women delighted in low, purple shoes, while shoes of two hues were not unknown. Slaves would be provided with shoes by their masters for hard work or winter wear.

The men invariably wore signet rings, but more for use than for ornament. The women carried sunshades very similar to the type now in use, though probably not collapsible, and quite likely the men who had no fears of being called effeminate by the women may also have sported them. The men also had caps, or hats not unlike low-crowned bowlers without the rim, as we often see Hermes wearing, though in his case the wings of his divine attribute are attached to it. The Greek took great pride in the care of his hair, and was unlikely to wear any head covering unless travelling or exposed for a long period to the heat of the sun. Neither sex objected to dyeing the hair, but the women did not plait, braid, or curl their hair, but might gather it together either over the crown, or as a bun at the back. Sometimes woman's crowning glory might take its due place over the brow, and then she might wear a bandeau, possibly of gold, as also a snood which would be of visible material.

In the athletic contests, or at the exercise of the gymnasia, the Greeks wore no clothes at all, and women were excluded from being present at these places, though we know this not to have been the case at the Greek colony of Cyrene in North Africa, and possibly elsewhere. In Dorian lands the women, or at least the maidens, had athletic exercises of their own, at which men could be present, but it is not clear whether the disrobing for their contests was the complete discarding of all clothes, though the probability is that such was the case, for the word is "denuding." It is also not clear whether in Dorian lands men and women exercised or danced simultaneously, and in the nude, but then Dorian customs differed so profoundly from Ionian, and also differed so much from tribe or city; depending largely on the purity of their antecedents, or the necessity of keeping their ascendency over their vassals.

CHAPTER V

THE HOME—THE WOMEN AND THE SLAVES

WOMEN play a part of paramount importance in the life and formation of the character of a nation. Those who study the science of political theory or history will have heard of the saying that if you want to know about the men of any country, you should study the womenfolk. In Athens, at least, the wives had little of such influence upon the men, but we must not forget the other saying that if a child has a good mother but a bad father, the chances are that the child will turn out well, but if, on the contrary, the child has a good father but a bad mother, we can expect a bad child as the result. So, bearing this in mind, we may consider that, for the good of the nation, it is the quality of the mothers that will assure its future. That hard-boiled mediaeval sage, Machiavelli, agrees with the importance of women, but he turns it to their discredit when he says that queens make better monarchs than kings do, for queens are advised by men, whereas kings are advised by women. Yet if this is the case, in the greatest age of Greek culture, the Golden Age of Perikles, it was Perikles' mistress Aspasia who was the power behind the throne, a woman of outstanding culture and wisdom, with immense prestige in spite of her irregular social position, and in spite of the fact that she was not even an Athenian by birth.

We hear next to nothing of the women of ancient Greece, but they were the "backroom girls" to whom was extended the care and maintenance of the sacred traditions and virtues of the race. To this, the upbringing of the children, their lives were dedicated and sacrificed.

The authorities who have written on the subject of the status of women in ancient Greece find it very controversial. They have to support their opinions by reference to treatises generally dealing with some other subject, by such writers as Platon and Aristoteles, by Xenophon in his *Oekonomika*, or by pointing to the quips of Aristophanes. Opinions are also supported by the legal cases.

We have already stressed how important it is, in weighing up the evidence, that the aspects should be contemporaneous, and we should note that when a new civilisation develops it progresses with accumulated momentum after it has passed its embryo stage. In the case of the ancient Greeks their civilisation was primarily a cultural one, whereas ours is a material one. Thus, what may have been normal custom in the time of Solon in 560 B.C. may have been strange in the time of Perikles in 460 B.C. and bear practically no relationship to the habits of a hundred years later, in about 340 B.C., in the period of the oratory of Demosthenes, when Aristoteles designated women as being, by nature, more or less a lower order of the human species.

The ancient Greek who might try to disentangle the conditions of present-day marriage would get many headaches, especially when comparing the systems of the Latin countries with the American and British way of marriage. He might find that in those very countries where marriages are arranged with a dowry basis, the resulting unity and bond is even closer than in countries where the young folk make their own choices. He might even shrewdly assess that in the States and in Britain, even if marriages are not actually parentally arranged, nonetheless in the higher levels of society they are more orchestrated than the young folk realise.

Athenian women did not get a square deal, yet at the same time there is no reason to think that the majority of unions did not result in close-knit, happy families. Personally I detest seeing birds in cages almost invariably too small even for the exercise of their wings, but I am generally told that such birds were born that way, that this is the only life they know, and that they are happy. That rather seems to sum up the attitude of the Athenians towards their women, from the time of Perikles to the time of the Macedonian kings.

It is difficult to know how much we can rely on Platon for our information on the Athenian general outlook on marriage. When he comments on what ought to be the case in his Ideal City, we can guess that it represents that which was not generally adhered to. Platon thinks that if a man had not married by the age of thirty-five, he ought to suffer the loss of civil rights and be fined. Platon categorically asserts that a man's choice should be in the interests of the city and not his own inclination. It is difficult to understand what chances he would have had of considering his own pleasure, if he had so little if any chances of seeing his bride before marriage. Platon, of course, may be referring to marriage with an alien, or to practices other than those in Athens.

The position in Sparta is very clear. The aged bachelor infringed the law, while the wife who was childless was actually enjoined to cohabit with another that she might have children. It was, however, not only the law and civic duty that constrained a man to marry but that obsession to leave someone behind to tend to the sepulchral duties and keep the memory alive, not only of oneself, but also of the forefathers, for at the very root of the Greek religion was ancestor worship, since in a sense the very gods and goddesses were but men and women who had been immortalised and canonised into the ancient form of saintship.

In Athens the women and their dowries were inseparable, and this was so very much the case, as we have seen, that on the death of the husband she reverted with her dowry to her nearest paternal relative. He could marry her, or he might allocate her suitably, with her dowry, to a husband chosen by him. In later law, her husband, who was her lord and master, could leave her with her dowry to whomsoever he wished by will. That was the law, but how it worked out in practice we do not know. If the person to whom she was left had been married in the meantime, the position is not clear. She might either be allocated by him, or more possibly she might revert to her nearest relative. We must remember that at the back of this, when the parents made a choice of a husband, the maiden had first to be introduced for approval and registration in the husband's section of the tribe. In earliest times the father could not even dispose of his daughter in marriage without the consent of his kinsmen, so that there must have been some curb on absolute power, and some protection for her against being allocated to someone entirely unsuitable.

Marriage Ceremony

An official engagement took place, attended by the parents of both parties, though it is most unlikely that the bride was present. The wedding was preceded by suitable sacrifices to the hymenal deities, apparently on the previous day. On the wedding day itself it was the universal practice for bride and bridegroom to bathe in waters fetched from some special spring which each individual city considered auspicious for the purpose.

The actual ceremony of marriage from its religious aspect seems to have consisted in the prenuptial sacrifices, while from the civil point of view there was not even any registration. On the wedding day the respective houses hung wreaths outside their doors, and after nightfall the bride left by carriage with her husband for his house, both dressed in their best, with chaplets on their heads, and accompanied by the best man. The husband would so far only have seen his bride's figure and not her countenance, for her face was veiled. This was perhaps wise as it might not only hide any grimaces she might be inclined to bestow upon him, but also on her mother-in-law, who would receive her in her new house.

The procession itself between the two houses would be accompanied by relations and friends singing the appropriate wedding hymns and accompanied by musicians and torch bearers. On arrival at her new house, the wedding feast would be laid on, and this feast went by the name which means marriage, for its purpose seems to have been the equivalent of registration. Those who participated at it would, if the need ever arose, be called upon as witnesses who had attended, and upon their testimony would depend not only her rights of widowhood but also the legitimacy of the issue.

The bride was allowed to remain at the feast, though still veiled, and female relatives were allowed to be present, no doubt seated apart. Who might be invited, and whether it also included friends, or whether the maidens, if invited, had to be veiled, we do not know for certain. At the conclusion of the feast the groom conducted the bride to her room, but probably left her there after symbolically sharing a quince. Even then she did not remove her veil, though she would be entertained by further singing and dancing. The interchange of wedding presents, as well as the gifts which would be received from friends, occurred only on the second day, "the day of discovery"—resulting from her unveiling.

The Wife's Duties

After marriage the wife's duties were those of managing the house, which art she might have to be taught if she were married fairly young, as was the case of Xenophon's wife. She would also have the complete responsibility of the upbringing of the children, though in the case of the boys only until the age of school attendance, which was seven. It was not the practice to let female slaves interfere. In this there is a difference with the Roman practice. The reason is that it became the custom from early times to ransom the Greeks taken prisoners of war, so that Greeks should not be slaves to fellow Greeks. Educated slaves were therefore most unusual. Exceptions of course there were, for we find the slave whom Themistokles sent to Xerxes to warn him that the Greeks were preparing to escape from the Bay of Salamis was also the trusted tutor of his sons.

Much of our knowledge of the actual status of women is learned from the *Oekonomika* of Xenophon, a word which means "household management." Xenophon, though an Athenian, lived in the region of Elis, close to Olympia, in Dorian lands, and was himself inclined towards the Dorian customs. He was of a pious Victorian type rather than imbued with Ionian gaiety of youth. Xenophon tells us of how he trained his young wife, after she had become used to him. We have some insight into the conditions of a woman at home when he tells her that it is among her duties to tend to the sick and ailing women of the household. The young wife replied that this would not be a chore, but on the contrary she would like doing it, for if she cares for them and looks after them when they are ill, then they will have more affection for her and be loyal to her.

In spite of the above, however we look at it, the relationship between the Athenian husband and his wife cannot have been that of love, affection, and esteem that we expect of present-day marriage. This does not apply to Dorian lands, where even clandestine cohabitation before marriage was not irregular.

In Dorian lands the husband was neither educated nor intellectual, though he may have been civilised. He did not feel, therefore, inclined to look down on his wife for being deficient in such qualities. He regarded his wife, in fact, with high esteem in the Homeric tradition. This, of course, applied not only to Sparta, Crete, Thessaly, and to some extent to Corinth, but also to the Dorian colonies of the Adriatic.

The practice at Thebes was much akin to Athens, though perhaps in that city women were held in somewhat higher esteem. In Aeolian lands, in general, women were given a standing between the very great freedom of the Dorians and the restrictions of the Athenians. We can remember that Sappho, the immortal poetess, was of Lesbos, which was racially an Ionian island, and that thus her conduct would scandalize Athenians, which may possibly have resulted in her calumny.

The women of the Greek cities in Ionia had much more freedom than in Athens, but with the reverse incidence of married and unmarried to the custom of the Dorian lands, for whereas the Dorians allowed the maidens freedom of intercourse, they were expected to be of a more chaste conduct on marriage. In Ionia the outlook was more what we would call Western, in that the maidens were restricted in appearance and behaviour but had greater liberties once they were safely married off.

Women's Legal Position

In Athens women had no legal standing at all in law and were therefore not able themselves to bring an action, but that is quite a different thing from saying that the law offered them no protection. Law and justice were greatly exalted, and women could rely on them. Should they be either neglected or badly treated they could expect that their blood relations would take the necessary legal steps on their behalf. This, however, still gave them no equality of any kind in the provisions of the law. Whereas the husband might commit adultery where and how he pleased with impunity from the law, it was a sin of such serious nature were the wife thus to behave that it was a grave offense for the husband to continue cohabiting with her. For such an offense the wife was reduced to having no protection other than if bodily harm were done against her, which would not include rape.

Slaves

The belief that Greek civilisation and culture were built up on slave labour, as has been said, is about as gross a misconception of economics as could possibly be stated. This is being said, and meant to be said, as an aggressive statement. The value of human manual labour will depend on the extent to which machinery and laboursaving devices can help it. In ancient Greece such material assistance was scarcely at all at their disposal, and almost disdained. Slaves were hardly "exploited," except in the Dorian lands where culture lagged behind.

With every pair of hands which may produce goods there is also a mouth to be fed. The market value of a slave will thus reflect the extent to which the value of his labour is in excess of his cost of maintenance. In Greece slaves were regarded more as an interest-bearing investment, and not for the purpose of administering to bodily comforts or pleasures, as was so much the case in Rome. The appetite of the Greeks for luxuries was so scant that this matter required but little attention. Though the houses of free citizens might well contain a goodly number of slaves, it would primarily be to attend to the economy which was based on provision for the year; the bottling of the wine, the preservation of figs, raisins, and such like matters. The slaves might also weave the cloth for the household requirements, a labour which was equally the competence of men as of women, on the large upright looms that were operated in a standing position. Slave labour would, of course, be used on the farms, while in the workshops of harness makers, potters, tinkers, and tailors (or perhaps we had better call them clothiers), they were also to be found.

Free men might sit on the same bench next to a slave. The free men would, of course, work for a wage, while the slave would be hired out possibly for a similar wage, though probably for a lower one as by reputation they were lazy. It was not unusual to allow the slave to make his own arrangements for pay, and see to his own maintenance, while contributing a set amount to his master. The master would thus regard such income as the interest on his outlay on the purchase of the slave.

The difference, therefore, in employing labour, as is the case today, for factory or office or household, as compared to the economy of slave labour, is precisely the same as the comparison of living in a house for which you pay rent, as compared to living in one you have bought or inherited. Of course this has no connection with the respective outlooks of the labour employer and the slave master, or of the employee and the slave. It is quite erroneous, however, to imagine that the system of slavery made any difference of any consequence to the free citizens in the matter of their leisure for artistic creation or philosophy. The fact that now you fire an incompetent employee or domestic and that then you sold him is, fundamentally, about the difference that existed between then and now in agricultural, industrial, domestic and national economy.

There were also the slaves of the Dorian cities and states, who were subjugated races. They were almost, in a sense, free men without civil rights whose main object of existence was therefore to free the citizens so that they could attend to their military avocations. They were not artisans. These slaves, such as the Helots of Sparta, although attached to particular masters, were really the possession of the State, and could not be sold outside it. Apparently they could not be separated from their families, and they might even possess property. Though in this respect the Helots might appear better off than the other type of slave of the non-Dorian cities and of Corinth, where they were the absolute property of their masters, they probably, and almost certainly, received harsher treatment from the less educated and uncultured Dorians.

To judge from the jokes of the comedies, the slaves were always lazy, ready for somewhat insolent repartee, and delighted in petty thefts. It seems that they were not treated with undue harshness, though an exception to this, in the case of Athens, was that of the conditions under which the slaves worked in the silver mines of Laurion, and for which purpose capitalist owners would hire them to the State.

Even in the case of the building of the Parthenon, which was erected at the expense of the Treasury, the system was for the contraction, or subcontraction of the various sections of work to be done, or portions of sections, such as the erection of one or two columns. Whoever undertook the job could utilize all free labour, or all slave labour, or part of one and part of the other. We have many details and we know that, in fact, the Parthenon was thus built. As was said earlier, this is another proof that it made no difference to the development of Greek culture that the institution of slavery existed.

Value of, and Law for, Slaves

The value of a slave would depend on his age and capacity. Though we know the price paid for slaves in the equivalent of silver or gold, it hardly gives us any basis of comparison on the cost of life index should we just report them as such. We might say that a common slave, of the very lowest type, might fetch about the equivalent of a hundred days' wages of a common free workman. A skilled artisan slave might fetch twice or three times that amount. The highest value might, perhaps, be for a talented girl citharist or flute player, or, in Corinth, City of the Courtesan, for outstanding beauty, which might command four or five times the value of a skilled artisan. The price of slaves never approached that which ruled in Rome, nor did the Greeks possess the huge number of them that the Romans did. We hear of one Athenian who hired out one thousand slaves to the silver mines as being most worthy of note. The Romans not only possessed far, far greater numbers, but they did not employ them industrially in the same way. Aristoteles, in fact, describes Greek slaves as "animated tools." Platon remarks that some citizens possessed fifty or more slaves, and from this we can gather that this number was already considered a great quantity, and more than would be employed for domestic use.

Women slaves were far less numerous. Procreation among slaves, other than the Helot type, was discouraged, as it would be uneconomical to rear them, and the children might well be girls.

There was a different law for the slave and for the free man, but nonetheless the slave did have a very considerable protection from the law, for in the first place he could not be put to death without a court license. A person who maltreated or struck a slave was liable to legal action. If the master maltreated a slave and he escaped and took sanctuary at one of the prescribed temples, of which there were quite a few, the master could be compelled to sell him to another owner. There were not infrequent escapes by individual slaves, though insurrections in Athens were largely confined to the mineworkers, whose treatment was certainly worse, and so much so that many of them were worked in chain gangs.

Slaves could earn their purchase money, but it does not seem that the owners were obliged to accept their offer. They could also be freed as recompense, but in either case they became only freed men, still owing allegiance to their former masters, who became their patrons. Slaves were sold at the slave market which was held once a month, and the normal way would be by auction rather than by private arrangement.

In Dorian lands the slaves might have to fight in the armies, but in Athens their military duties seem to have normally been confined to carrying their masters' armour. It is not clear whether slaves were used for rowing in war vessels as well as the commercial vessels which relied more on their sails than on their oars. It surely must have been the case that the men at the oars were also slaves, for in Classical times, in the days of Perikles, the usual man-of-war was a trireme with three tiers of rowers, with a total complement of some two hundred. When we see that at the time of Themistokles there were some two hundred men-of-war, this might represent over thirty-five thousand rowers, or forty thousand men with the marines, which would mean a little more than the total male free citizens, though not a complete impossibility if we have reckoned the complement average too high. The time of Themistokles was a little prior to the time when mercenaries became common.

Social Welfare

One of the aspects of modern civilisation which hardly existed in any part of Greece was that of organised social welfare.

Social welfare, as we know it, can be considered as entirely an innovation of the last one hundred years. In comparatively recent times a new spirit of liberalism has swept the world. America abolished slavery. Florence Nightingale gave nursing a new respect. Lord Shaftesbury initiated legislation which protected the working classes, freeing women and children, for instance, from going down in the mines.

Lack of social welfare would have affected the children of the poor rather than the aged, for in ancient Greece there was always respect for the latter. In the case of the poorest families, an infant girl might well be exposed, probably at some temple, in the hope that a compassionate person might see the child and adopt it. Upon this aspect it is difficult to pass judgment for, whereas it shows a harshness that we do not expect of Greek parents, it also brings out the fact that there were compassionate persons who might take pity.

Broadly speaking the legislation for the protection of the individual, especially in Athens, was so immense that there were next to no decrees of a social-welfare nature. If, however, there were infringements, protection would be granted by the courts. Assistance, except for burial at the expense of the city, would be more a matter of concern of the deme or tribe than of the city.

PART IV
ALEXANDER AND AFTER

CHAPTER I

THE SPREAD OF GREEK CIVILISATION

IN THE last chapter of the first part of this book we dealt most cursorily with the history of Greece from the Peloponnesian War to the time of Alexander the Great, since it had little bearing on the development of Greek culture and civilisation. In this final chapter history has even less bearing, yet there is considerable interest for it deals with the events which canalised and somewhat transformed that civilisation which was to become our heritage.

In the year 356 B.C., when Alexander was born in Macedon, Athens was having trouble with most of her allies, and did not come out too well, with the result that internal recriminations followed. Thebes was fighting strenuously with her northern neighbour Phokis, and the latter was helped by King Philip of Macedon, so that she emerged for the time being as victorious. It was not much later, however, that Philip helped Delphi to crush Phokis, much to the disgust of Athens.

This was the time when Demosthenes, the great Athenian orator, devoted himself with passion to attacking King Philip, for he had sensed the astute diplomacy of the Macedonian king. He considered that it was permeated with crafty unscrupulousness, and that his imperialism was aimed at loss of liberty for the Greek cities. There

are two sides to each question, and we must not take it
for granted that those who did not follow Demosthenes
were not equally patriotic, though their views might be
diametrically opposed, and possibly less farsighted. Of
these, "old man" Isokrates was an example, and he was
of the old school, one who remembered the good old days.
When he died, King Philip was victoriously marching southwards towards the Peloponnesos. This was two years before the accession of Alexander the Great; Isokrates was
in his ninety-ninth year.

Isokrates looked back to the good old days and longed
for them again. All his early youth and rising manhood
had been spent during the Peloponnesian War, and the
rest of his life had seen the continued jealousies of the
Greek cities, and the struggles of one after the other with
ambitions of supremacy. To him King Philip seemed the
answer to his prayer, a man who might unite the Greek
cities together in bonds of friendship, and lead them against
the Persians. Thus he thought that Athens, Sparta, Thebes,
Phokis and the other contending cities, while keeping their
love and pride for their city, might also find the larger
conception of patriotism in Hellenism. Perhaps Isokrates
may have been right. Perhaps, in spite of the guile of King
Philip, his admiration for Greek, and especially Athenian,
culture may have been such that the dream of Isokrates
might have been fulfilled. Had not King Philip been killed
after subduing the Greek cities and obtaining their confidence and allegiance, he might well have granted them
the full measure of civic liberty that they required.

Alexander the Great not only changed the political geog-
raphy of the ancient world but he changed its political
outlook, and this we can surmise was largely due to the
fact that Aristoteles was his tutor. King Philip, his father,
and other Macedonian kings before him, were great ad-
mirers of Greek culture and they looked southward with
envy. They would have liked to elevate their rough farmers
to follow the Greek ideal. The Macedonian kings had had
their right contended to participate in the Olympic Games,
but had substantiated it and had been accepted as Hellenes,
but this does not tell us to what extent it would have

THE SPREAD OF GREEK CIVILISATION

applied to other Macedonians. The very fact that the Macedonian kings had an entourage which was known as "the Kinsmen" rather indicates that those who did not belong to it, and were of the mountain tribesmen, neither were nor would have been accepted as Hellenes. Some authorities indicate that the Macedonians were Dorians, while others affirm that although they were definitely Aryans, they were neither Dorians nor Achaeans, and as proof of this bring forward what we know of their language. This language, however, was never referred to by the Greeks themselves as a foreign language, but as a dialect, or perverted form of the Hellenic.

The influence of Aristoteles on Alexander must have been preponderating. To Aristoteles men were the most civilised of animals, and of men the Greeks were the most civilised, and he was interested in everything that was of this world, and beyond it. To the Greeks, the world was divided into two: Greeks, or barbarians. To Aristoteles the Greeks were but part of the world.

Alexander believed devoutedly in the gods, yet later he allowed himself to be revered as a god by the Greek cities, so that what might be treated otherwise as irregular, or what we would today call undemocratic, could receive constitutional blessing. Alexander could no longer believe that the gods lived on Mount Olympos, for Aristoteles would have told him that men had climbed to the summit and disproved it. When Alexander also got to know the vast expanses from the Caspian to the Punjab, and to the Arabian Gulf, and had sighted the mighty range of the Himalayas, he could no longer consider the gods as being purely Greek nationals. Alexander also found that the Greek cities of Asia Minor had prospered beyond what was possible for the cities of Greece itself, and had shown no particular yearning to be liberated by the Macedonians. Thus he finally dispersed the military contingents sent by the cities of Greece. He went on, ever victorious. Though he became satisfied with his conquests as a student of Aristoteles he never felt satisfied in his capacity as an explorer.

There came a time when his men felt that they had had enough of privations and of the heat of the desert,

and they forced him to turn back to more civilised and
habitable parts. It thus came about that he formed an
empire into a kingdom of his own, almost estranged from
Macedon, where his mother Olympia no longer held his
esteem or affection. He set about to fuse his new kingdom into one unit with one nationality, and over which
he would be the king of the whole civilised, inhabited world.
No doubt, if he had lived, he would have tried to extend
his kingdom to embrace the West. He still admired Greek
culture above all else, and sent many gifts to Athens, but
he no longer wished his kingdom to be Greek, or Macedonian, and so he did everything possible to induce his
men to marry the local inhabitants and, indeed, he succeeded in this to a large extent. He himself married a
Persian wife and wore Persian clothes, and protected all
religions and priests within his domains. He favoured
Persian customs, and the womenfolk led not only the
slightly less secluded life that the wives of the Macedonian
soldier-farmers enjoyed, when compared with the Athenians, but the comparative emancipation of the Persian races.

Within the thirteen years of his life in the Middle East,
without ever returning to Macedon, the races that became subordinate to him no longer looked to him as a
conqueror or as an usurper, but as their very own "Great
King." At the same time Alexander did spread Greek
civilisation, for the conquering army had not only been
mainly Greek, but he had brought Greek learning, Greek
artists, and Greek engineers and technicians from Syracuse and elsewhere.

Athens could hardly now think of herself as the dominant city, nor could she visualize the inhabited world as
constituted of the Classical community-type cities. Alexander, in spite of his outstanding genius as a soldier and
leader of men, and perhaps greater genius as a statesman
and administrator, was becoming unbalanced towards the
end. He had fits of temper, caused either through heredity
from his mother Olympia, through malaria, or through
bouts of excessive drinking, or all three. Nonetheless, he
carried out many great undertakings. He built magnificent
roads with relay services throughout his empire, and he

also constructed fast ships, making his world a busy hive of commerce linking the East, Egypt, and the Middle East in trade, so that Corinth and Athens could no longer feature as the outstanding entrepôt centres of the world.

When Alexander died, in his thirty-third year, he had not left the mantle of his authority sufficiently vested in any one person, and his empire was divided among his generals who are historically known as "The Successors." At first they held it in trust, but soon dropped all semblance, and the empire disintegrated. Rhodes, as an independent entity, became powerful for two or three generations, the proud possessor of the greatest fleet, and Pergamos, in Asia Minor, became an independent city, outshining Athens in splendour and rivalling her in learning. Of the big realms under the successors, it was only Egypt under the Ptolemies that flourished for very long. We have seen how the Museum was founded and how the city begun by Alexander became the centre of ancient learning.

The cities of Greece still remained under the hegemony of Macedon for some years. In 281 B.C., at a time when there was dissension for the throne of Macedon itself, some of the cities of the Achaean League on the southern shores of the Gulf of Corinth managed to expel the Macedonian garrisons and assert their freedom. This league had existed in the time of Herodotos, and had then been considered as of twelve cities, confederated mainly for religious purposes. After Helike had been submerged by a tidal wave at the beginning of the fourth century B.C., Aegion had become their capital, as the centre for solemn worship and sacrifices at the temples of Zeus and Demeter. The Achaean cities had managed to use this bond to hang together and remain outside the alliances of the more famous cities. These were quarrelling for prestige and supremacy, but we hear little of the Achaean cities, partly because they were not so great, and moreso because history is not interested in cities and states that live normal, uneventful, and peaceful lives, any more than the newspapers of today are interested in normal, commonplace people. They had, however, even before the Macedonian conquest, obtained the respect and esteem of the rest of Greece for their integrity and sincerity of purpose.

In 277 B.C. Aegion again took the lead, but this time the aim was political and the confederation was closely knit, forming united states on the principles that have since been adopted by Switzerland and the United States of America. Each city that applied for membership and which was admitted acquired voting rights. The government became entirely federal, and the federal officers and magistrates resided in the federal capital, and it was thither that ambassadors from outside cities and lands were sent. No member city was allowed to send ambassadors of its own, or even accept gifts from outsiders. Whereas every male citizen of thirty years or over could speak at the convocations, the decisions were carried out by the member cities, each of which had its own vote. Soon Sikyon and Corinth joined the league, and these were followed by Epidauros, Troezen, and Megara, and then by Argos and Megalopolis, and later by other cities of the Peloponnesos, with the exception of Sparta, Elis, and three others. Later still, Salamis joined, and also Aegina, and possibly even for a short time Athens.

*The Achaean League thus became very powerful, and consolidated itself by adopting common standards of the calendar, of weights and measures, and of money. It is interesting to interpose here that Greek measures were based, as they are today, on parts of the body: the thumb knuckle (the inch), the span of the hand (the foot), the elbow to hand tip (the ell), and the pace. Whereas the Romans did likewise, the Greek measurements were slightly longer than the Roman equivalents by approximately 6 per cent.

As well as the Achaean League there were other leagues, such as the Aeolian, and the Thessalian. The conflicts are no longer of cities but of leagues. Even the leagues gradually had to respond to the interests, intrigues, and pressures from without, from Egypt, Macedonia, and the Middle East.

The Achaean League lasted for many decades, and though there was some dissension among the members towards

THE SPREAD OF GREEK CIVILISATION 251

the end, and some of the generals did not show sound judgment, it was the old story of Spartan inability to co-operate that gave the Romans the opportunity to intrigue and finally overthrow Greek liberty by the capture of Corinth in 146 B.C., first making the confederacy a Roman province under the name of Achaia.

When the Romans conquered Greece, precisely two centuries after the time when Philip of Macedon was receiving the leadership of the Greek cities at the same spot—that is, Corinth—they could hardly have been more cultured than the rough Macedonian farmer-soldiers, and were certainly more domineering overlords and had less respect for their fellows. Just as in the case of the Macedonians, yet even more so, the conquerors were finally conquered by the higher civilisation of the Greeks.

By the time of Julius Caesar, less than a hundred years later, the standards of refinement in Rome itself were Greek. The Romans tried to emulate Greek art and avidly absorb Greek science and philosophy. They sent their sons to Athens to be educated, and at times even Greek was spoken in Rome in polite society, where the works of the Greek dramatists were read. There was much, too, of Greek civilisation that the Romans furthered, and though they did not produce any great art, they contributed to architecture, and added encyclopaedic additions to knowledge, without, however, attaining any semblance of the Greek humanities.

The next historical stage in the transference of the Greek store of civilisation and culture to modern Europe is the decision of the Roman Emperor Constantine to leave Rome and establish his capital in the old Greek colony of Byzantium, which he renamed Constantinople. The Roman emperor ordered houses which were the replicas of the residences of many of the great Roman patricians, to be built in Byzantium, whither he forced them to migrate, and he founded there the Eastern Roman Empire. The basic population, however, was Greek, and many years had not gone by before the new empire, too, became Greek in everything but name, though even in this, it is historically known as the Byzantine Empire. The Byzantine Empire lasted a thousand years, finally falling in A.D. 1453 to the Ottoman invaders.

After the establishment of the Eastern Roman Empire, a dark age fell on Italian lands and most of Western Europe, while Byzantium itself prospered and spread over many lands, with a highly developed material civilisation based on Christianity.

The courts of the Byzantine emperors were among the most magnificent that have ever been known, and luxury and self-indulgence reached such a high pitch that the strength of the empire was sapped and could neither resist the onward surge of the Turks nor the raids of the uncultured Northerners, so that even before the actual fall of Constantinople many had to flee from the European Balkan provinces. They sought refuge in Greece, and particularly in the isle of Crete, where they had in turn to contend with the ravaging crusaders. The crusaders did, however, bring back with them to Western Europe much knowledge of what they had seen and heard, and this was followed up by a flight of Greeks themselves when the Turks advanced further to capture Greece and Crete. It was these Greeks who brought to Italy the rebirth of learning and culture, or the Renaissance. Once more Greek thought and art were admired and copied, and emulated in Italy so that the great Italian painters, thus inspired, reached heights not surpassed today, and literature received a new impetus and stimulation. It is not generally known but a poem of an epic nature has been found in Crete which so resembles the *Divina Commedia* of Dante that it would be astonishing if it were not its inspiration.

Conclusion

It is now time to bid farewell to the ancient Greeks, and having been introduced, let us hope that you will meet them again and again and get to know them better. Let us first revert, however, to the dear lady whom we mentioned at the very beginning of the first chapter, who, when she was told that this book was being written, asked,

"What good can the ancient Greeks do for us now?" She was told that they were interesting, entertaining, and fascinating, but, as she certainly will not have read this book, it will not apply to her. Yet, what good can they do for us now? You may have drawn your own conclusions, but may I here be allowed to add an opinion. They taught us to think. They taught us how to think. They taught us of what and about what we should think. However much scientists try to pursue new materialistic paths, made perchance out of broken crockery and flying saucers, it is to the ancient Greeks we must turn for clarity of thought, which they invented and which had not existed at all in all the wondrous and fabulous civilisations before them.

The ancient Greeks assessed the value of things for the contentment, spiritual and otherwise, of the human race. They thought logically, spiritually, rhythmically, in sculpturesque form, scientifically, mathematically, and in every other form, but especially ideally, and in terms of beauty.

If we turn backward and look upon the winding paths that we have been following, whose forward signposts point to the ultimate grave, might we not find that if they are those laid down by the creative thought of the Greeks, our lives would be fuller and richer, more contented and serene, than they would be if we followed those which modern civilisation is so apt to pursue.

PRINCIPLE HISTORIC PERIODS

First traces of Mesolithic	6000 – 5000	B.C.
Neolithic	3800 – 2800	"
Early Helladic	2800 – 2100	"
Middle Helladic	2100 – 1600	"
Late Helladic (or Mycenaean)	1600 – 1100	"
Protogeometric	1100 – 900	"
Geometric	900 – 700	"
Late Geometric (or Oriental Influence)	700 – 600	"
Archaic	600 – 480	"
Classic	480 – 330	"
Hellenistic	330 – 146	"
Greco-Roman	146 – 240	A.D.

INDEX

— A —

Academy, the, 63, 167, 173, 174, 175, 176, 196
Achaean, pre-, 35, 201
Achaean gods, 18
Achaean League, 10, 182, 249, 250
Achaeans, 17, 19, 20, 23-24, 35, 46, 51, 54, 160-61, 247
Achaia, 251
Acoustics, 143
Acropolis, 7, 13, 43, 78, 90, 98, 120, 125, 128, 133, 134, 135-36, 137, 142, 153, 217, 218
Actors, 142, 144, 146, 186
Aegean(s), 5, 13, 15, 28, 30, 39, 83
Aegean Sea, 31
Aegeus, 28, 30
Aegina, 134, 182, 185, 250
Aegion, 182, 249, 250
Aeolian(s), 20, 23, 52, 82, 103, 150, 236
Aeolian League, 250
Aeschylos, 142-43, 145-46, 151
Aesculapius, 37
Aesopos, 151
Agamemnon, 14, 15, 25, 26, 27
Ageladas, 123
Agesilaos, 168
Aghia Traida, ix
Agones, 64
Agora, the, 3, 73, 80, 97, 99, 100, 128, 129, 136, 153, 162, 213, 214-17; excavations, 219; museum, 80, 219; of Elis, 182
Agoranomos, 203
Agraffes, 157
Agrigento, 55
Akadēmeia, 63, 167, 173
Akkadian civilization, 13; language, ix
Akragas, 55
Albion, 57
Alexander the Great, 57, 71, 94, 105, 114, 151, 152, 156, 175, 196, 227, 245, 246-49
Alexandria, 71, 108, 112, 161, 163, 164, 176-77, 249
Alkibiades, 68, 102-3, 168, 207, 221
Almighty Zeus, 63, 125
Alphabet, 13
Alpheos, 60
Amber, 51, 57
American School of C l a s s i c a l Studies, ix, 19, 219, 220
Amphictyonic Council, 65, 105
Amphissa, 59
Amphitrite, 39
Amphora, 153-54, 155
Anabasis, the, 168
Ancestor worship, 233
Apelles, 152
Aphaea, 134
Aphrodite, 37, 39-40, 119, 185

"Aphrodite": of Knidos, 127; of Milos, 122
Apollo, 36
Apollon, 7, 8, 36, 39, 41, 59, 65, 76, 97, 119, 134, 197, 210
Apostle Paul, the, 136
Arcadia, 6, 48, 58
Arcadian legend, 126
Arch, Roman, 131
Archaeological Museum (Athens), 120, 122, 125, 157
Archaeologists, ix, 14, 24-32
Archaic sculpture, 119-20, 121
Archimedes, 173, 177
Architecture, 128-39
Archons, 45, 72, 78, 144, 157, 189, 214, 224, 226
Areios Pagos, 217
Ares, 37, 41
Arete, 208
Argive(s), 19, 75, 121-25
Argive Plain, 19
Argive school, 122, 125
Argos, 13, 38, 47, 75, 81, 97, 105, 121, 135, 182, 194, 250
Ariadne, 30, 31
Aristeides, 86, 96, 97, 98
Aristodemos, 49
Aristomenes, 49, 50
Aristophanes, 147-48, 203, 209, 232
Aristoteles, 57, 106, 107, 112, 162, 165, 174-75, 232, 240, 246, 247
Armour, 228
Art, 113-15, 140, 152
Artemis, 37, 39, 48, 134
Artemissia, 91
Aryan stock, 19; Aryans, 247
Asculepius, 210
Asia Minor, 10, 13, 14, 23, 51, 52, 53, 58, 82, 97, 134, 150, 160, 247
Asklepios, 37, 135
Aspasia, 99, 205, 231
Astarte, 39
Astronomy, 112, 162
Athena (Athene), 37, 42-44, 77, 79, 100, 131, 136-37, 140, 157, 228
"Athena and Marsyas," 126
Athena Ergane, 43
Athena Nike, 138
"Athene, Bringer of Victory," 137
Athene of the Parthenon, 122
Athene Parthenos, 42, 126
Athene Promachos, 42, 79, 125

Athenian(s), 9, 20, 21, 22, 28, 41, 55, 60, 68, 70, 78-79, 80, 82, 83, 84, 86, 89, 93, 104, 114, 147, 155, 184, 187, 190, 191, 201, 205-7, 213, 221
Athenian Empire, 193
Athens, 3, 4, 8, 11, 13, 21, 22, 23, 28, 29, 41, 43, 51, 58, 67, 70, 71-73, 77, 82, 83, 85, 86, 87, 90, 92, 95, 97, 99-101, 103-5, 107, 128, 134, 135, 157, 169, 181, 183-84, 185-87, 190, 191, 193, 196, 203, 204, 212, 233, 237, 245, 246, 248, 249
Athinai, 43
Athletic games, 58, 118, 230
Attalos II, Stoa of, 218-19
Attic: Plain, 136; soil, 154; stage, 77; sunlight, 125
Attica, 6, 7, 13, 20-21, 43, 45, 90-91, 99, 101, 142, 183
Attire, Greek, 227-29
Authorship, introduced to Greek plays, 142

— B —

Babylonians, 13
Bacchus, 37, 41, 141
Banquets, 210, 223-24
Barbarians, 11, 23, 81, 100
Basic Year, 61
Beauty aids, 228
Bibliotheke, the, 176
Black Sea, 11, 51, 68, 168, 182
Boreas, 90
Bracelets, 157
Britain, 51, 57
British Museum, ix, 80, 122, 137, 138
Bronze statues, 119, 124-25
Burials, 155, 209
Byron, Lord, 150
Byssos, 227
Byzantine architecture, 130
Byzantine Empire, 252
Byzantium, 53, 65, 125-26, 130, 182, 189, 251-52

— C —

Caesar, Julius, 57, 168, 177, 251
Calendar, 177, 212
Candles, 226
Cape Sounion, 90, 134
Caps, 229

INDEX 257

Carthage, 54-56
Carts, four-wheeled, 195
Caryatids, 137
Caskey, Prof. John L., ix, 19
Cassiderean Isles, 51
Centaur, 6
Ceramics, 68, 153-56
Cerberus, 209
Ceres, 37
Chalkidike Peninsula, 83, 174
Chaplets, 224
Chariot racing, 59, 62, 196
"Charioteer, The" (Delphi), 122, 125
Charon, 42, 209
Children, 35, 47, 78, 222-23, 235, 240, 242
Chiton, 227-29
Chlamys, 228
Choros, 142
Chorus, 142, 146, 186, 201
Christianity, 112, 164
Chronology, 177
Churches, Greek, 130-31
Circe, 14
Citadel (Acropolis), 128
"City," the, 113, 186
Civic centre, 129, 214, 219
Cleopatra (wife of Philip II), 106
Clothing, 227-29
Clusium, 54
Cnossos. *See* Knossos
Coal, 178
Cohabitation, 205, 233
Coins, 156
"Cold tables," 223
Colonies, Greek, 52-55
Colour: in sculpture, 123; in painting, 152
Comedy: 140, 146, 147; Middle Comedy, 148; Old Comedy, 147; writers, 149
Commercial Exhibition Hall, 129
Communal feeding rooms, 47, 188
Competitive games, 225-26
Concert Hall, 135-36
Constantine, Emperor, 251
Constantinople, 53, 68, 125, 130, 131, 251
Corcyra (Corfu), 48
Corinth, 9, 39, 40, 48, 52, 58, 81, 106, 119, 134, 142, 181, 185, 189, 205, 239, 240, 249, 250, 251
Corinth: Gulf of, 20, 21, 59, 182; Isthmus of, 22, 29, 87, 88, 101, 195
Couch, for reclining at meals, 221, 222
"Crater" bowl, 225
Cretans, 13, 16, 27, 31, 58, 188, 189
Crete, ix, 15, 18, 19, 21, 27, 29, 30, 31, 39, 51, 58, 142, 188, 190, 236, 252
Crimea, 23, 53
Croesus, 74-77, 82
Cycladic civilisation, 15
Cyclopean giants, 14
"Cyclops, The," 146
Cyprian, the (Aphrodite), 39
Cyprus, 39
Cyrene, 53, 182, 230
Cyrus the Younger, 75-76, 168
Cythera, 39
Cytherean, the (Aphrodite), 39

— D —

Danaos, 13
Dances, 77, 84, 85, 141-42, 146, 156, 190
Dante, Alighieri, 252
Dardanelles, 11, 14
Darius, 78, 82, 85
Darwin's theory, 163
Death, Greek attitude towards, 208
Deigma, The, 129
Delos: 39, 97, 98, 184; Confederacy of, 97, 185
Delphi, 21, 38, 39, 52, 53, 59, 64, 65, 66, 75, 76, 78, 89, 90, 105, 118, 119, 122, 134, 197, 245
Delphi, Oracle at, 46, 49, 64, 65-67, 76, 90, 207
Delphic Amphictyony, 105. *See also* Amphictyonic Council
Delphic Stadium, 64
Demeter, 35, 36, 39, 119, 141, 249
Demigods, 6, 37-38, 117
Democracy, 72, 172, 185, 187
Democracy Stele, 219
Demokritos, 163
Demos, the, 147
Demosthenes, 99, 105, 203, 232, 245-46
Devil, the, 173
Dialogue, introduced into plays, 142

Dictaean Cave, 18
Dido, Queen, 54
Didyma, 134
Dionysia, Great, 41, 77, 142, 190, 207
Dionysos: 37, 40, 41, 119, 140-41, 142, 145, 147; theatre of, 135-36
"Diskobolos," the, 126
Dithyrambs, 141-42
Divina Commedia, 252
Divorce, 204
Dodona, 65, 119, 135
Dorian, 58, 65, 67, 140, 142, 160, 227, 228, 260
Dorians, 20-21, 23, 46, 48, 51-52, 67, 147, 188, 189, 247
Doric: 67, 137, 161, 228; Doric column, 132-33, 134, 139
Double Axes, Hall of the, 31
Dowry, 204, 213, 232, 233-34
Drakon, 72, 192
Drama, 140, 143, 146, 149
Dramatists, 143, 149
Dress, 220, 226
Dryads, 38

— E —

Earrings, 157, 227
Earth Mother, 117
Eastern Roman Empire, 125, 130, 251
Eating, customs of, 221
"Ecclesiazusae," 148
Eclipse, 162
Education, 14, 142, 148, 151, 189, 190
Egypt, 13, 16, 46, 53, 87, 108, 168, 176, 181, 249, 250
Elektron (alloy), 156
Eleusinian Mysteries, 103, 135, 141, 196, 207, 208
Elgin, Lord Thomas, 137
Elian (s), 60, 62, 63
Elis, 48, 61, 182, 236, 250
Elpinike, 100
Emblematic sculpture, 119
Emperors: Constantine, 251; Hadrian, 77, 134; Justinian, 111
Entertainment, at a symposion, 224
Epaminondas, 104
Ephessos, 134
Ephors, x; of Sparta, 47
Epidauros, 135, 250

Epiros, 65
Eponymos, 157
Eratosthenes, 177
Erechtheion, 133, 136-37
Eretrians, 82, 84, 85
Ergane, Athena, 43
Eros, 38, 40
Ethics, 171, 175
Etruscan, 54, 55, 155
Euboea, 82, 101
Euclid, 112, 162
Euklides, 177
Euripides, 115, 145, 148, 177
European civilisation, 51, 55
Eurotas Valley, 21
Euxine Sea, 68
Evans, Sir Arthur, 15-17, 31

— F —

Fables (Aesop), 151
Fabrics, 226-27
Father of the Gods, 34, 36, 117
Fawns, 141
Foods, 189, 199, 215, 221, 222, 223-24
Footwear, 229
Foreigners, status of, 193
Freewomen, attendance at theatre, 144
Frieze, 132, 138
"Frogs, The," 148, 209
Fuller's earth, 221
Funeral customs, 209
Furumark, Arne, ix, 17

— G —

"Gadfly, The," 166
Galleons, 195
Game, as food, 221, 222
Gamelion, 214
Ganosis, 124
Garlands, 62
Garments, 226-29
Gelo, 55
Geometric Period, 45, 132
Glass, 154
Gnomon, 222
God: of the Hebrews, 36; the unknown God, 136
Gods and goddesses, 3, 6, 33-44, 149, 208, 210, 233
Gold, 156
Golden Fleece, 28
Golden Horn, 182

INDEX

Gordon, Prof. Cyrus, ix
Graces, the, 39
Great Dionysia, 41, 77, 142, 190, 207
Great Festival (at Corinth), 40
Great God, 36
Great King, 56, 81, 82, 90, 97, 99, 103, 181
"Great King" (Alexander), 248
Great Panathenaea, 208; Great Panathenaic Festival, 81
Greco-Roman period, 108
Greek architecture, 128-39; art, 2, 107-8, 112-13, 114; coins, 156; drama, 140-48; language, 161; poetry, 115-16, 148-51; sculpture, 2, 117-27
Greek Orthodox Church, 130, 131
Greenhill's translation, 210
Gymnasia, 64, 129, 190, 222, 226, 230
Gymnastics, 142
Gymnos, 69

— H —

Hades (Pluto), 37
Hadrian, Emperor, 77, 134
Hair, care of the, 229-30
Halikarnassos, 91
Hall of Ceremonies, 136
Hall of the Double Axes, 31
Hamilcar, 55
Harmonics, 190
Hats, 229
Hebraic background of Christianity, 112, 164
Helen of Troy, 14
Helike, 249
Helladic civilisation, 15, 21, 28
Hellespont, 14, 83
Helots, 46, 47, 49, 50, 88, 89, 98, 185, 189, 239, 240
Hephaistion, 219
Hephaistos, 37, 38, 40, 133
Hera, 36, 38, 75, 117, 119
Heraion, 117
Herakles, 20, 29, 32, 38, 61, 63, 117
Heraklidae, 117, 121
Heraklieia, 189
Hercules, 38, 117
Herkleia, 189
Herm, 42, 103, 119
Hermes, 37, 42-43, 122, 209

"Hermes" of Praxiteles, 123, 127
Herodotos, 2, 51, 75, 82, 87, 91, 249
Hesiod, 149, 150, 207
Hestia, 37, 41
Hetairae, 4, 99, 145, 200, 204, 205, 224, 228
Hexapolis, 10
Hieroglyphics, ix, 17
Himation, 228
Himera, battle of, 55, 63
Hipparchos, 115
Hippias, 78, 114, 120
Hippodamos, 129, 196
Hippokrates, 163
Hippokratic Oath, 210-11
Hittite language, ix, 17
Homer, 3, 8, 13, 14, 20, 23, 25, 34, 38, 39, 40, 54, 61, 77, 115, 149, 160, 190, 208, 222, 236
Homosexuality, 150
Horse collar, invention of, 196
Hoplites, 88, 98, 186
House, Greek, 220-21
House of the Muses, 150
Hydra, the, 20
Hygeia, 210
Hyperborean, 59

— I —

Iacchos, 41, 141
Iceland, 57
Icon, 139
Iconoclastic religion, 120
Ictis, 57
Idea, the, 171
Ideal, the, 171
Ideal City, 182, 233
Ideal State, 172
Idolatry, 119
Iktinos, 134, 137-38
Illiad, 13, 14, 77
Illyrians, 65
Immortality, 165
Immortals (Xerxes'), 88
Indo-European, 17, 18, 19, 160
Ionian(s), 20, 23, 53, 57, 78, 82, 99, 103, 128, 133, 135, 149, 159, 161, 197, 201, 230, 236, 237
Ionian school (of sculpture), 121
Ionic column, 132, 133, 135, 137, 138; Ionic portico, 136
Iris, 42
Irish Sea, 57

Isokrates, 246
Isthmus of Corinth, 22, 29, 87, 88, 101, 195
Italy, 50, 54, 55, 56, 155, 157, 164
Ithaca, 14
Ithome, 49, 98
Ivy, 141

— J —

Jason, 28
Javelin, 62
Jewelry, 123, 157, 227, 229
Julius Caesar, 57, 168, 177, 251
Juno, 36
Jupiter, 36
Jury, 169, 185, 193
Justice, administration of, 190-94
Justinian, Emperor, 191

— K —

Kadmos, 13
Kaida, 47, 50
Kallikrates, 137
Kantion, 57
Kastalian Spring, 59, 65
Kekrops, 13, 43
Kerberos, 209
Kerkyra, 48, 101
Kimon, 71, 86, 92, 98, 100
Kleobis and Bito, 75
Knidos, 127
Knossos, 15-18, 27, 28
Kodros, 21-22, 45-46, 72, 73
Kolophon, 163
Kopais marshland, 68
Kore (korai), 121
Koroebos, 61, 69
Korrina, 151
Kottabos, 225-26
Kouros, 120
Krater, 154, 225
Krimissa, battle of, 56, 63
Krissa, 59, 65
Krissean Plain, 59, 64
Kronos, 36
Kroton, 164

— L —

Labours of Herakles, 20, 27, 31
Labrys, 31
Labyrinth, the, 29, 30, 31
La Fontaine, Jean de, 151
Lakedaimonia, 21, 48
Lakonia, 21, 48

Lamps, 226
Language, Greek, 160-62
Lars Porsena, 54
Laurion, 87, 239
Law courts, 148, 167, 169, 190
Laws, The, 172
Leda, 38
"Leiturgies," 144, 186, 193
Lekythos, 155, 209
Lenaia, 77
Leonidaeon, 135
Leonidas, 88, 89
Lerna, ix, 19-20
Lesbos, 150, 182, 236
Lethe, river of forgetfulness, 209
Life after death, 208
Linear Script A, ix, 17, 18
Linear Script B, ix, 17, 18, 45
Lion Gateway, 26
"Liquid Fire," 177
Logic, 174
Lord God (Poseidon), 36
Louvre, the, 122
Lyceum, the, 174, 176, 177
Lydia, 53, 75
Lydians, 76, 82, 162, 199
Lykeion, the, 174
Lykourgos, 46, 47
"Lysistrata," 148

— M —

Macedon, 182, 205, 245, 247, 249
Macedonia, 11; Macedonians, 78, 105-6, 247
Macedonian Empire, 106
Macedonian phalanx, 106
Machiavelli, 231
Marathon, 29, 51, 71, 78, 84, 86, 129, 152, 155
Marble, 124, 132, 134, 196
Mardonius, 83, 87, 91, 92, 94, 120, 183
Marinatos, Spyros, x
Marriage, 202, 204, 232-35
Mars, 37
Marseilles, 54, 56, 57
Marsyas, 126
Masked actors, 142
Massilia, 54, 56, 182
Mathematics, 173, 174
Matondidae, 21, 46
Medes and Persians, 53, 55, 56, 75-76, 81, 82, 162, 164, 181
Medicine, 163, 177

INDEX

Mediterranean Sea, 9, 13, 18, 51, 56
Megale Hellas, 55-56, 60-61, 155, 161, 164, 182
Megalopolis, 135, 182, 250
Megara, 73-74, 182, 189, 250
Megara, Sicilian, 140
Megarians, 147
Menander, 148
Mercenaries, 85, 168, 184
Mercury, 37
Messenians, 48-49, 98, 116, 182
Metropolitan Museum (New York), 120
Mileto, 162
Miletos, 82
Milos, Aphrodite of, 127
Miltiades, 84-86, 92, 98, 100
Minerva, 37
Minoan(s), 15, 18, 25, 45, 51, 154
Minos, 16, 29, 30, 58
Minotaur, 29, 31
Mirrors, 157
Mitylene, 185
Mnemonics, 162
Mnesikles, 137-38
Moloch, 31
Money, 156, 250
Months, length of, 212
Mosaics, 221
Mother City, 52, 53, 63
Mount Athos, 83, 87
Mount Helikon, 6, 38, 149
Mount Hymettos, 132
Mount Ithome, 56, 98
Mount Lykabettos, 135, 136
Mount Olympos, 6, 11, 35, 41, 65, 247
Mount Parnassos, 31, 38, 59
Mount Pentelicon, 132, 195
Mount Taygetos, 48
Murray, Gilbert, 148
Muses, the, 6, 38, 149
Museum, the (at Alexandria), 176, 177, 249
Music, 190
Mycenae, 3, 14-15, 17, 18, 31, 34, 45, 181, 267
Myron, 122, 123, 126-27
Mysteries, Eleusinian, 103, 135, 141, 196, 207, 208

— N —

National Archaeological Museum of Athens, 120, 122, 157

Nea Polis (Naples), 55
Nemea, 118, 182
Neo-Platonism, 112
Neolithic Age, 15, 19, 219
Neptune, 36
Nereids, 38
Nestor, 17
New Year's Day, 212
"Nike Apteros," 137-38
Nikias, General, 102
North Wind (Boreas), 90
Numerals, 173
Nymphs, 6, 37-38, 48

— O —

Obols, 144, 166, 209
Odeion, 135-36
Odysseus, 14, 24, 209
Odyssey, 13, 14, 77
Oekonomika, 168, 232, 236
Old Testament, 33
Olive oil, 154, 183, 215, 223
Olive tree, planted by Athena, 43-44
Olympia, 38, 58, 59, 60, 61, 64, 67, 102, 117, 118, 119, 122, 182
Olympia(s) (Alexander's mother), 106, 248
Olympiad, 12, 60-62, 69, 117
Olympian gods, 34, 36-37, 41, 43, 141, 160, 166, 206
Olympian Zeus, 77, 122, 126, 133
Olympic Games, 46, 60-64, 81, 117, 121, 129, 144, 151, 246
Onyx, 125
Optics, 177
Oracle, 21, 52, 58, 65, 76, 90, 203, 207
Orca, 57
Orders (columns), 132
Oreads, 38
Orkneys, 57
Orpheus, 38
Orthodox Church, Greek, 130, 131
Ostracism, 80, 95
Ottomans, 252
Ouranos, 36
Owl, 42, 157

— P —

Pack animals, 195
"Painted Arcade," 129
Painting, 152
Palaestra, 64, 201

Palermo, 55
Pallake, 202
Pallas Athena, 42
Pan, 7, 37, 44, 48
Panacaea, 210
Panathenaea, 77, 81, 208
Pandemos, Aphrodite, 40
Pankration, 62
Pankratists, 64
Panorma (Palermo), 55
Paphos, 39
Parian marble, 132, 134
Paris, prince of Troy, 14
Parliament, Athenian, 185
Paros, 86, 132, 182
Paros, Isle of, 195
Parthenon, 7, 70, 122, 123, 125, 133, 134, 136, 138-39, 239-40
Parthenos, Athene, 42, 126
Paul, the Apostle, 136
Paul, king of the Hellenes, 219
Patina, 124
Patronage, of art, 113-14, 115
Pausanias, 25-26, 122, 127, 182
Pederasty, 169, 201
Pegasos, 36
Peisistratos, 74, 75, 77-78, 114, 120, 133, 142
Pelopidas, 104
Peloponnesian cities, 45, 117, 250; Peloponnesians, 13, 90
Peloponnesian War, 101, 103, 107, 113, 138, 146, 197, 246
Peloponnesos, x, 5, 14, 17-19, 23, 28, 31-32, 35, 38, 39, 48, 58-59, 121, 134-35, 140, 182, 246
Penelope, 14
Pentathlon, 62
Pentelicon marble, 132, 195
Pergamos, 108, 176, 181, 218, 220, 249
Perikles, 3, 5, 70, 86, 93, 98, 100, 102, 113, 115, 128, 129, 133, 135, 144, 147, 152, 155, 185, 186, 203, 205, 219, 231, 232, 233, 240, 241
"Perioeki," 184
Peristyle, 220
Persephone, 36, 119
Persia, 5, 98, 107
Persian wars, 2, 51, 71, 100
Persians, 45, 53, 55, 56, 70, 75, 81, 90, 92, 113, 120, 134, 151, 154, 164, 181, 183, 246
Phalanx, 106
Phaleron, 85

Phallophori, 146
Phallophoros, 146
Phallus, 141, 147
Pharaoh, 16, 53, 176
Pheidias, 63, 115, 122, 123, 125-26, 138, 139, 145, 151
Pheidon, 48, 105, 121
Phidipides, 85
Phigalia, 134
Philip II, 105, 186, 245, 246, 251
Philopater, 195
Philosophy, 114, 158-70
Phoenicia, 13
Phoibus Apollon, 39, 76
Phokaia, 53, 56
Phokis, 13
Pindar, 107, 116, 151, 191
Pindos Range, 20
Piraeus, the, 73, 86, 96, 101, 107, 128-29, 183, 185, 193, 196
Plataea, 84, 92
Platon, 63, 112, 144, 164, 165, 167, 171-74, 182-83, 194, 203, 208, 232, 240
Plouton (Pluto), 37
"Plutus," 148
"Poesis," 149
Poetics, 175
Poetry, 115, 148-50, 162
Poikile Stoa, 129, 152
Polis, the, 172
Politics, 162, 175
Polykleitos, 123
Population, 181, 183-84, 185
Porsena, Lars, 54
Poseidon, 36, 38-39, 43, 58, 74, 85, 119, 122, 125, 131, 134, 136
Pottery, 20, 45, 153-55, 183
Praxiteles, 122, 127, 145
Printing, 178
Promachos Athene, 42, 79, 125
Propylaea, 125, 137, 153
Proserpine, 36
Prytaneion, 214
Ptolemaeus Philopater, 195
Ptolemies, 108, 176, 249
Punic City, 56
Punjab, 107
Pylos, x, 17
Pythagoras, 164, 167, 171, 173, 208
Pytheas, 56-57
Pythia, 66
Pythian Apollon, 21, 39, 52, 65, 78, 105, 197, 203

INDEX

Pythian Games, 58, 59, 60, 64-65
Pythian Oracle, 21, 22, 52, 76, 203
Python, 39, 65

— R —

Racing, 59, 62, 196
Renaissance, 252
Republic, The, 172
Residence tax, 194
Rest days, 212
Rhea, 36
Rhodes, 50, 108, 181, 249
Riddles, 199, 225
Roads, 196, 248
Rock of the Acropolis, 43, 78
Rockefeller, John D., 218
Roman: arch, 131; conquest, 10, 13, 108; law, 191
Romans, 21, 125, 141, 200, 205, 240, 251
Rome, 54, 55, 56, 114, 182, 238
Rosetta stone, ix
Rota, 84
"Rule, The," 123

— S —

Sacred Flame of the Mother City, 53
Sacred Unwritten Volumes, 24
Sacred Way, 196
Saint Michael's Mount, 57
St. Sophia, 131
Salamis, 51, 55, 63, 71, 73, 90-91, 250
Samos, 164, 182
"Sample, The," 129
Sandals, 129, 222, 229
Sappho, 116, 150, 236
Sardinia, 54
Sardis, 76, 82
Saronic Gulf, 195
Satraps, 82, 187
Saturn, 36
Satyrical drama, 146
Satyrs, 37, 38, 48, 77, 127, 141
Schliemann, Heinrich, 3, 15, 18, 24-27
Schools of philosophy, 162-64
Science and scientists, 158, 161, 163-64, 166, 173, 174, 176-77
Scientist, first, 175
Scilly Isles, 57
Scotland, 57
Scribes, 186

Scripts, Linear, ix, 17, 18, 45
Sculpture, 117-27
Scythian police, 186, 216-17
"Second tables," 224
Senate: of Athens, 72, 129, 214; of Sparta, 47
Shakespearean drama, 145
Ships, 194, 195
Sicilian Megara, 140
Sicily, 50, 51, 54, 55, 56, 57, 60, 61, 68, 102, 103, 133, 148, 161, 182, 187
Signet rings, 229
Sikyon, 182, 250
Six Cities of Asia Minor, 10
Slaves and slavery, 178, 184, 186, 192, 193, 200, 203, 213, 216, 221, 223, 224, 226, 235-41
Slippers, 229
Sokrates, 100, 112, 129, 148, 164-67, 168, 169-70, 171, 205, 208, 216
Solon, 72-77, 86, 95, 149, 183, 194, 232
Sophists, 148, 166, 214
Sophokles, 145-46
Soul, the, 171
Sounion, 85, 90
Sounion marble, 134
Sparta and the Spartans, 21, 22, 27, 46-47, 48-50, 60, 69, 78, 82, 84, 87, 90, 94, 96-98, 102, 104, 105, 107, 113, 116, 142, 157, 168-69, 181, 184, 187-89, 190, 207, 233, 236, 239, 246, 250
Stadium, 64, 134
Stage, 142-43
Stagyros, 174
Stoa, Poikile, 129, 152
Stoa of Attalos II, 218-19
Strabo, 57
Styx, River, 42, 209
"Successors, The," 249
Suffragettes, 148
Sumerians, 13
Susa, 84
Symposia, 190, 199, 206, 213, 216, 224-26
Syracuse, 54, 55, 79, 102, 103, 125, 151, 157, 172, 177, 181, 184, 189, 216, 248
Syssitia, 188, 189

— T —

"Tanten," the, 120

Tegea, 182
Teleology, 162
Tellon, 74
Temples, Greek, 129, 130-32, 133-34
Tetralogies, 146
Thales, 162
Theatres, 41, 77, 134-35, 140, 142, 144, 199
Theban, 89, 100, 151, 206
Thebes, 68, 81, 94, 104, 106, 181, 182, 194, 236, 245, 246
Themistokles, 86, 89-91, 96-97, 128, 236, 241
Theodosius, 191
"Theogonia," 149
Thermopylae, 71, 87-88
Theseion, 133
Theseus, 24, 28-32, 38, 58, 133, 183
Theseus (city), 135
"Thesmophoriazusae," 148
Thespis, 77, 142, 146
Thessalian League, 250
Thessaly, 8, 11, 87, 91, 150, 189, 236
Thrace, 11, 41, 83, 102
Thrasyboulos, 104
Thucydides, 2, 101, 157, 197
Thule, Isle of, 57, 65
Timber, 195
Tin, 51
Tiryns, 182
Toasts, at a banquet, 225
Tonic, 164
Torches, 226
Tragedies, 142-43, 145
Tragōidia, 142
Tragos, 77, 142
Transmigration of the soul, 164
Transport, 194-96
Trapezous, 182
Tribes, 19, 78, 84, 185, 214, 242
Trireme, 194-95
Troezen, 28, 31, 182, 250
Trojan War, 4, 15, 20
Troy, 12-15, 18, 52; siege of, 12, 23; site of, 25, 26
Tunis, 54
Tyrant(s), 55, 104, 187
Tyrseni, 54, 155
Tyrtaeos, 49, 116

— U —

Uranus, 36
Urn, burial, 209
Utopia, ideal, 172

— V —

Vaphio, 27
Vatican copies (of statues), 127
Venetians, 139
Ventris, Michael, ix, 17
Venus, 37
Verse, 149, 161
Vesta, 37
Victories, Winged, 127, 138
Vulcan, 37

— W —

War God, 37
Warrior Goddess, 37, 44
"Wasps, The," 148
"Water-stealer," 191
West Country (Cornwall), 57
White Iron Islands, 51
Windows, absence of, 220
Wine, 37, 40, 77, 141, 154, 183, 190, 213, 223, 225, 226, 238
Women, 16, 35, 48, 96, 113, 144, 148, 150, 151, 157, 172, 182, 188, 192, 221, 227, 228, 229, 230, 231-34, 235-37, 238, 248
Wooden Horse, 14
"Wooden Walls," 89
Writing, knowledge of, 13

— X —

Xanthippos, 86, 96, 98, 100
Xenophanes, 163
Xenophon, 167-68, 232, 235, 236
Xerxes, 85-86, 87, 88, 90, 91

— Z —

Zeus, 16, 18, 34, 35, 36, 37, 38, 42, 43, 63, 65, 117, 119, 122, 126, 133
Zeus, Olympian, 77, 122, 126, 133
Zeus Keraunobolos, 125